Rev. Edward J. M[...]
569 Burnt Creek [...]
Lilburn, GA 30247

W9-BLA-420

S.B.C.
House on the Sand?

David O. Beale

UNUSUAL PUBLICATIONS
Greenville, SC 29614

LIBRARY
BRYAN COLLEGE
DAYTON, TENN. 37321
131764

S. B. C. House on the Sand?
by David O. Beale
© 1985 Bob Jones University
Greenville, South Carolina 29614

ISBN: 0-89084-281-7
All rights reserved. No part of this book may be
reproduced in any form, except for brief quotation
in a review, without written permission from the
publisher.
Printed in the United States of America

LIBRARY
BRYAN COLLEGE
DAYTON, TENN. 37321

Dedication

To My Church History Students

Contents

Chapter Five: Southern Seminary Continued—
The Fall into Apostasy

Preface

It has been my constant desire in the writing of this book to make it as helpful and convincing as possible. There is a glossary, and the several appendixes at the end of the book define more fully those terms which the text mentions and which are unfamiliar to or misunderstood by many. I have tried as much as possible to use source material from Southern Baptist publications, so I have constantly referred to the SBC *Annuals,* 1845-1984, the various state convention newspapers, and the bulletins from the various schools and institutions. All of the references to the *Christian News* have been Religious News Service releases. Other publications by individuals outside the Convention were cited only when I could not obtain a Southern Baptist source.

As a Baptist I have with great interest observed the Southern Baptist Convention for many years. Brought up in a rural Southern Baptist church, I will always appreciate the host of godly people in the Southern Baptist Convention who love the Lord and who care enough about the future to study their great Baptist heritage and to evaluate contemporary men and movements on the basis of the infallible Word of God. The motivation behind this book is love for the people of God, not the love of "heresy-hunting," which runs totally against my "grain." I believe that there are multitudes of dedicated grassroots Southern Baptist people who respond positively to truth and who abhor falsehood. This book's purpose is to allow Southern Baptist leaders—pastors, editors, and educators—to tell their own story. It is my prayer that the reader will also measure what he reads about the Southern Baptist Convention in this book by the Word of God. I trust that eternity will prove wrong anyone who may view this work as the product of a malicious heart. As a Fundamentalist, I love the people of God as well as the Word of God.

David O. Beale

Greenville, South Carolina
1985

Acknowledgements

I am indebted to Dr. Russell Kaemmerling, editor of the *Southern Baptist Advocate,* and Dr. William Powell, editor of the *Southern Baptist Journal,* for their help in providing pertinent information for this book.

This book would not have been possible without the Religious Information File (commonly known as the Fundamentalism File) in the Mack Library of Bob Jones University. Joseph Allen and his staff who maintain this file have consistently helped to keep me informed concerning news releases. I am especially grateful to Robert Franklin and his staff at *FAITH for the Family* magazine for their labor and pertinent suggestions.

I probably would never have entered into this endeavor at all had not Dr. Bob Wood, Executive Vice President of Bob Jones University, encouraged me.

Part I:
Historical Background

Chapter One
Southern Baptists in Conflict

On August 28, 1984, Dr. Roy L. Honeycutt, president of Southern Seminary in Louisville, spoke to an overflow audience of cheering students, faculty, staff, and visitors at opening convocation. Honeycutt, a leading liberal spokesman, was declaring a "holy war" against the whole conservative movement within the Southern Baptist Convention (SBC). This war, however, declared or undeclared, has a long and dramatic history, and this book attempts to tell the story.

The Real Problem

Wallie Amos Criswell, Baptist legend and pastor of First Baptist Church in Dallas for more than forty years, [1] has clearly pinpointed the problem. As long ago as 1962, Dr. Criswell, whose church is the largest congregation in the SBC, [2] was crying, "The fruits of liberalism are plain

1

and simple to see; just open your eyes and look; they are decay and death."[3] Dr. Criswell is successor to the famous pastor George W. Truett. In 1970, when Criswell was president of the SBC, the Sunday School Board published his own key book, *Look Up, Brother!* In this book, Dr. Criswell uses the example of a professor in a Southern Baptist school who told his class that they should not preach from some books of the Bible. After ridiculing the Song of Solomon, the professor concluded, "If I were making up the Bible and had a choice of including in it *Playboy* magazine or the Song of Solomon, I would choose *Playboy* magazine."[4]

The Baptist Standard, the official organ of the Texas Baptist Convention, has revealed that "in some of these schools there are Unitarian teachers. . . . There are some Roman Catholic teachers. . . . There are some Jews teaching in Baptist institutions. . . . It is possible that there might be found an atheist on some Baptist school faculty." The article raises a legitimate question: "Shall we tell him he is free to use a Christian institution to destroy the faith of our youth just because he doesn't believe in God?"[5] When Broadman Press published Dr. Criswell's book *Why I Preach That the Bible Is Literally True* (1969), sixty-four SBC Bible professors signed a resolution seriously objecting to its publication by the official SBC press. [6] More recently, Dr. Criswell told reporters, "I don't understand why our denominational leaders seek to cut down in every way those who defend the infallibility and the inerrancy and inspiration of the Bible and at the same time liberals are taking away our institutions one by one and they say nothing about it."[7]

All will agree that the SBC is in a state of turmoil, and many laymen are wondering exactly what is going on. Is the problem just a matter of ecclesiastical politics with various factions vying for power? Or are there real theological issues at stake? More important, what is ahead for the largest Protestant denomination in the world? These are questions which every concerned Southern Baptist should be considering.

Definition of Terms

There is a sad lack of understanding among lay people today regarding the current religious situation, and the blame must rest to a great degree on the media, who have constantly misused terms and distorted the real picture. The average person is repeatedly barraged with words like "Fundamentalist," "conservative," "moderate," and "Liberal," but more than likely he has only a very vague idea of what they mean.

Take for instance the term *Fundamentalist*, which one hears applied to such diverse leaders as the Ayatollah Khomeini, Jim Jones, and Sun Myung Moon. In reality, none of these three can properly be called by that name. Fundamentalism is historically a movement within orthodox Christianity which accepts the Bible as the inerrant Word of God (as Christians have done for two thousand years), defends the doctrines that the Bible teaches, and refuses to work or be identified in any way with those who attack the Bible and its teachings.

Let us take a look at some of the other terms that are currently bandied about. Today there are three major groups within the SBC. First, there are the *Liberals*. Liberalism itself divides into three subgroups: old-line Liberalism or Modernism, Neo-liberalism, and Neo-orthodoxy. The older Liberalism or Modernism is the theological position which rejects any or all of the Bible as the absolute Word of God; denies the supernatural elements of the Bible; denies the deity and substitutionary atonement of Christ; and perpetrates the anti-scriptural doctrines of the universal fatherhood of God, the universal brotherhood of man, and the social gospel as the answer to man's needs. Neo-liberalism, which emerged about 1935, is an attempt to preserve the basic tenets of Liberalism while clothing them in conservative-sounding terminology. Various events had occurred which discredited the optimism and free-handed misuse of the Bible which the old Liberalism exhibited, so with Harry Emerson Fosdick they decided that "the Church must go beyond Modernism." In point of fact it was simply the same old Liberalism clothed in a more attractive garb of conservative-sounding terminology, intended to be more palatable to the average lay person. Neo-orthodoxy, whose founding father was Karl Barth (1896-1968), tried a different approach with the same purpose. Accepting the liberal view of the Scriptures, Karl Barth attacked Fundamentalists for "worshipping a self-sufficient paper pope." While claiming to preserve the "message" of the Bible, neo-orthodox men deny many of the literal *facts* of the Bible. They assert that while many of the events related in the Bible did not actually occur in history, they teach us what is true in a higher realm. What is so deceptive about Neo-orthodoxy is that this so-called "higher realm" is merely a theological fog bank into which Neo-orthodox spokesmen flee (often secretly) when discussing what the Bible teaches. Many do not realize that these church leaders are speaking in a non-literal realm when they use such terms as "virgin birth," "resurrection," and "second coming."

Most Liberals today embrace a combination of Neo-liberalism and Neo-orthodoxy. All Liberals reject the doctrine of biblical inerrancy or infallibility (i.e. that the Bible is without any mixture of error), which both Scripture and historic Christianity have affirmed. Reporters and journalists often refer to a Southern Baptist as a "moderate," but this is deceptive, for they are almost always speaking of one who is left of center and committed to liberal tenets. (See Appendix 4 for further discussion of Liberalism and its teachings.)

The second major group within the SBC today is the *New Evangelical* movement. New Evangelicalism is the religious mood or attitude which advocates dialogue with Liberals and infiltration into apostate institutions. Harold J. Ockenga coined the term in 1948 and explained that New Evangelicals are a "new breed" who repudiate the doctrine of separation and call for more social involvement and serious theological dialogue. Today, reporters and journalists often confuse New Evangelicalism with Fundamentalism; this is a serious mistake. The early leaders of New Evangelicalism—Carl F. H. Henry, Edward Carnell, Bernard Ramm, Gleason Archer, and others—identified themselves as a "new breed" and stated

4

forthrightly that they were in fact repudiating Fundamentalism. The two movements stood worlds apart, and they remain worlds apart, even though reporters constantly cloud the issue.

Fundamentalism is that historic position which maintains an unwavering allegiance to the inerrancy and authority of the whole Bible; affirms the foundational truths of Christianity which have most often come under attack—the Trinity, Christ's incarnation, virgin birth, substitutionary atonement, bodily resurrection, and second coming, the new birth through instantaneous regeneration, the resurrection of the saints to eternal life, and the resurrection of the wicked to final judgment and eternal punishment; and practices the biblical doctrine of holiness or separation from *all* apostasy and willful practices of disobedience. Fundamentalists believe that the scriptural criteria for fellowship are genuine belief in and consistent obedience to Christ and the Bible. While Fundamentalists reject the teaching of "sinless perfection" in this life, they regard the doctrine of biblical fellowship as a fundamental part of the doctrine of God's absolute holiness—separation (sanctification) from the world, from false religion, and from every practice of disobedience to God's Word. Fundamentalists believe that the Scriptures instruct Christians to separate from deeds of darkness (I John 2:15-17; II Corinthians 6:15-17:1), from false teachers (II John 9-11; I Timothy 6:20-21), and from professing Christians who practice disobedience (Matthew 18:15-18; II Thessalonians 3:6, 14-15). (See Appendixes 2 and 3 for further discussion of the history and doctrinal position of Fundamentalism.)

The New Evangelical movement's "stay-in" philosophy has made the mainline, separatist-Fundamentalist movement progressively more conspicuous. Contrary to general opinion, the commonly designated list of "cardinal doctrines of the faith" alone can no longer properly identify mainline Fundamentalism. Fundamentalists still embrace these truths as much as ever, but New Evangelicals generally believe the same list. When Fundamentalists began publishing their conviction that the mainline denominations were unsalvable, both

Liberals and New Evangelicals began attacking the doctrine of *holiness*—a term which in both Hebrew and Greek carries the basic meaning of "separation" or "sanctification" from sin. Fundamentalists believe that apostasy and disobedience to God are sins. (See Appendix 1 for a more detailed discussion of New Evangelicalism's origin and meaning.)

The third major group in the SBC today is the *silent majority*—the thousands of laymen and pastors who pay the bills. Many of these have repeatedly expressed to me that they would love to see a single book which clearly defines theological and ecclesiastical terms and presents a general survey of the Southern Baptist battles of the twentieth century. This is the purpose of this book—to place in the hands of both pastors and laymen a handbook of reference materials relating to the present conflicts.

The Graf-Wellhausen Historical-Critical Method (JEDP)

One of the major "props" upon which liberal theology rests is the Graf-Wellhausen historical-critical method of interpretation, and the reader must have an idea of its view of the Bible if he is to understand the dangerous threat that Liberalism poses for the SBC. Is the Bible the inspired Word of God, without any mixture of error? Did Moses write the Pentateuch as the Bible claims, or are this and other large sections of Scripture simply a patchwork of exaggerated oral tradition handed down by bigoted Jewish nationalists? If the Bible is unreliable in these areas, then how can we depend upon it in other areas, such as the person of Christ and the New Birth?

In essence the historical-critical method assumes that the Bible is not a trustworthy and straightforward record which God revealed to "holy men" who "spake as they were moved by the Holy Ghost" (II Peter 1:21); rather, each of the books of the Bible is made up of stories which were gradually put together and altered as time went on. The term "JEDP theory" is often used to refer to this approach because the letters J-E-D-P stand for the four supposed sources which were put together over a period of centuries to form the first five books of the Bible. The name "Graf-Wellhausen method" is taken from the names of two nineteenth-century German critics, K. H. Graf (1815-1869) and Julius Wellhausen (1844-1918), who assigned dates to these imaginary sources of the Pentateuch.

If one accepts the historical-critical method, then the historical accuracy of the Bible is out of the question: Moses could not have written the Pentateuch, even though Christ Himself ascribes it to him; Deuteronomy was a pious fraud passed off on the people of Josiah's day as an ancient work of Moses. (See Appendix 4 for further discussion of the history and conclusions of the historical-critical method.)

Liberalism and the SBC

You may ask, "What does all of this have to do with me as a Southern Baptist?" The fact is that the Graf-Wellhausen historical-critical method is now a standard assumption in Southern Baptist colleges and seminaries and even in the official literature published by the Sunday School Board. Among those who have done most to popularize the Graf-Wellhausen historical-critical method and to introduce these views subtly to American laymen are the authors of the *Broadman Bible Commentary* and more recently the *Layman's Bible Book Commentary*, both of which the Southern Baptist Broadman Press publishes and Southern Baptist Bookstores aggressively promote. The official Southern Baptist Sunday School Board has been publishing such views for twenty-five years with no words of caution. Consequently, Southern Baptist institutions are now completely saturated with hypotheses which have no basis in fact or Scripture, but which good people now assume to be Scripture truth.

This situation in the SBC is a definite cause of concern, and it prompts us to recall the parable of the Lord Jesus in Matthew 7:24-27:

> Whosoever heareth these sayings of mine, and doeth them, I will liken him unto a wise man, which built his house upon a rock: And the rain descended, and the

floods came, and the winds blew, and beat upon that house; and it fell not: for it was founded upon a rock. And every one that heareth these sayings of mine, and doeth them not, shall be likened unto a foolish man, which built his house upon the sand: And the rain descended, and the floods came, and the winds blew, and beat upon that house; and it fell: and great was the fall of it.

Today Southern Baptists who are aware of the problems outlined above are asking some searching questions: Are there deadly diseases of apostasy and compromise still running rampant and unchecked within the SBC? Is it creeping Liberalism or is it controlling Liberalism? Is there really a malignant cancer within the body? If so, is a complete diagnosis and removal now possible, or is the disease terminal? Is conservatism actually gaining in strength within the SBC? With all of the warring factions within the Convention, will a split occur? These are questions which the following chapters will endeavor to answer. Was the Convention actually founded upon the solid rock of God's Word? And, if so, has the structure ever shifted from that original foundation? Is the house now resting on sinking sand as the lightnings of controversy flash across the ecclesiastical skies and as the winds and rains of conflict beat vehemently upon it?

Endnotes

1. Dr. Criswell's church has 23,000 members and an annual budget of over eight million dollars. Though seventy-five years of age, Criswell is still serving as pastor as this is being written. He was born on December 19, 1909.

2. "W. A. Criswell: A Case Study in Fundamentalism," *Review and Expositor,* Winter 1984, pp. 107-31.

3. *First Baptist Reminder,* June 15, 1962 (the weekly bulletin of the First Baptist Church in Dallas).

4. Wallie A. Criswell, *Look Up, Brother!* (Nashville: Broadman, 1970), p. 83.

5. *The Baptist Standard,* December 12, 1962.

6. *Tulsa Daily World,* March 16, 1969; see also W. A. Criswell's *Look Up, Brother!,* p. 72.

7. *Presbyterian Journal,* November 3, 1982, p. 5.

Chapter Two

Early History and Basic Structure of the Southern Baptist Convention

The 140-year-old Southern Baptist Convention is the largest evangelical or Protestant denomination in the world. During the fiscal year October 1, 1982, through September 30, 1983, 36,531 churches with 14,185,454 members contributed $272,571,144 to the SBC Cooperative Program. Southern Baptists now support over seventy educational institutions of higher learning. At the June 1984 SBC meeting in Kansas City, Missouri, the six seminaries alone reported a total of 14,020 students; one of these, Southwestern, is the largest seminary in the world. [1]

No longer limited to the southern United States, Southern Baptists are now organized in all fifty states and Canada. Organized in 1845, this sprawling ecclesiastical machine has an intriguing history of great men and women, of noble goals and achievements, and of heated battles and skirmishes resulting in both glorious victories and heartbreaking defeats. The story unfolds as more of an adventure than a mere history.

Baptists in America Prior to 1845

Both the First Baptist Church in Providence, Rhode Island, and the First (now United) Baptist Church in Newport, Rhode Island, share the distinction of being the oldest Baptist churches in America. Both originated about 1638. Roger Williams, first pastor of the Providence church, and Dr. John Clarke, first pastor of the Newport church, played vital roles in the colony's earliest history.

Nevertheless, with Puritan Congregationalists hostile to Baptist views of "individual soul liberty," Baptist churches' growth in New England was slow during this period. It is not surprising that the middle colonies, rather than New England, became the center of Baptist activity. In the absence of any "established" state church, the Philadelphia area, with its policy of religious toleration under the Quakers, became the center for the earliest organizational efforts. In 1707 five local churches established the Philadelphia Baptist Association, which in 1742 adopted the Philadelphia Confession of Faith. While Baptists first appeared in the South as early as 1683, when William Screven from Maine established the First Baptist Church at Charleston, South Carolina, there was very little real growth in the South until after the Great Awakening of the eighteenth century.

Daniel Marshall and Shubael Stearns, both from Connecticut, came to Christ under George Whitefield's preaching in New England. Becoming Separate Baptists, that is, separate from the "Standing Order" of established Congregational churches, these men brought the Great Awakening to the South and in 1755 planted a Separate Baptist church at Sandy Creek, North Carolina. Stearns served as pastor. The church is now a Southern Baptist church and is near Route 49 between Liberty and Ramseur in Randolf County, North Carolina. Noting this movement of his converts into Baptist ranks, George Whitefield reportedly lamented, "Lo! My chickens have become ducks." Within three years the Sandy Creek church had established two others, and the three congregations totaled 900 members. Daniel Marshall moved on to Georgia where he established the first Baptist church in the colony—the Kiokee Baptist Church, now a Southern Baptist church near Appling, in Columbia County, Georgia (near Augusta). This "farmer-preacher" Baptist movement in the South resulted in phenomenal church growth. The "Regular" Baptist churches which had been established in the South prior to the Separates' arrival were generally less evangelistic, but beginning in Virginia in 1787, the two groups eventually united throughout the southern region of the country.

Baptists formed their first national organization in Philadelphia in 1814; it was called the General Missionary Convention of the Baptist Denomination in the United States of America for Foreign Missions. It was commonly known simply as the Triennial Convention because it met once every three years. Richard Furman, pastor of the First Baptist Church of Charleston, South Carolina, served as its first president.

Origin of the Southern Baptist Convention

While many factors—social, cultural, economic, political, and religious—contributed to the mid-nineteenth century separation of Baptists in the South from those in the North, three factors demand special mention. First, the Baptists in the South, with their frontier setting, favored more centralization in their organized work; Baptists in the North favored a loose structure of autonomous societies. Second, Baptists in the South, with their revivalist-Separatist heritage, favored a more aggressive evangelism than did their northern brethren. Finally, there was the issue of slavery, which served as the catalyst to complete the separation.

Although the Triennial Convention had attempted to establish a noncommittal policy regarding slavery, Baptists in the South felt that they were receiving unequal treatment in the expenditure of funds and in the approval of missionary candidates. The Baptists of the South finally set up a test case by recommending to the Board of the Home Mission Society James E. Reeves, a Georgia slaveholder, as a missionary to the Cherokee Indians. The Board rejected Reeves by a seven-to-five vote. The southern brethren soon met in Augusta, Georgia, and on May 8, 1845, established the Southern Baptist Convention.

The Baptists in the North did not organize the Northern Baptist Convention until 1907; in 1950 they renamed themselves the American Baptist Convention, which in 1972 became the American Baptist Churches in the USA. Southern Baptists have never seriously considered any formal union with the "Northern" Baptists. While the latter have tended to conceive of their denomination as simply a loose structure within which the local churches operate, Southern Baptists have strengthened their early trend toward centralization. Moreover, Southern Baptists manifest a stronger sense of unity and loyalty to their own convention than do the "Northern" Baptists toward theirs. The Southern Baptist Cooperative Program, established in 1925, is the very heart of this complex organization.

Structure of the Southern Baptist Convention

The Seventy-Five Million Campaign of 1919-1925 was the forerunner of the Cooperative Program. The purpose of this campaign was to raise $75 million in five years to provide missionary, educational, and benevolent relief both at home and in war-torn countries suffering from the aftereffects of World War I. It was largely a social emphasis, and even Southern Baptist Fundamentalists such as J. Frank Norris [2] originally supported this effort because it was the Southern Baptists' answer to the interdenominational "church union" movement represented by such groups as the Federal Council of Churches, the Edinburgh Conference, the Foreign Missions Conference, and the Inter-Church World Movement. The Southern Baptists' Seventy-Five Million Campaign raised $58,591,713 but left Convention agencies drained of their own operating funds. It laid the foundation, however, for the Cooperative Program which Southern Baptists officially formulated on May 13, 1925, at their convention in Memphis, Tennessee.

The Cooperative Program was the practical solution to a financial crisis; it made good business sense, and it was completely voluntary on the churches' part. Its purpose was to serve as a channel for funding mission ministries. Money given by the churches was to be divided evenly between state-convention ministries and the national Southern Baptist Convention ministries. The most recent definition of the Cooperative Program appears in the 1979 SBC *Annual:*

> The Cooperative Program is a financial channel of cooperation between the state conventions and the Southern Baptist Convention which makes it possible for all persons making undesignated gifts through their church to support the missionary, education, and benevolent work in their own state conventions and also the work of the Southern Baptist Convention. [3]

Theoretically, Southern Baptist work operates on four separate levels, with the *local church* as the basic unit. Then the *district associations* represent churches located within city or county boundaries. On the third level, there are thirty-seven organized *state conventions.* In some areas such as New England and the Northwest, where Southern Baptist work is not so strong, several states cooperate through a single convention. Under the jurisdiction of each state convention come such ministries as Baptist hospitals, homes for the aged, orphanages, state colleges, and recreational retreats. Election of trustees for the various institutions occurs at the annual state conventions. Most of the state conventions publish their own newspapers or "state papers." The fourth level of organization is the national body, the SBC proper; it consists of "messengers" from the local churches. Since, theoretically, every local church affiliated with the SBC is autonomous and the local church's authority is never "delegated," representatives at sessions of either the state conventions or the SBC are designated as "messengers" rather than delegates. Each church is allowed one messenger, then one additional for every 250 members or for each $250 contributed to the work of the Convention.

A maximum of ten messengers can come from each church, and they must come only from "churches in cooperation with the SBC and contributing to its causes." Today, the depth of a church's true loyalty is measured by the percentage of its offerings it contributes to the Cooperative Program, and no one is considered a loyal Southern Baptist who does not give regularly to the Program. Corporations under the jurisdiction of the SBC (national level) include the Home and Foreign Mission Boards, the Sunday School Board, the Annuity Board (retirement), the Radio and Television Commission, the Christian Life Commission, the Stewardship Commission, and the six seminaries. It has been controversy, however, which has shaped the very nature of the SBC as it appears today, whether observed from the local, district, state, or national level.

Overview of the Battles

The two major nineteenth-century controversies involved the anti-missions movement and the landmark movement. The three major twentieth-century battles have been these: the Fundamentalist Versus Evolutionist Controversy, which peaked from 1921 to 1926; the Conservative Versus Modernist Controversy, which focused on Ralph Elliott from 1961 to 1963 and on the *Broadman Bible Commentary* from 1969 to 1972; and the Inerrancy Versus Errancy Controversy, which exploded in 1979 and continues today. [4] The evolutionists were victorious in the first battle, the Modernists in the second, and the errantists are doing quite well in the contemporary conflict.

Endnotes

1. *Annual,* SBC, 1984, pp. 72, 73, 170-83.

2. J. Frank Norris declared that "the biggest thing that Baptists have ever undertaken since the days of John the Baptist is for Southern Baptists to raise Seventy-Five Million Dollars in the

next few years for all missionary and benevolent enterprises around the world. . . . First Baptist Church will get in the campaign and every member in it" (*Searchlight,* September 25, 1919, p. 1).

3. *Annual,* SBC, 1979, p. 30; cited also in the 1983 *Annual,* p. 43. Helpful discussions on the Cooperative Program appear in *Baptist History and Heritage,* October 1982, p. 41f. and *Baptist History and Heritage,* July 1982, p. 55f.

4. A brief but valuable discussion on the twentieth-century battles appears in *Baptist History and Heritage,* April 1981, p. 12f.

Chapter Three

J. Frank Norris in Historical Perspective

Norris and the Evolutionists

The Southern Baptist Convention originated in 1845 with 4,126 churches. They more than tripled that number in their first thirty-five years. By 1925 there were 27,517 churches; that year, however, 3,176 churches left the SBC. It took twenty-five more years to regain the number of churches that withdrew in 1925. The controversy was evolution, and the seeds of toleration were germinating.

In 1919 Fundamentalist J. Frank Norris, pastor of First Baptist Church in Fort Worth, Texas, began leading an attack against Baylor University professors Grove S. Dow, C. S. Fothergill, and W. P. Meroney, and others who were teaching evolution. Baylor's president, S. P. Brooks, defended these faculty members who had published pro-evolution materials and whose salaries Southern Baptists were paying. To the Fundamentalists' chagrin, however, George W. Truett, pastor of First Baptist Church of Dallas, and Lee Scarborough of Southwestern Baptist Theological Seminary in Fort Worth led a counter-attack against the Norris movement.

Scarborough published a tract called "The Fruits of Norrisism," and in 1922 the Tarrant County Baptist Association expelled Norris. The following year, the Texas state convention refused to seat a lone messenger from Norris's church, and in 1924 it officially ousted both Norris and his church for their lack of a "spirit of unity," which involved their refusal to use SBC literature. It may be that both Truett and Scarborough would have stood more strongly with the Fundamentalists if Norris himself had set a more biblical example for the movement.

The ouster did not stop Norris. He had been a thorn in Baylor's side even in his student days when he had led a protest rally to oust President O. H. Cooper. As recently as 1923 Norris had conducted at the World's Christian Fundamentals Association a dramatic mock trial of several Texas colleges. Now he would continue his protest outside the Convention. Fundamentalists, led by Norris, did force Professor Dow and a few of his colleagues out of Baylor, and immediately Norris launched an all-out attack against the denomination's foremost Darwinist— Wake Forest College president William L. Poteat. The controversial Norris, however, was not to repeat his act successfully outside of Texas. Opposition to Norris would continue to arise from scholarly conservative circles.

Edgar Y. Mullins, president of Southern Baptist Theological Seminary in Louisville, Kentucky, was responsible for making the hypothesis of evolution acceptable in Southern Baptist institutions. Mullins, a leading Southern Baptist theologian and president of the SBC (1921-1923), openly endorsed President Poteat of Wake Forest. Addressing the 1923 SBC, Mullins argued that evolution could be accepted as a "working hypothesis of science" without destroying "the supernatural element in the Christian religion." [1]

Mullins followed the same policy when in 1925 he chaired the seven-man committee which formulated the Baptist Faith and Message, the first SBC confession of faith. C. P. Stealy, [2] the only anti-evolutionist on the committee, tried but failed to get a single anti-evolution clause into this statement of faith. He failed even to have the phrase "and not by evolution" added to article three of the confession. [3]

Southern Baptist Convention president George W. McDaniel, pastor of First Baptist Church in Richmond, Virginia, avoided an open rift at the 1926 SBC meeting in Houston by including in his address a remark condemning "every theory, evolution or other, which teaches that man originated in . . . a lower animal ancestry." The nearest thing to a conservative victory was the passing of a simple resolution that the McDaniel Statement become the "sentiment of this convention." [4] Three days later, a resolution was presented "that this convention request all its institutions and Boards and their missionary representatives" to sign the McDaniel Statement. Mullins, along with Lee Scarborough, led a successful campaign to make these proposals non-binding. "Baptist liberty" became a byword.

C. P. Stealy led the Oklahoma state convention to withhold undesignated Cooperative Program funds from Southern Baptist seminaries whose faculties refused to sign the McDaniel Statement. In two years, however, the state released these funds—even though only one seminary had faculty members who had signed the statement. By this point, the Fundamentalists had lost the war; they would now be unable to prevent a liberal takeover. Within two years, these controversies at the annual SBC meetings would cease. Once evolution became acceptable in "scholarly" Southern Baptist circles, the slide into rank Liberalism, with its higher critical methods, was inevitable. For example, at the SBC meeting in Birmingham, Alabama, in 1931, Dr. John W. Phillips, pastor of First Baptist Church of Mobile, Alabama, was the speaker on May 13. In this sermon, which Phillips published and distributed in advance, he asserted that the Old Testament sacrifices were "ghostly forms of ancient superstition. . . . a relic of paganism." The popular liberal pastor asserted that the New Testament writers actually misunderstood Christ's teaching and incorporated errors into their writings. In spite of conservative protest, the messengers elected Dr. Phillips to the vice presidency of the SBC for the following year. [5] As for J. Frank Norris, even most Fundamentalists eventually shunned him and his controversial tactics.

Norris and the Fundamentalists

Southern Baptist authors sometimes depict J. Frank Norris as a founder of Fundamentalism.[6] However, Fundamentalism as a religious movement actually originated in the North, which was the main scene of its activities for the first fifty years of its existence. (See Appendixes 2 and 3). Fundamentalism (the movement, that is, though not the name) originated in the fourth quarter of the nineteenth century, nearly half a century before Norris's rough and tumble bouts with the evolutionists in the twenties.

Mainline Fundamentalism is not a "Norris movement"; it is a movement which simply tries to reach out to people, embraces the whole Bible as its absolute and infallible authority, and endeavors to practice scriptural holiness as the only means of achieving true joy and bringing the greatest glory to a holy God.

Endnotes

1. *Annual,* SBC, 1923, pp. 19-20; see also the *Biblical Recorder,* March 28, 1923, p. 5. The *Biblical Recorder* is the North Carolina Southern Baptist state paper. Also see E. Y. Mullins, "The Dangers and Duties of the Present Hour," the opening address at the SBC, Kansas City, Missouri, May 16, 1923.

2. C. P. Stealy was editor of the *Baptist Messenger,* the Oklahoma Southern Baptist state paper.

3. *Annual,* SBC, 1925, pp. 71-76.

4. *Annual,* SBC, 1926, p. 18.

5. *Annual,* SBC, 1931-1932, p. 68; published sermon by J. W. Phillips.

6. *Review and Expositor,* Winter 1982, pp. 63-103; see especially p. 87.

PART II:

Southern Baptist Seminaries and Colleges

The Southern Baptist Convention operates four of the five largest seminaries in the world. The six Southern Baptist seminaries will appear in sequence according to their founding dates. The first two, Southern and Southwestern, were established as staunch, conservative institutions, and for that reason their early histories receive more attention in the following chapters. Every Baptist deserves to know the grand heritage of these two oldest schools. New Orleans had a short history of exclusive conservatism before becoming a mixed school of conservatives and Liberals. The last three seminaries, however, were founded with a bent towards Liberalism; these are Golden Gate, Southeastern, and Midwestern.

Chapter Four

Southern Baptist Theological Seminary

Southern Baptist Theological Seminary (SBTS) opened in Greenville, South Carolina, in 1859 with twenty-six students. The school remained in Greenville for eighteen years, then moved to Louisville, Kentucky, in 1877 with eighty-nine students. The earliest years of the school's history were indeed glorious. The four original faculty members—James P. Boyce, John A. Broadus, Basil Manly, Jr., and William Williams—were outstanding spiritual and scholarly giants who provided dignity and poise to the institution's character. These four pioneers stood adamantly for the full inspiration, total inerrancy, and absolute authority of the Scriptures. Basil Manly, Jr., who became a Christian after reading the life of Jonathan Edwards and whose father was the pastor of the oldest Baptist church in the South—First Baptist of Charleston, South Carolina—expressed his own strong convictions in *The Bible Doctrine of Inspiration Explained and Vindicated.* [1] A closer look at early SBTS leaders should further illustrate the integrity of the institution's original character.

James Petigru Boyce (1827-1888)

James P. Boyce was converted in 1846 in a revival meeting at Charleston's First Baptist Church. The well-known Richard Fuller was the visiting preacher who had the joy of baptizing young Boyce, who was just then at home for spring recess from Brown University. Boyce later studied under Charles Hodge at Princeton Theological Seminary, then went on to serve as pastor of the Baptist church in Columbia, South Carolina, and professor of theology at Furman University in Greenville.

Boyce became "chairman" of SBTS's original faculty (1859-1888); the trustees named him the school's first "president" in 1888, the year that he died. He was president of the Southern Baptist Convention from 1872 to 1879 and again in 1888. Scholarship, humility, and leadership characterized his ministry. During the dark days of the Civil War, when the seminary was unable to pay Boyce's salary, a railroad company offered him $10,000 a year— a vast sum in those days—to become the company's president. Boyce sent his reply: "Thank the gentlemen for me; but tell them I must decline, as I have decided to devote my life, if need be, to building the Southern Baptist Theological Seminary."[2] President Boyce published his strong views on the Bible in his *Three Changes in Theological Institutions* (1856) and later in his *Abstract of Systematic Theology* (1887). Dr. Boyce was building upon the solid rock.

John Albert Broadus (1827-1895)

John A. Broadus had taught Greek at the University of Virginia, where he served as pastor of the Charlottesville Baptist Church. Forsaking a promising, brilliant future in the Old Dominion (Virginia), Dr. Broadus went to Greenville, South Carolina, to help pioneer the founding of SBTS. Here he served as Professor of New Testament and Homiletics from 1859 until his death in 1895 and as president from 1889 to 1895. Long remembered for his practical wisdom, Dr. Broadus kept alive the old proverb that there are three basic requisites for founding an institution of learning: brains, books, and bricks: "Our brethren usually begin at the wrong end of the three b's; they spend all their money for bricks, have nothing to buy books, and must take such brains as they can pick up. But our brethren ought to begin at the other end of the three b's." [3]

Southern Seminary held her first commencement in 1861; then the Civil War broke out, and the school closed, not to reopen until after the war. Early in the summer of 1865, Chairman Boyce conferred with his colleagues concerning the threatening end of the seminary's existence. Here, it was Dr. Boyce who soberly advised, "Suppose we quietly agree that the seminary may die, but we'll die first." When the school did reopen on November 1, it was with only seven students. In Homiletics, Dr. Broadus had only one student, and he was blind. Dr. Broadus gave this student the best that he had. The carefully prepared lectures for that blind brother became the basis of one of Dr. John Broadus's classic works, *On the Preparation and Delivery of Sermons* (1870).

Other works by Broadus include his well-known *Commentary on the Gospel of Matthew* (1886) and his *Memoir of James Petigru Boyce* (1893). He amplifies his strong views on biblical inerrancy in his *Paramount and Permanent Authority of the Bible* (1887). Dr. Broadus built upon a solid rock.

The Toy Case

Crawford Howell Toy, a brilliant, young Southern Seminary student, made a profession of faith in Christ and was baptized by Dr. Broadus, who took this Old Testament scholar under his wings until he graduated. Following the Civil War, young Toy studied in various German universities, then returned to join the SBTS faculty in 1869. It was not the same Crawford H. Toy, however, who had sat at the feet of John Broadus. Toy had changed; he now had a quiet tolerance toward Liberalism. Soon, however, Toy would give a supportive voice to his now silent views. [4] Broadus himself tells the story:

Dr. Toy became a pronounced evolutionist and Darwinian, giving once a popular lecture in Greenville to interpret and advocate Darwin's views of the origin of man. About the same time he became acquainted with Kuenen's works on the Old Testament, presenting the now well-known evolutionist reconstruction of the history of Israel and relocation of the leading Old Testament documents. These works, and kindred materials coming from Wellhausen and others in Germany, profoundly interested Dr. Toy. . . . If the Darwinian theory of the origin of man has been accepted, then it becomes easy to conclude that the first chapter of Genesis is by no means true history. From this starting-point, and pressed by a desire to reconstruct the history on evolutionary principles, one might easily persuade himself that in numerous other cases . . . the Old Testament account is incorrect. This persuasion would seem to the critic to justify his removing various books and portions of books into other periods of the history of Israel, so as to make that history a regular evolution from simpler to more complex. For example, it is held that the laws of Moses cannot have arisen in that early and simpler stage of Israelitish history to which Moses belonged, but only in a much later and more highly developed period. . . . Then the passion grows stronger for so re-locating and reconstructing as to make everything in the history of Israel a mere natural evolution. [5]

Recognizing and honestly admitting that he had departed from the historic Christian position on the total inerrancy of the Bible, Toy in 1879 submitted a letter of resignation which the trustees accepted. This was only two years after the seminary's move from Greenville to Louisville. Dr. Broadus describes the scene of Toy's departure at the Louisville railway station: "Throwing his left arm around Toy's neck, Dr. Boyce lifted the right arm before him, and said, in a passion of grief, 'Oh, Toy, I would freely give that arm to be cut off if you could be where you were five years ago, and stay there.'"[6]

Toy went on to become Professor of Hebrew at Harvard. He even joined the Unitarian Church there in Cambridge, Massachusetts, and the Unitarian Sunday

School Board published one of his books.[7] It is difficult to imagine that at one time Crawford Toy had considered giving his life on the mission field. In fact, Toy and Lottie Moon, the famous Southern Baptist missionary to China, had seriously considered marriage. Rejecting Crawford's proposal the same year as his resignation from the seminary, Lottie regarded his theological ideas as untenable. She had carefully read the books which Toy had recommended to her; this is evident from the marginal notations in her copies. A relative asked her in her later years if she had ever been in love; Lottie Moon answered, "Yes, but God had first claim on my life, and since the two conflicted, there could be no question about the result."[8]

Lottie Moon spent forty years in China, and in 1888 she wrote a desperate appeal for more missionaries, which resulted in a great Christmas offering which has now become tradition in Southern Baptist life. In the midst of one of her deepest trials Lottie wrote, "I hope no missionary will be as lonely as I have been." When the Chinese suffered famine, she starved with them. Literally starving, Lottie Moon collapsed and died aboard a ship in Kobe, Japan, on Christmas Eve, 1912. Many Baptists today have never seriously considered the biblical principles for which Miss Moon lived and died.

For many years now SBC schools have accepted and propagated the same views which Lottie Moon had so sacrificially rejected. For years, the Southern Baptist Sunday School Board in Nashville has endorsed, published, and promoted views identical to those of Crawford Toy. In fact, views far more radical than Toy's appear regularly in Broadman Press materials, as later chapters of this book will amply demonstrate. Over the years the constant assault from Satan's insidious arsenal of deception has gradually conditioned the silent majority to tolerate views which Southern Baptist pioneers once regarded as heretical and dedicated their lives to combatting. It is vital that Southern Baptists learn this lesson from their history.

William H. Whitsitt (1841-1911)

Before joining Southern Seminary's faculty, William H. Whitsitt had been a chaplain in the Civil War and had served as a Baptist pastor in Albany, Georgia. He was a SBTS professor from 1872 to 1899 and the seminary's third president from 1895 to 1899. His resignation resulted from a controversy over baptism.

Whitsitt, a dedicated historian, traveled to England and made intensive studies into Baptist origins. Concluding that English Baptists had not discovered and practiced immersion until 1641, Whitsitt published his findings in *Johnson's Universal Cyclopaedia.* Unwilling to tolerate such "innovative research," Southern Baptist pastors rose up in protest. The SBTS trustees asked for and received Whitsitt's resignation.

Edgar Young Mullins (1860-1928)

Edgar Y. Mullins is the transitional figure who represented a shift among many Baptists from an absolute view of verbal, plenary inspiration to more pragmatic and tolerant views. With him the great house began to shift from its historic rock. Mullins had served as a pastor in churches in Kentucky, Maryland, and Massachusetts before joining the SBTS faculty. A generally "conservative" Bible scholar, Mullins taught theology and authored several books; [9] he served as SBTS's fourth president from 1899 until his death in 1928. He also served as president of the Southern Baptist Convention from 1921 to 1923. [10]

His book *Christian Religion in its Doctrinal Expression* (1917), though generally conservative, places great emphasis upon experiential theology. Influenced by the psychologist-philosopher William James (1842-1910), Mullins allowed his work to be dominated by *pragmatism,* the teaching that the truth of a doctrine must be tested by its practical consequences. His was an inductive approach into the Bible on the basis of religious experience, rather than a deductive approach based upon the revealed precepts of God's Word (pp. 49-81). The *Review and Expositor* carried a review of Mullins's book as late as 1984 and described it in glowing terms.

John Richard Sampey (1863-1946)

Graduating from SBTS in 1885, John R. Sampey became Dr. Broadus's assistant and also served as librarian. Sampey soon became the leading Southern Baptist Old Testament specialist of his day. As Professor of Hebrew and Old Testament, he published his firm belief in the Mosaic authorship of the Pentateuch and in the prophet Isaiah's genuine authorship in the book which bears his name.[11] Dr. Sampey, however, with a gentlemanly tolerance, typical of old Southern Baptists, opened the door for new views to enter—views which the professor's own students would carry to radical extremes.

In 1922 the *System Bible Study* appeared; this claimed to be a compilation of Bible helps "by many of the world's greatest Bible scholars." In this popular book, Dr. Sampey wrote the "historical digest" of the Old Testament books. In his discussion of the Genesis account of creation, Sampey takes the "long-day" view of creation and capitulates to the theistic evolutionists' view:

> The fact that the creation of the sun is placed in the fourth day is proof that we do not have in this chapter a strictly scientific account of the events sketched; for no modern scientist would place the creation of the sun after that of the earth. While the scientist must admire much in this sketch of the creative process as anticipating some of the views of modern students of nature, he would not interpret the Hebrew story as a cold and scientifically accurate account of the order of events. It is a popular account with the emphasis on the religious element, attention being drawn to the Divine activity throughout the story. The long creative process is compressed within the limits of a week of days. The author evidently wished to put emphasis on the observance of the Sabbath.[12]

Dr. Sampey succeeded Broadus as a member of the International Uniform Sunday School Lesson Committee, on which he served for forty-six years. He was president of SBTS from 1929 to 1942 and president of the SBC from 1936 to 1938. He was generally a sound, conservative man, with a glowing testimony of his salvation experience, but Dr. Sampey, along with Dr.

Mullins, allowed the camel to get his nose into the denominational tent.

Archibald Thomas Robertson (1863-1934)

Dr. A. T. Robertson–America's greatest Greek scholar– was Professor of Greek and New Testament Interpretation at SBTS for forty-six years, from 1888 to his death in 1934. A prolific author of forty-five books, [13] "Dr. Bob," as his students called him, repeatedly defended the authenticity, authority, verbal plenary inspiration, and inerrancy of the whole Bible. Liberals have long desired to claim Dr. Robertson for his erudition, but his books are completely void of liberal views. It is true that he would not associate himself with the J. Frank Norris movement, but neither would many other Fundamentalists.

Dr. Robertson did dedicate his *Word Pictures in the New Testament* to Adolf Deissmann of Berlin, "who has done so much to make the words of the New Testament glow with life," as the dedicatory page states. It is also true that in his book *The New Citizenship* Dr. Robertson appeals to the works of social gospel advocates Washington Gladden and Walter Rauschenbusch. However, Robertson never strays beyond biblical revelation, and he expresses his regret that Rauschenbusch failed to emphasize personal salvation. [14]

As for his attitudes toward the new evolutionary views, Dr. Robertson quietly agreed with Drs. Mullins and Sampey in their opposition to Fundamentalists' efforts to ban the teaching of evolution from the public schools. Never once, however, does any trace of sympathy toward evolution itself appear in his many books. It was only a rare moment during a small, informal classroom discussion that Dr. Robertson reportedly expressed a sign of intimidation toward Darwinism. According to one of his students' shorthand notes, Robertson allegedly made the following statement, apparently in answer to a student's question: "I am willing to believe in it [evolution], I rather do, but not in atheistic evolution ... I say, write 'God' at the top, and what if He did use evolution? I can stand it if the monkeys can. . . . If He did do it that way, He still did it."[15] The quotation, however, seems completely inconsistent with Dr. Robertson's extensive writings. Since he could have simply been speaking facetiously and since the context of the remark can never be known, no one should ever attempt to use that student's hastily written notes to prove anything. We note the matter here only because it appears in Dr. Robertson's official biography by Everett Gill.

Endnotes

1. Basil Manly, Jr., *The Bible Doctrine of Inspiration Explained and Vindicated* (New York: A. C. Armstrong and Son, 1888); see also his article "Why and How to Study the Bible," *Western Recorder,* September 4, 1879. This was the Kentucky Southern Baptist state paper.

2. Porter Routh, *Chosen for Leadership* (Nashville: Broadman, 1976), p. 18.

3. John A. Broadus, *Memoir of James Petigru Boyce* (New York: A. C. Armstrong and Son, 1893), p. 153.

4. See George William Gardner, "Class Notebook for Old Testament Interpretation under C. H. Toy," Fall 1876. This notebook rests in the treasure room at Southwestern Baptist Theological Seminary's Fleming Library.

5. Broadus, op. cit., pp. 260-61.

6. Ibid., pp. 263-64.

7. C. H. Toy, *The History of the Religion of Israel* (Boston: Unitarian Sunday School Society, 1894).

8. Irwin T. Hyatt, *Our Ordered Lives* (Cambridge, Mass.: Harvard University Press, 1976), p. 99.

9. Most significant are *Christianity at the Cross Roads* (Nashville: Sunday School Board of the SBC, 1924); *The Christian Religion in Its Doctrinal Expression* (Valley Forge, Pa.: Judson Press, 1917); and *Freedom and Authority in Religion* (Philadelphia: The Griffith and Rowland Press, 1913); see also his *Axioms of Religion* (Valley Forge, Pa.: Judson Press, 1908).

LIBRARY
BRYAN COLLEGE
DAYTON, TENN. 37321

10. For an excellent discussion of E. Y. Mullins, see L. Russ Bush and Tom J. Nettles, *Baptists and the Bible* (Chicago: Moody Press, 1980), pp. 286-303.

11. John R. Sampey, *The Heart of the Old Testament: A Manual for Christian Students* (Nashville: Sunday School Board of the SBC, 1909), pp. 73-74 and 168-70.

12. *System Bible Study* (Chicago: The System Bible Co., 1922), p. 51.

13. A. T. Robertson's major titles include these: *A New Short Grammar of the Greek Testament; A Grammar of the Greek New Testament in the Light of Historical Research; The Minister and His Greek New Testament; An Introduction to the Textual Criticism of the New Testament; Studies in the Text of the New Testament; Luke the Historian in the Light of Research; Paul and the Intellectuals; Paul's Joy in Christ; The Glory of the Ministry;* and *Making Good in the Ministry.*

14. A. T. Robertson, *The New Citizenship: The Christian Facing a New World Order* (New York: Fleming H. Revell Co., 1919), pp. 145-57.

15. Everett Gill, *A. T. Robertson: A Biography* (New York: Macmillan Co., 1943), p. 181.

Chapter Five

Southern Seminary Continued—The Fall into Apostasy

Southern Baptist Theological Seminary Presidents Ellis A. Fuller and Duke K. McCall Invite Liberalism

Southern Baptist Theological Seminary finally fell into apostasy under the administration of her sixth president, Dr. Ellis A. Fuller—president from 1942 to 1950. It was Fuller who had George A. Buttrick bring the E. Y. Mullins Lectures in 1943. Buttrick was the liberal pastor of the Madison Avenue Presbyterian Church in New York City. Liberalism came swiftly upon Southern Seminary; this was only nine years after A. T. Robertson's death. Fuller then brought in Dr. John Mackay, the liberal president of Princeton Seminary, to lecture in 1947, the same year that he brought Dr. Nels F. S. Ferré to deliver the Julius B. Gay Lectures at Southern.

Nels F. S. Ferré: Ferré was the blaspheming, apostate Professor of Christian Theology at Andover Newton Theological School (a Northern Baptist Convention seminary) at Newton Centre, Massachusetts. Ferré published his 1947 SBTS lectures as the book *Pillars of*

32

Faith. On page 48 he asserted that both the canon and the inspiration of the Scriptures are open questions. "To many," said Ferré, "the way in which the Bible is indiscriminately worshiped is offensive to their intelligence and finer sensitivity" and "many of us cannot honestly accept the unintelligent use made of the Bible by many who profess to love it the most." On page 95 he denied the claim for "Bible accuracy in matters of science and history." Setting himself up as a judge over the morality of the Bible, the lecturer scorned "the outworn morality of parts of the Old Testament."

As conservatives launched their attacks against Ferré's presence at Southern Seminary, President Fuller and his colleagues pleaded that they had been unaware of the professor's teachings. Ferré, however, had widely published his views in three major books between 1942 and 1946. In *The Christian Faith,* published in 1942, Ferré denied that Jesus is "a supernatural Saviour with an eternally pre-existing personality" (page 34). On page 102 he said, "God differs from all men, including Jesus, in that His personality alone is eternal and the Creator of all other personalities." Ferré charged that Fundamentalists had perverted such doctrines as the virgin birth by taking them literally (page 103). Ferré admitted that he did "not teach the pre-existence of the personality of Jesus. . . . The historic personality of Jesus was fully human" (page 110).

In his book *Return to Christianity* (1943), Ferré spoke positively in favor of Marxism and socialism and castigated the historic Christian faith. [1] It is no wonder that ten years later, in the January 15, 1953, issue of the Communist *Daily Worker*, Nels Ferré's name would appear as a signer of an "Appeal for Amnesty" for eleven Communist Party leaders. Even in his third book published prior to his speaking at SBTS, Ferré had embraced and expounded Kierkegaardian Existentialism, which denies the reality of biblical absolutes. This book, *Faith and Reason* (1946), would become a text at Southern Seminary.

As other books by Ferré rapidly appeared after 1949, the author, who was now Professor of Philosophical Theology at Vanderbilt University, became very much in demand as a speaker at Baptist gatherings—north and south. In his *Christianity and Society* (1950), Ferré embraces Marxism throughout. For example, he asserts that "Marxism may be God's means to Christian fulfillment in history" (p. 239). The following year, Ferré published his *Christian Understanding of God*, in which he asserts, "We have no way of knowing that Jesus was sinless" (p. 186). On page 191, he adds, "Mary, we remember, was found pregnant before her engagement to mild Joseph. Nazareth was hard by a Roman garrison where the soldiers were German mercenaries. Jesus is . . . reported throughout. . . the history of art . . . to have been blond. . . . Hence Jesus must have been the child of a German soldier! After all, . . . such is the experience of many girls near military camps. . . . Who can deny that such a conjecture *could* be true?"

Nels Ferré would go on to publish his *Sun and the Umbrella*, which he described as "a parable for today." According to Ferré's parable, people once lived in an "old barn," very wide but with a low ceiling and no windows. That was the "House of Legality," lighted by dim, smoky "Lamps of the Law." Then one day a prophet came (Jesus) and announced that there was a bright light outside this old barn. So they killed this "imposter," but some, like the New Testament apostles, came out of the House of Legality. However, they could not stand the bright sun (full knowledge), so they built themselves umbrellas to keep off the sunlight. These hindering umbrellas were belief in such "superstitions" as Christ's deity, virgin birth, substitutionary atonement, and second coming. In Ferré's parable one young man (evidently the author himself) goes out into the sunshine, discarding all the umbrellas; he urges others to do likewise. Here are sample quotations from *The Sun and the Umbrella*: "The use of the Bible as the final authority for Christian truth is idolatry" (p. 39). "Jesus never was nor became God" (p. 112). "Hinduism is good and wise" (p. 117). There can be "the Hindu branch of the Church of the living God" (p. 122). The book's jacket carried an endorsement from Dr. Edwin McNeill Poteat, Southern Baptist minister of Pullen Memorial Baptist Church in Raleigh, North Carolina.

Poteat was a "consulting editor" of the infamous *Interpreter's Bible.* [2]

The Interpreter's Bible: SBTS president, Dr. Ellis A. Fuller, not only brought apostate speakers to the seminary but as a consulting editor helped to produce and promote this twelve-volume set which appeared between 1951 and 1957. Contributors included general editor George A. Buttrick, Henry Sloane Coffin from Union Theological Seminary in New York, Elmer G. Homrighausen from Princeton Seminary, and the Methodist Bishop Gerald Kennedy.

Volume one says "the evidence is clear" that books of the Bible "contain inaccuracies, inconsistencies, interpolations, omissions, over-statements, and so forth" (p. 16). Moreover, "Isaiah is not one book, as a cursory reading of the Bible would assume, for there is a gap of centuries between the end of ch. 39 and the beginning of ch. 40" (p. 168). In the same volume of this set which Baptist Bookstores across the nation still stock and promote, the God of Genesis is a local deity which the Hebrews picked up in Hebron. Most of Genesis is mere legend (p. 442f.). In the "explanation" of the Day of Atonement in Exodus 12, the *Interpreter's Bible* simply depicts the Hebrews as cruel, vile savages who received pleasure from cutting the throats of struggling little lambs and watching hot blood spurt (pp. 917-18).

The New Testament volumes show no more fidelity than the Old Testament ones. Volume seven, for example, rejects miracles such as the feeding of the 5000 and Jesus' walking on the water (pp. 127-28). In fact, some of the Gospel accounts of Christ's resurrection supposedly "contain legendary details" such as Jesus eating "boiled" fish (p. 144). Southern Baptist newspapers such as the *Baptist Program* carried ads (some full-page) to promote this set which offends Bible believers everywhere. Dr. Ellis Fuller endorsed the *Interpreter's Bible* and served on its editorial board. Toleration for apostasy leads to support of apostasy. The sequence seems to be silence first, then sympathy and support. A little leaven leavens the whole lump. The general editor of the *Interpreter's Bible*, George A. Buttrick, soon accepted an invitation from another

Southern Baptist institution, New Orleans Baptist Theological Seminary, to speak at their Pastors' Conference.

Duke K. McCall, a Furman University graduate, had been president of New Orleans Baptist Theological Seminary from 1943 to 1946 and Executive Secretary of the SBC Executive Committee from 1946 to 1951. McCall was president of SBTS from 1951 to 1982; he continues to serve as the institution's chancellor. [3] Less than a year before McCall's retirement from the presidency, a SBTS trustee admitted that this man had led the institution into the mainstream of Liberalism and even into cooperation with the World Council of Churches. [4] Further discussions of McCall, who has also served for years as president of the Baptist World Alliance, will appear throughout the remainder of this book. For more than thirty years this man has been at the helm of the SBTS.

Eric C. Rust: When President Duke K. McCall brought Dr. Eric Rust to teach philosophy at Southern Baptist Theological Seminary in the 1950s, Rust had already published his liberal views in his *Christian Understanding of History* (1947) and *Nature and Man in Biblical Thought* (1953). In the latter work Rust, writing as Professor of Biblical Theology at Crozer Theological Seminary, had said this regarding the Genesis account of creation: "The Old Testament begins with two myths of creation, both of which reflect elements from the pagan mythology of surrounding peoples" (p. 20).

Addressing the 1959 Pastors' Conference at the Southern Baptist-supported University of Richmond, Rust offered his opinions on the stories of Noah and the ark and the Garden of Eden. These accounts, says Rust, are merely parables or myths, never intended to be taken literally:

> I have a smart cookie of a girl who, two years ago, came home from high school where she'd been doing biology, and she had been to Sunday School (not where Dr. Polhill and I are members or he was pastor and I was member, but at another church nearer our home where the pastor is not so dead honest and a lot of the

36

teachers ought never to be teaching, at least not high school girls like her) and she came to me, and she said, "Daddy, how did Noah get all the animals in that silly little ark?" *"Well, I guess that's a parable,"* I said. "I wonder very much whether Noah ever lived in that sense." So she said, "Well, wait a minute. What do you mean?" "Well," I said, "I guess there's (uh) (this is what Albright says, by the way, too,) I guess there was a kind of historical basis in the story. When the glaciers retreated and the glacial age finished, the ice melted, and tremendous floods came down upon the plains. Why, our Appalachian hills are a result of that here. And slowly the earth got flooded and men had to do something to escape, and some built boats. *And obviously, more than one man built a boat* because there was Noah among the Jews and among the Babylonians there was Utnapishtim and you should go all over the world, and you find this kind of story appearing about people who built boats to escape from the flood. So, quite obviously, there was a primordial flood, and some people escaped in boats. But," I said, "this story has been lifted up deeper than a mere historical happening. It has become revelatory of three things."

The Garden. Well, was there a Garden? Now if I listen to what the scientist tells me, I can't say yea or nay. I mean, this is, there may have been a garden. But after all, as my young hopeful said the other day, well, about two years ago when I told her about Noah, "Well, that means that the story of the Garden is a parable, too, Daddy," I said, "Yes." She said, "Well that explains where Cain got his wife from." Now, really, I mean if there was only one Adam created and Eve was made out of his rib, well, heaven help us, ever counted your ribs to find out? I mean this seriously, I mean . . . *You see, take it literally, and you land yourself* (uh) *you make yourself a laughing stock for intelligent people.* But that doesn't mean you have to cast this out. Spiritually, it's true. Parabolically, it's true. [5]

In his book *Science and Faith* (1967), Rust embraces evolutionary views and reduces the first eleven chapters of Genesis to the non-historical. [6] The above are only samples of this Southern Baptist Theological Seminary professor's message to young seminary students entrusted to this institution's care. A discussion of Rust's contribution to the *Broadman Bible Commentary* appears in chapter fourteen.

T. O. Hall: Another McCall-administration faculty member at Southern Baptist Theological Seminary was Dr. T. O. Hall, who in 1953 published his neo-orthodox views of the Bible. He wrote that "the writers of holy scripture had vital experiences with God. Having come to know Him by experience, they were led to record these experiences. This is not the Word of God. It is a record of it."[7]

Conference Speakers—Robert J. McCracken and H. H. Rowley: From the earliest days of Duke K. McCall's presidency, he brought in notoriously liberal speakers. For example, the chief speakers for the 1955 Southern Baptist Theological Seminary E. Y. Mullins Lectures (March 8-12) were Dr. Robert J. McCracken, who was the liberal Harry Emerson Fosdick's successor at Riverside Church in New York City, and Dr. H. H. Rowley, professor of Old Testament in England's University of Manchester. Rowley's Southern Seminary lectures soon appeared in a new book, *The Unity of the Bible*, which reveals his "historical-critical method." The professor instructed his Baptist audience that "none of the main documents on which the Pentateuch rests can have been compiled until long after the time of Moses.... There is little which we can with confidence ascribe to Moses."[8] The list of radical speakers has continued to the present day.

William E. Hull

After graduating from Southern Baptist Theological Seminary, William E. Hull continued his studies at the University of Göttingen in Germany, then returned to become Professor of New Testament Interpretation at Southern Seminary. His Southern Baptist Theological Seminary inaugural address appeared in the *Review and Expositor* in 1965. In this message, which Hull entitled

"The Relevance of the New Testament," the professor argues that the Scriptures are simply not "relevant" beyond their own historical setting. "Liberals and conservatives alike," asserts Hull, "have had to learn the stubborn truth that there simply is no . . . timeless revelation which transcends the historical particularity in which it was originally expressed."[9] Hull uses the typical terminology of Neo-orthodoxy. "The Christian message in any age," argues Hull, "is seen not as a set of self-contained, timeless propositions, but as the address of God set over against the world in dialogue, a confrontation in which truth is disclosed in encounter."[10] It may come as a surprise to Southern Baptists who believe that God delivered an absolute, unchanging, once-for-all message to discover that Hull says, "Our message today is not . . . the same as the New Testament message, any more than our modern world is identical with the first century world."[11] Therefore, concludes this Southern Seminary professor, "We are not to say to Louisville the same thing that Paul said to Corinth."[12]

In 1969 Dr. Hull received a promotion; in his published inaugural address as the new Dean of the School of Theology, he acknowledged his indebtedness to radical theologians such as Rudolf Bultmann, Emil Brunner, Sören Kierkegaard, C. H. Dodd, and Dietrich Bonhoeffer. These were the theologians who had led William Hull to move on beyond those "who in the name of 'classical learning' or the 'sole sufficiency of the Bible' or the 'historical Baptist position' would have us only study the past."[13]

In 1970 Hull preached a sermon at the Crescent Hill Baptist Church in Louisville, where many of the SBTS faculty and students have their membership. In this published message, entitled "Shall We Call the Bible Infallible?," Hull went to great lengths to deny the Bible's inerrancy. "The infallible text is a theory, not a reality," said Hull.[14] The message concludes that "it is not wise to call the Bible infallible."[15] This sermon appeared in *The Baptist Program,* a magazine distributed to Southern Baptist leaders at every level. The magazine's editor, W. C. Fields, soon received a promotion by the Executive

39

Committee of the SBC, while the SBTS trustees elevated Hull himself to the position of Provost.

When William E. Hull finally resigned in 1975 to become pastor of First Baptist Church in Shreveport, Louisiana, President Duke McCall was careful to explain that Hull was not fired. Southern Seminary has never repudiated a single proposition which Hull taught. [16] He remains a popular speaker at Southern Baptist gatherings, and his published materials receive wide promotion. For twenty-one years Hull freely taught his radical ideas at Southern, and he has enjoyed the prestige of being an author of the *Broadman Bible Commentary.*

E. Glenn Hinson

Dr. E. Glenn Hinson was Professor of Church History at SBTS for more than twenty years before his recent move to Wake Forest University. [17] He helped to establish Baptist Peacemaker, an organization whose purpose is to silence the conservatives in the SBC.

In his book *Jesus Christ* (1977), Hinson agrees with liberal higher critics who attack the Gospel miracles: "A number of modern scholars have discounted the healing narratives and miracle stories, ascribing them to primitive mythology and early Christian embellishment. Some embellishment undoubtedly occurred" (p. 66). In a remarkable statement in chapter 5, Hinson asserts that the early church corrupted the teachings of Christ: "Comparative study of his parables and other sayings in Gospel parallels turns up evidence of embellishment, changes of audience, hortatory use by the Church, influences of the Church's situation, and allegorization. Form critics have pointed out that this process of modification preceded the written documents. Indeed, Jesus' sayings circulated as independent pericopae over a thirty to fifty year period before being collected, the churches still expecting his return. A delay of Christ's return, or Parousia, finally forced the writing down of his words but not before they had undergone considerable reshaping. What was written down, therefore, represented the mind of the early Church much more than the mind of Jesus himself. When sifted,

it leaves little that one can confidently attribute to Jesus
himself"(p. 78). Hinson further asserts that "Jesus himself
had no consciousness of 'divinity'" (pp. 83-84), and that
"the risen Christ had not a physical but a spiritual body.
Flesh and blood, Paul contended, cannot inherit the
kingdom of God"(p. 111).

Frank Stagg

Dr. Frank Stagg, a SBTS graduate, taught for many
years at New Orleans Baptist Theological Seminary before
joining Southern Seminary's faculty. [18] Until his recent
retirement, Stagg was SBTS's "Senior Professor of New
Testament Interpretation." A reporter in 1981 cited
Professor Stagg's unreasonable, blistering attack upon the
conservative view of a young earth: "The theory that God
made a young earth (not more than 10,000 years old!) to
look old (instant antiquity!) invites the deplorable idea
that God cannot be trusted." [19]

Broadman Press had published Stagg's Liberalism
back in 1962 in his *New Testament Theology*, in which
he clearly propagates the ancient heresy of modalism,
which denies the distinct personalities of the Son and
Spirit. This view asserts that there is only one divine
person—the Father. The Son and Spirit are simply
"modes" or manifestations of the Father, and they are in
no way distinct from the Father. They have no distinct
identification. Stagg explains:

> The Spirit is the continuing presence of Jesus Christ
> (John 20:22). Paul could write of the risen Christ and
> the Holy Spirit in such a way as to make the terms
> almost interchangeable (Romans 8:9f.). The New
> Testament knows God as Father, Son, and Holy Spirit,
> yet it knows God as one alone. One may suggest that
> in his transcendence he is known as Father, in his
> immanence as Holy Spirit, and in his ultimate presence
> and self-disclosure as Son. Yet to raise metaphysical
> questions and to offer rationales about the Trinity is
> to attempt to go beyond the New Testament. Its writers
> only knew that the "incredible" had happened: the God
> of the ages had visited earth in the person of Jesus of

41

Nazareth, and after the death of Jesus he continued his presence as the Holy Spirit. It is the uniqueness of the New Testament that the Father and the Spirit are understood in terms of Jesus Christ (pp. 39-40).

Using the phrase "God as Father, Son, and Holy Spirit," however, is far from asserting "God the Father, God the Son, and God the Holy Spirit," which Stagg and most other Liberals would avoid.

This Broadman publication denies the propitiating or satisfactory aspect of Christ's atonement: "Because propitiation is so linked to pagan ideas of the appeasement of God, it is not suitable for translating New Testament ideas. Expiation is not satisfactory, but it is not so definitely linked to pagan usage. It is not sound exegesis to obscure by the pagan idea of propitiation or appeasement the biblical emphasis upon the initiative of God in man's salvation" (p. 140). Stagg goes to great lengths to attack the historical Christian doctrine of Christ's work of satisfaction, as expressed by great men such as John Calvin: "Calvin taught that God was our enemy until he was reconciled to us by Christ, writing that Christ satisfied and propitiated the Father—'by this intercessor his wrath has been appeased.' But this is Calvin, not Holy Writ! . . . The Father does not need to punish the Son in order to win the right to forgive. . . . Sin in the New Testament is not viewed as an entity which can be offset by a good act; it is a broken relationship which must be restored, a sickness which must be cured" (p. 141). Says Stagg, whose salary came from the sacrificial gifts of Bible-believing Southern Baptists, "It goes far beyond the writer of Hebrews to add the idea that this death was an appeasement or satisfaction offered to the Father" (p. 144). After all, he adds, "In modern sports, a player may be taken from the game and be replaced by a 'substitute.' But Jesus never becomes our substitute in that sense" (p. 145).

Frank Stagg remains a popular Southern Baptist speaker. In 1984, for example, he addressed a SBTS "Woman's Conference."[20] He also wrote the commentary on Matthew in the *Broadman Bible Commentary*.

Dale Moody

Dr. Dale Moody taught as Senior Professor of Christian Theology at SBTS from 1948 to 1983. He denies the historicity of much of the Old Testament. Adam, Eve, Cain, and Abel "are only representative," according to Moody. Defending evolution, he once asked, "Why should conservative Christianity attempt to rule out the long biological process?"[21]

In his book, *The Word of Truth*,[22] Moody exalts such radicals as Paul Tillich and Friedrich Schleiermacher. Most of the book is a blatant attack on conservative theology and an endorsement of liberal European theologians. Moody had studied under Emil Brunner in Germany and had established neo-orthodox teaching at SBTS.

Ironically, conservative Southern Baptists tolerated Dale Moody's radical theology at Southern Seminary for thirty-five years, but when he published a denial of the doctrine of "eternal security," the Arkansas Baptist Convention rose up in protest, passing a resolution demanding Moody's resignation. After all, they insisted, some things are "worth fighting for." Moody's controversial material appears in his *Word of Truth* (pp. 348-65), published by Eerdmans in 1981. The SBTS trustees "relieved" Dale Moody of his teaching responsibilities as of July, 1983, with a full-pay "leave of absence" for one year.[23] Following his year's paid vacation, Moody decided against resuming his faculty position. After all, Southern Baptists had found something "worth fighting for." Moody continues, however, to teach his radical theological views in Baptist churches across the country.

Roy Lee Honeycutt

In 1982 Dr. Roy L. Honeycutt succeeded Duke McCall as president of SBTS. Honeycutt's liberal theology had appeared even in the 1960s, while he served on the editorial board of the *Broadman Bible Commentary*; he wrote the commentary on Exodus in volume one of this set while serving as Professor of Old Testament at Midwestern Baptist Theological Seminary.

Under Honeycutt's leadership, SBTS became the only seminary offering a master's degree in social work. In March 1984, the trustees approved twelve faculty additions for this new "School of Church Social Work." [24] Honeycutt, who recently declared a "holy war" against the conservative movement within the SBC, began his broad social appeal early in his administration. In 1983, for example, the SBTS "Ethics Club" invited an avowed homosexual, Samuel F. Dorr, to speak; Dorr was president of a local chapter of "Dignity/Integrity," a national homosexual organization. [25] Southern has also become the first Southern Baptist seminary to hire a woman to teach theology. Her name is Dr. Molly Marshall-Green, and she has served at least one church as pastor. [26] Honeycutt hired an ordained woman chaplain and has recently expressed his plans to get more women faculty and to do all that he can to promote their place in the ordained ministry. [27]

One of Honeycutt's most recent additions to his faculty is Kenneth L. Chafin, the new Carl Bates Professor of Christian Preaching. Chafin has been one of the most outspoken opponents of the conservative movement within the SBC. As President Roy Honeycutt himself recently wrote, "One charge to which Southern Seminary has never been guilty is that of being 'Fundamentalists.'" [28] As long ago as 1966 the *Baptist Challenge* documented some of Honeycutt's own liberal views, such as his claim that there are different levels of morality in the Bible, the Old Testament having the "lowest level." [29] Other outspoken Liberals such as Dr. Wayne Ward remain on Honeycutt's faculty. Ward clearly denies that the Bible is the infallible Word of God. [30] The 1984 SBC *Annual* lists him as Professor of Christian Theology at Southern Seminary (p. 411).

The Hollyfield Thesis

In 1976 Noel Wesley Hollyfield, Jr., wrote his thesis for the Master of Divinity degree at SBTS. The study is entitled "Sociological Analysis of the Degrees of 'Christian Orthodoxy' Among Selected Students in the

Southern Baptist Theological Seminary." A committee composed of G. Willis Bennett (chairman), E. Glenn Hinson, and Henlee Barnette read and approved the thesis. Their official approval indicates that they believed that the research was accurate and that its conclusions were valid.

Hollyfield's thesis strongly suggests that Modernism is having a devastating effect upon the students at Southern Seminary. Using thirty-seven questions, he polled between 9 and 10 percent of the student body and formulated several statistical tabulations. The chart on page 46 represents my own key findings from Hollyfield's research.

These figures generally indicate that Southern Seminary does not produce faith. It destroys faith. A look at just the Master of Divinity students alone suggests the following: 9 percent lost their faith in the existence of God while in seminary; 24 percent lost their faith in Jesus as the divine Son of God; 21 percent lost their belief in miracles; 24 percent lost their belief in the existence of the devil; 22 percent lost their belief in life beyond death; 33 percent lost their belief in the virgin birth; and 25 percent lost their belief that it is absolutely necessary to believe in Christ to be saved. The more education students receive at Southern Seminary, the less likely they believe that the Bible is true. [31]

Other Liberals on Honeycutt's Faculty

Other well-known Liberals on Honeycutt's faculty include Joseph A. Callaway, Page H. Kelley, John Joseph Owens (all of whom contributed to the *Broadman Bible Commentary*), and Paul D. Simmons, who lobbies for the pro-abortion movement.

Cooperative Program Support

The 1984 SBC *Annual* reports that this seminary received $4,649,927 from God's people through the Cooperative Program during the previous fiscal year (p. 73). Denominational leaders are projecting higher sums

Summary Data from the Hollyfield Thesis

Questions and Answers	Diploma Students	First Year M.Div.	Final Year M.Div.	Ph.D. & Th.M.
I know God really exists, and I have no doubt about it.	100%	74%	65%	63%
Jesus is the Divine Son of God, and I have no doubt about it.	100%	87%	63%	63%
I believe the miracles actually happened just as the Bible says they did.	96%	61%	40%	37%
The Devil actually exists: Completely true.	96%	66%	42%	37%
Probably true.	4%	18%	26%	15%
Probably not true.	0%	12%	23%	32%
Definitely not true.	0%	5%	9%	15%
There is life beyond death: Completely true.	100%	89%	67%	53%
Jesus was born of a virgin: Completely true.	96%	66%	33%	32%
Probably true.	4%	17%	33%	37%
Probably not true.	0%	14%	21%	15%
Definitely not true.	0%	2%	12%	15%
Jesus walked on water: Completely true.	96%	59%	44%	22%
Do you believe Jesus will actually return to earth some day? Definitely.	100%	79%	56%	53%
How necessary for salvation do you believe the following to be:				
Belief in Jesus as Saviour: Absolutely necessary.	100%	85%	60%	59%
Holding the Bible to be God's truth: Absolutely necessary.	73%	42%	33%	21%

for the coming years. The SBTS publication, *The Tie,* recently itself revealed inner links between this seminary and the Southern Baptist Cooperative Program. According to the March/April 1983 issue, five of the nine staff members of the SBC Stewardship Commission are alumni of SBTS and 45 percent of this school's budget comes directly from the Cooperative Program. It is amazing that Southern Baptist conservatives still claim that they are actually purging the seminaries. Even Duke K. McCall continues on as Southern Seminary's chancellor.

Endnotes

1. Nels F. S. Ferré, *Return to Christianity* (New York: Harper and Brothers, 1943); see especially page 66. Such attitudes permeate the entire book, however.

2. George A. Buttrick, ed., *The Interpreter's Bible*, 12 vols. (Nashville: Abingdon Press, 1951-57).

3. Harold Lindsell, *The Bible in the Balance* (Grand Rapids: Zondervan, 1979), pp. 121-25, 353-56. This is an excellent and thorough discussion of McCall by a Southern Baptist author.

4. *Southern Baptist Journal,* July/August 1981, p. 9.

5. Taped message by Eric C. Rust, published in part in *Southern Baptist Journal,* October 1980, p. 6. The emphasis is by the editor of the Journal.

6. Eric C. Rust, *Science and Faith* (New York: Oxford University Press, 1967); see also his *Christian Understanding of History* (London: Lutterworth Press, 1947); *Salvation History* (Richmond, John Knox Press, 1962); and *Evolutionary Philosophies and Contemporary Theology* (Philadelphia: Westminster Press, 1969).

7. *The Faith,* September 1953.

8. H. H. Rowley, *The Unity of the Bible* (Philadelphia: The Westminster Press, 1955), p. 21. For a more complete list of liberal E. Y. Mullins Lecturers, see *The Tie*, November/December 1984, p. 3. This is a Southern Baptist Theological Seminary publication.

9. *Review and Expositor*, Spring 1965, p. 190. Hull's relativistic philosophy and neo-orthodox theology had appeared even earlier in the *News Leader* of Richmond, Virginia, February 7, 1961, in which he launched a blistering attack upon Fundamentalism's absolutes.

10. *Review and Expositor*, Spring 1965, p. 192.

11. Ibid., p. 194.

12. Ibid., p. 195.

13. William E. Hull, *The Integrity of the Theological Curriculum* (Louisville: The Southern Baptist Theological Seminary, 1969), p. 5. This was the published version of Hull's inaugural address.

14. *The Baptist Program*, December 1970, p. 17. The Southern Baptist Sunday School Board had also used Hull to write the "Commentary on the Gospel of John," in Vol. 9 of the *Broadman Bible Commentary*, in which he applies the liberal Documentary Hypothesis to the Gospels.

15. *The Baptist Program*, December 1970, p. 18.

16. Additional documentation of William E. Hull's Liberalism appears in Harold Lindsell's *Bible in the Balance*, pp. 158-62; see also Lindsell's *Battle for the Bible* (Grand Rapids: Zondervan, 1976), pp. 93-95.

17. The 1984 SBC *Annual* (p. 44) lists E. Glenn Hinson as Professor of Church History at Southern Baptist Theological Seminary. This was the same year in which he moved to Wake Forest University.

18. The 1981 SBC *Annual* (p. 403) lists Frank Stagg as Senior Professor of New Testament Interpretation at Southern Baptist Theological Seminary.

19. *The Times-Picayune/The States-Item*, August 8, 1981. See also Harold Lindsell's discussion of Frank Stagg in his *Bible in the Balance*, pp. 154-57.

20. *The Tie*, November/December 1984, p. 9. This is a publication of Southern Baptist Theological Seminary.

21. *Review and Expositor*, Summer 1967, p. 345; see also Harold Lindsell's discussion of this article in *Bible in the Balance*, pp. 162-65.

22. Dale Moody, *The Word of Truth* (Grand Rapids: Eerdmans, 1981); see also Carl F. H. Henry's review of this work by Moody in *Eternity*, October 1981, p. 42. Henry concludes that the book is too liberal, especially on the doctrine of inspiration.

23. *The Capitol Voice*, July 1, 1983, p. 4.

24. *The Tie*, May/June 1984, p. 1.

25. *Southern Baptist Advocate*, May 1983, p. 2.

26. *Southern Baptist Advocate*, February/March 1984, p. 1f.; the 1984 SBC *Annual* lists Dr. Molly Marshall-Green as Assistant Professor of Theology (p. 411).

27. Ibid., p. 12.

28. *The Tie*, November/December 1984, p. 4.

29. *Baptist Challenge*, February 1966.

30. Wayne E. Ward and Joseph F. Green, eds., *Is the Bible a Human Book?* (Nashville: Broadman Press, 1970), pp. 71-82; see also William A. Powell, *The SBC Issue & Question* (Buchanan, Georgia: Baptist Missionary Service, Inc., 1977), pp. 100-121.

31. For another study of the Hollyfield thesis, see Harold Lindsell's *Bible in the Balance*, pp. 172-75.

Chapter Six

Southwestern Baptist Theological Seminary

Southwestern Baptist Theological Seminary came into existence as a result of a day of prayer and meditation in the life of B. H. Carroll as he rode a train in west Texas. As the plan for the seminary unfolded, the man of God stood to his feet in the speeding train car. It must have been an impressive sight to other passengers: a crowded railroad coach and a great tall preacher with flowing white beard, standing like an Old Testament prophet, completely unaware of the people around him and seeing only the mission which God had set before him.

Benajah Harvey Carroll (1843-1914)

B. H. Carroll had begun his adult life as a skeptic. Following his experiences with life and death in the Civil War, however, twenty-two-year-old Carroll accepted Christ after hearing the final sermon of a neighborhood Methodist brush-arbor revival.

So rapid was his spiritual progress that only twelve years later the SBC asked Carroll to deliver the annual Convention sermon. For twenty-nine years Carroll served as pastor of the First Baptist Church of Waco, Texas, and for thirty-two years he was Professor of Bible and Theology at Baylor University. In 1905 he reorganized the theology department of Baylor University into Baylor Theological Seminary. In 1907 the Texas Baptist Convention authorized the separation of the seminary from the university and gave it a new name, Southwestern Baptist Theological Seminary, and a separate board of trustees. The seminary received her charter in 1908 and moved from Waco to Fort Worth in 1910, with B. H. Carroll serving as the first president until his death in 1914. In 1925 control of the seminary passed from the state convention to the SBC.

Carroll held staunchly to the verbal, plenary inspiration, full inerrancy, and absolute authority of the complete Bible, and he expressed these views repeatedly in thirty-three published volumes, including his *Interpretation of the English Bible.* [1] Shortly before his death, Carroll related the following to his soon-to-be successor, Dr. Lee R. Scarborough:

> You will be elected president of the seminary. I want you, if there ever comes heresy in your faculty, to take it to your faculty. If they won't hear you, take it to the trustees. If they won't hear you, take it to the conventions that appointed them. If they won't hear you, take it to the common Baptists. They will hear you. . . . I charge you in the name of Jesus Christ to keep [the seminary] lashed to the old Gospel of Jesus Christ. [2]

Lee Rutland Scarborough (1870-1945)

Lee Scarborough served at Southwestern from 1908 until his death in 1945. He was professor of evangelism, becoming the school's second president in 1914. He helped to establish the SBC's Cooperative Program in 1925. Dr. Scarborough was a conservative man—very evangelistic, warm, and practical, but his attitude of tolerance toward Liberals and his opposition to Fundamentalism helped to pave the way for the ultimate sellout of the SBC to apostasy.

Other Early Southwestern Leaders

In her earliest days, Southwestern had an array of such great, Bible-believing men of God as these: A. H. Newman, the noted Baptist historian, who also served as dean; C. B. Williams; Calvin Goodspeed; J. D. Ray; J. J. Reeve; James B. Gambrell; Walter T. Conner, who during thirty-nine years of service wrote twelve books expressing his strong belief in the Bible's inerrancy and authority; and of course Harvey E. Dana, Professor of New Testament who in 1923 published his *Authority of the Holy Scriptures: A Brief Story of the Problems of Biblical Criticism.* In 1930 Dr. J. B. Cranfill collected B. H. Carroll's lectures on inspiration, and Fleming H. Revell published them under the title *The Inspiration of the Bible.* Southwestern has a glorious heritage indeed.

The Fall into Apostasy

Southwestern, with more than 5,000 students, is the largest seminary in the world. Most observers consider it the most conservative of the six Southern Baptist seminaries. As early as 1928, however, J. M. Price, who taught sociology for ten years at Southwestern, published his *Christianity and Social Problems,* which expressed major social-gospel ideas such as the church's duty to establish the "kingdom of God" on earth by Christianizing the social order. [3] While Price, teaching under the Scarborough administration, was by no means a complete Modernist or Liberal, he was attracted to the tolerant and liberalizing trends of his day. During the 1940s Southwestern began using occasional liberal guest speakers such as Dr. E. T. Dahlberg, chairman of the Executive Committee of the Federal Council of Churches (now the National Council of Churches). It was much later, however, that Southwestern's faculty or administration began publishing liberal views. Even today there is still a very conservative element at this seminary, but it is definitely a mixed multitude, with strong men serving as window dressing for error.

In the 1950s Dr. Charles A. Trentham served for seven years as Professor of Systematic Theology at Southwestern.

Trentham, a Southwestern graduate, had taught in Baylor University's Department of Religion, and he would go on to become the pastor of the First Baptist Church in Knoxville, Tennessee. Trentham, however, publicly declared his opinion that any reference to the Bible as the infallible and authoritative Word of God is a "heresy." The Virginia Baptist Convention's official organ, the *Religious Herald,* quoted the professor as saying, "This is our heresy; we have made claims for the Bible which it does not make for itself. Let us remember that heresies are not always beliefs that are totally false. There may be an overemphasis on a part of the truth which claims to be the whole truth. The part of the truth which is being overemphasized today is that the Bible itself is the Word of God and as such is the infallible authority in religion."[4] Trentham was once hailed as "one of the most dynamic and influential preachers in the Southern Baptist Convention. . . . He has contributed many articles to various Southern Baptist periodicals and is the author of two books. . . . He has served his denomination as a member of various Boards, Committees, and Commissions. He carries a heavy schedule of speaking engagements at schools, churches, and denominational gatherings." That quotation comes from an official brochure from Midwestern Baptist Theological Seminary in Kansas City, Missouri, promoting Trentham's 1963 H. I. Hester Lectures there. There is no reason to assume that Dr. Trentham formed his views about the Bible after serving as Southwestern's Professor of Theology; he had received his graduate training at Southwestern.

Broadman Press published *Worthy Is the Lamb* (1951) by Ray Summers, Southwestern's Professor of New Testament. In this commentary on the book of Revelation, Summers denies that the apostle John wrote the book, and he constantly attempts to explain away its prophetical nature. To Summers, almost all of the book of Revelation is mere history. Summers later joined Baylor University's Religion Department and contributed an article in volume eight of the *Broadman Bible Commentary,* in which he attacks the doctrine of the Bible's inerrancy (p. 48).

W. Boyd Hunt

In the book *Is the Bible a Human Book?*, edited by Wayne E. Ward and Joseph F. Green and published in 1970 by the Southern Baptist publishing house, Broadman Press, there is a chapter entitled "What is Inspiration?" by Dr. W. Boyd Hunt, Professor of Theology at Southwestern. Hunt's entire chapter is an attack on the Bible's inerrancy. [5] He confuses such terms as *inspiration* and *illumination* (pp. 123-24) and employs typical neo-orthodox terminology. Says Hunt, "No matter how much we stress that the Bible is the Word of God, only the Holy Spirit today can make it the Word of God for us" (p. 125). The 1984 SBC *Annual* lists Dr. Hunt as "Distinguished Professor of Theology" at Southwestern (p. 413).

Kenneth L. Chafin

Dr. Kenneth L. Chafin, long-time pastor of South Main Baptist Church in Houston, Texas, has been Professor of Evangelism at both Southwestern and Southern Seminaries. He has served as Director of the Evangelism Division of the SBC Home Mission Board, and for fifteen years he held the deanship of the Billy Graham Schools of Evangelism. An outspoken opponent of biblical inerrancy, Dr. Chafin joined Southern Seminary's faculty as Professor of Christian Preaching. The 1984 SBC *Annual* lists him as a trustee of Southwestern (p. 366). Chafin had participated in the National Convocation of Christian Leaders, August 25-29, 1980, on the campus of Stanford University, a gathering billed as "a unique and exciting ecumenical effort by Catholics and Protestant leaders." Chafin also endorsed Robert Schuller's heretical book *Self-Esteem*. This appears on the book's cover.

Harry Leon McBeth

Dr. Harry Leon McBeth, presently the Professor of Church History at Southwestern, has long been known for his attacks against historic Fundamentalism. "Fundamentalism," says McBeth, "is a fighting faith ... angry, militant and narrow. Generosity, tolerance or simple kindness has too often been foreign to fundamentalism."[6]

John P. Newport

Dr. John P. Newport became vice president for Academic Affairs and Provost at Southwestern in 1979. As recently as February 1978, however, Newport had delivered a series of "Lectures on Christian Theology" at Stetson University, a Southern Baptist school in De Land, Florida. Here he had clearly denied the historic Christian doctrine of the soul's immortality. Said Newport, "Despite some people's opinion, the Bible does not teach . . . natural immorality."[7]

Newport is a director of the North American Paul Tillich Society. Tillich, a German theologian, came to America in 1933 when the Nazis forced him into exile. He taught in several liberal institutions in the United States, including Union Theological Seminary in New York City, Harvard University, and the University of Chicago. Paul Tillich was perhaps the most influential heretical theologian in America. He died in 1966 at the age of eighty. In 1984 Word Books published John P. Newport's book *Paul Tillich,* edited by Bob E. Patterson, Professor of Religion at Baylor University. While castigating Tillich's critics, Newport praises Tillich and his doctrines. As far back as 1973, however, at least two books appeared which revealed Tillich's personal lifestyle. One of these books was *Paulus* by Rollo May, and another was *From Time to Time* by Hannah Tillich, Paul Tillich's wife. These books reveal that Paul Tillich was a whoremonger, an adulterer, a pornographer, and a religious infidel. Paul Tillich denied such cardinal doctrines as the Trinity, and Christ's deity, incarnation, atonement, and bodily resurrection. Dr. John Newport concludes that Tillich's system "is surely one of the most significant contributions to Christian thought in this century" (pp. 219-20). In his preface, Newport said, "I am indebted to Russell Dilday of Southwestern Seminary for the constancy of his friendship and encouragement." Dilday is the seminary's president.

The late Huber L. Drumright, who taught and served at Southwestern for over twenty-five years and who knew John Newport well, once told Dr. Bill Powell this: "If Newport becomes Vice-President for Academic Affairs, Bill, you can mark Southwestern Seminary off." The *Southern Baptist Journal* refers to Newport as "the most dangerous man in our SBC."[8]

According to the 1984 SBC *Annual*, Dr. John P. Newport continues to hold his positions of high leadership at Southwestern (p. 415).

President Russell H. Dilday, Jr.

Dr. Russell H. Dilday, Jr., has been Southwestern's president since 1978. He openly attacks the doctrine of the Bible's inerrancy. For example, to a *Denver Post* reporter he said, "Whether the Bible is inerrant is of little concern to the Southern Baptist in the pew. . . . The Bible never misleads us in its message but maybe in technicalities."[9] In 1982 the Church Training Department of the SBC Sunday School Board published Dilday's book *The Doctrine of Biblical Authority,* in which he argues not only against using the term *inerrancy* but also against any sort of creedal statement. After reviewing Dilday's book, Harold Lindsell concluded that it is extremely weak doctrinally. When Dr. Dilday presented his book at a Church Training Doctrine Conference in Nashville, his audience cheered and clapped. One Sunday School Board employee stood and said that Dilday's views made him proud to be a Southwestern graduate and that he could "hardly wait for Dr. Lindsell's review of the book, God forbid that he should live that long." Laughter and more clapping followed that remark.[10]

Less than seventy-two hours after conservative Charles Stanley's 1984 election to the presidency of the SBC, Dilday was predicting to the media that Stanley would be a one-term president and that he himself was beginning immediately to work for that defeat in 1985.[11]

Cooperative Program Support

The 1984 SBC *Annual* reports that Southwestern

SOUTHWESTERN SEMINARY

Seminary received almost $6.5 million from the Southern Baptist Cooperative Program during the previous fiscal year (pp. 73 and 181). This is in spite of the fact that liberal views continue to find a welcome at this institution. Professor Bob Patterson of Baylor recently said the following in a lecture there sponsored by the Texas Baptist Christian Life Commission: "If creation is allowed equal time in our classroom, it will destroy all of science."[12] It is a tragedy indeed that an institution with such a grand heritage has now fallen into the very pits of apostasy, and even worse is the fact that God's people are helping to promote it and to support it. The Bible-believing men who remain on the faculty are serving as window dressing for error. How "can two walk together, except they be agreed" (Amos 3:3)?

Endnotes

1. B. H. Carroll, *An Interpretation of the English Bible.* This set was first published by Revell in 1913 under the title page imprint of the Sunday School Board of the Southern Baptist Convention. In 1942 Broadman bought the copyright from Revell. Those early volumes, edited by J. B. Cranfill assisted by J. W. Crowder, were incomplete. Crowder, Carroll's assistant, had the remaining material (mostly from the Old Testament poetical and prophetic sections), and in 1947 Broadman began copyrighting a "New and Complete" edition. In 1973 Baker Book House of Grand Rapids, Michigan, reprinted Broadman's 1948 edition in six volumes, but the Baker reprint preserved the pagination and format of the earlier seventeen-volume set.

2. Lee R. Scarborough, *Gospel Messages* (Nashville: Southern Baptist Sunday School Board, 1922), pp. 227-28. Many Fundamentalists would disagree with Dr. Carroll's advice to Scarborough. Dr. Bob Jones's advice is this: "If you find heresy on your faculty, don't wait for committees to argue about it. If heresy is present, purge it out the very day you discover it, before it can destroy a young person's life" (telephone interview, February 9, 1985).

3. J. M. Price, *Christianity and Social Problems* (Nashville:

Southern Baptist Sunday School Board, 1928), preface, pp. 90-103, 224-39. Price was also head of Southwestern's Department of Religious Education, created in 1915.

4. *Religious Herald,* November 1963; see also the *Maranatha Gospel Messenger,* July 1968. Charles A. Trentham was by 1963 dean of the Department of Religion at the University of Tennessee, where he could express his true feelings with more "academic liberty."

5. Wayne E. Ward and Joseph F. Green, eds., *Is the Bible a Human Book?* (Nashville: Broadman Press, 1970), pp. 120-29; for discussions of other chapters in this book, see my chapter 14 on Southern Baptist literature.

6. *Baptist Messenger,* May 18, 1978. This is the Oklahoma Southern Baptist state paper.

7. William A. Powell, Sr., "Liberalism Brews Within the Southern Baptist Convention," *Fundamentalist Journal,* February 1983, p. 20f. (Powell is a Southern Baptist writer.)

8. *Southern Baptist Journal,* January/February 1985, p. 4; see also March 1985, p. 1f.

9. Cited by William A. Powell, loc. cit.

10. *Southern Baptist Journal,* March/April 1983, p. 1f.; see also *Christian News,* May 2, 1983, p. 2.

11. *Southern Baptist Advocate,* July/August 1984, p. 15.

12. *Southern Baptist Advocate,* Spring 1982, p. 3.

Chapter Seven

New Orleans Baptist Theological Seminary

New Orleans Baptist Theological Seminary was established in Louisiana in 1917, and until 1946 it was called Baptist Bible Institute. From the time of its transition into an official "seminary," however, Liberalism has been present at New Orleans.

Frank Stagg

Frank Stagg, whose radical Liberalism is discussed in chapter 5, was Professor and Chairman of the New Testament Department at New Orleans for many years before becoming Senior Professor of New Testament Interpretation at Southern Seminary in Louisville. A recording of one of his lectures during the 1950-51 session at New Orleans Seminary proves beyond doubt that even then Frank Stagg was denying the verbal inspiration of the Bible and the priestly work of Christ. In this recording, Stagg argues that "Jesus is not our mediator. . . . God in Christ is our Redeemer, our Saviour, and there is no mediator."[1] Of course, this is consistent with Stagg's doctrine of modalism which would appear later in his *New*

Testament Theology (1962). New Orleans Seminary's president, Roland Q. Leavell, publicly defended Stagg, and the school has never repudiated any of the professor's views.

New Orleans Baptist Theological Seminary Endorses George A. Buttrick

Dr. George A. Buttrick, general editor of the liberal, twelve-volume *Interpreter's Bible* (1951-57) and Professor of Preaching at Garrett Theological Seminary, Northwestern University, was the main speaker at the Pastors' Conference at New Orleans Seminary that took place June 13-17, 1966. Buttrick's modernistic stance was well known. He had been Professor of Christian Morals at Harvard; he had been president of the Federal (now National) Council of Churches. The whole country knew him as the pro-communist political activist who helped to sponsor a program for the Emergency Civil Liberties Committee, a group which the House Committee on Un-American Activities cited in 1958-59 as being a Communist front. Buttrick's reputation in both political and theological circles had gone before him.

He had edited the four-volume *Interpreter's Dictionary of the Bible,* which Abingdon Press in Nashville published in 1962. This work is typical of liberal thought. In volume two, for example, "Mark is the folk book of the folk called Christian" (p. 449). In volume four there is an attack on the doctrine of Christ's resurrection: "The earliest records do not speak specifically of the empty tomb, and this has in consequence been held to be a subsequent embellishment or materialization of a tradition that originally knew nothing of it. It is, however, often overlooked how insistently they speak of the full tomb" (p. 45).

George Buttrick had clearly expressed his own theological views as far back as 1934, in his *Christian Fact and Modern Doubt,* published in New York by Charles Scribner's Sons. Here he claims that the Bible is not the infallibly inspired Word of God which it claims to be (pp. 157-58). He says that Darwinian evolution has proved the book of Genesis, "with its Garden of Eden and its story of a rib," too ridiculous for anyone to take seriously. Buttrick sneers at such Pauline passages as I Corinthians 15:22 (p. 59). He lists what he thinks are "contradictions in the Bible" and concludes, "Probably few people who claim to 'believe every word of the Bible' really mean it. That avowal held to its last logic would risk a trip to the insane asylum" (pp. 160-62). Buttrick appears completely ignorant of the mass of scholarly literature by Bible-believing conservatives. He charges the Old Testament with teaching "low ethical standards" (p. 163). To Buttrick, the books of Obadiah and Revelation are no more inspired than the apocryphal books (p. 170); Bible believers are guilty of "bibliolatry" (p. 171), and "their favorite campground is Daniel," which is "not prophecy, but history masquerading as prophecy" (p. 172). The author scorns and sneers at the doctrines of original sin and the atonement of Christ. The God of the Bible, concludes Buttrick, has "earned the verdict of the French sceptic: 'Your God is my Devil' " (pp. 173-75). After all, adds Buttrick, "A God who punishes men with fire and brimstone through all Eternity would hardly be Godlike. He would be almost satanic in cruelty and childlike in imagination—like a nasty little boy pulling off the wings of a fly" (p. 283).

The president of New Orleans Baptist Theological Seminary openly defended George A. Buttrick's presence there. That president was Dr. H. Leo Eddleman, who would later become the first president of W. A. Criswell's Center for Biblical Studies. However, Buttrick had not only been accepted at New Orleans; he had been a featured speaker at their annual Pastors' Conference, and conservatives would not soon forget this.

Theodore R. Clark

After studying under Dr. Stagg and receiving his doctor's degree at New Orleans Seminary, Theodore R. Clark taught at this school for more than ten years. In 1959 Macmillan in New York published Clark's *Saved by His Life,* one of the most blasphemous books ever published. Filled with blatant infidelity, this book denies Christ's

61

deity and substitutionary atonement and scorns the inspiration of the Bible. To Clark, those who sing and believe the old hymns are guilty of "Jesusolatry," a kind of "Jesus cult." Such hymns include the following: "How Firm a Foundation," "Pass Me Not," "Safe in the Arms of Jesus," "Living for Jesus," "We Would See Jesus," and "Jesus Saves"(pp. 11 and 59-69). Says Clark, "Christianity must restudy its position and make whatever readjustment is necessary"(p. 11). For example, the hymn "Nothing but the Blood of Jesus" is "a most serious distortion of the Christian faith" (p. 22), and the hymn "Are You Washed in the Blood?" is "crude and even repulsive" to Clark (p. 59). He attacks belief in the inerrancy of the Bible as "a form of idolatry" (p. 125) and adds, "We must not speak of the Bible as the Word of God . . ., that is, in the sense that it consists of infallible revealed truths given to men in written form" (p. 130). Clark even revives elements of Gnosticism, an ancient heresy which taught that Christ was a heavenly being who was a separate person from the man Jesus. He asserts that the Spirit came upon Jesus but that Jesus was not the Christ (chaps. 2 and 8). He viciously assaults the doctrine of the efficacy of Christ's blood (pp. 22-38).

After much conservative protest, New Orleans Seminary finally dismissed Dr. Theodore R. Clark in March 1960. Offering only vague reasons for letting Clark go, the trustees agreed to pay the professor's salary for another year after his dismissal. They offered to review him for rehiring "on or before the expiration of a five-year period"; after all, Dr. Clark had been teaching his views as Associate Professor of Theology at New Orleans Seminary since 1949. For over a decade, Clark had freely expressed these views, and Bible-believing Southern Baptists had helped pay his salary. Now in 1960, the trustees were simply under fire; they still kept Clark's own teacher, Dr. Stagg.

Fisher H. Humphreys

Broadman Press in Nashville published *The Death of Christ* by Fisher H. Humphreys in 1978. The book offers a historical overview of the major views of the atonement, and the author freely expresses his own ideas as well. According to the book's jacket, Humphreys has been Professor of Theology at New Orleans Seminary since 1970; he is also a New Orleans graduate. The author seems ignorant of the doctrine of salvation in the book of Hebrews. He asserts, "I do not know of anyone today who naturally assumes, as the writer of Hebrews did, that sins can be washed away only by the blood of sacrifices" (p. 38). However, the writer of Hebrews states emphatically that the blood of bulls and of goats can *never* take away sins (9:12; 10:4). After casting aspersion upon the integrity of the Holy Scriptures, Humphreys states, "I believe it is unwise to seek for a 'necessity' for the cross. It is quite possible to affirm and clarify the importance of the cross without speaking of it as necessary" (p. 55). Obviously the professor thinks himself wiser than the writer of Hebrews, who says, "Without shedding of blood is no remission" (9:22). Humphreys even denies the substitutionary atonement of Christ. "We cannot accept Calvin's view of substitutionary punishment," he asserts. Then he adds, "No illustration can be given, so far as I can tell, which makes vicarious punishment morally credible to men today." To Humphreys, it "seems morally outrageous that any judge would require a substitute. However noble the substitute's act might be, the judge's act seems despicable" (p. 61). Here is an infidel theologian who has set himself up as a judge of the God of heaven. Thinking his own morals greater than God's, Humphreys castigates the Bible doctrine of vicarious atonement as "morally outrageous" and "despicable."

Yet, Bible-preaching Southern Baptists continue to pay the salaries of Fisher H. Humphreys and scores of Liberals like him, and it was Broadman Press's Cooperative Program money which published his infidel book. Every Southern Baptist supports this kind of apostasy whether he agrees with it or not. The 1984 SBC *Annual* lists Humphreys as still holding the position of Professor of Theology at New Orleans Seminary (p. 409). [2]

The Social Gospel

New Orleans Seminary has launched a new emphasis towards the old social gospel. Dr. M. Thomas Starkes, for example, made the following statement at a 1983 meeting of state Christian Social Ministries directors: "There is more biblical evidence for doing social ministry than there is for our traditional evangelism."[3] The 1984 SBC *Annual* lists Dr. Starkes still as Professor of Christian Missions and World Religions at New Orleans (p. 409).

Cooperative Program Support

The people of God helped contribute $4,554,789 to New Orleans Seminary in the fiscal year 1982-83, and thus pay the salaries of men like Fisher and Humphreys.[4]

Endnotes

1. *The Faith and Southern Baptists,* March 1952, p. 5. This article cites and discusses the Stagg recording in detail.

2. See also *Christian News,* May 19, 1980, p. 13.

3. *Southern Baptist Advocate,* March/April 1983, p. 15.

4. *Annual,* SBC, 1984, p. 73.

Chapter Eight

Golden Gate Baptist Theological Seminary

Golden Gate Theological Seminary was established in Mill Valley in the San Francisco area of California in 1944. It has been liberal from its inception.

Bishop James A. Pike at Golden Gate

Golden Gate Seminary has hosted an array of modernist speakers. The school's paper, the *Span*, reported in April 1963, for instance, that "California Bishop of the Episcopal Church, James A. Pike, was the recent speaker in chapel services on the seminary campus." Pike was an outspoken radical, long known for his deep involvement in the occult, which even his mysterious death later seemed to confirm. Merrill F. Unger's book *The Mystery of Bishop Pike,* published by Tyndale House in 1971, relates the complete story of this controversial and unorthodox bishop.

James Dunn Speaks Against Military

In 1979 Dr. James Dunn, director of the Southern Baptist Christian Life Commission of Texas, spoke at

Golden Gate Seminary. Revealing his anti-militarism, Dunn announced the following to the seminary students: "Probably some of you here, who are studying to proclaim the gospel of peace, are keeping bread on your table through an industry that denies the gospel of peace. Our world has enough kill power. . . . Half of all the scientists in the world are in some way related to the so-called defense industries. And, the U. S. has become the arms monger of the world." [1]

Robert L. Cate

On April 9, 1974, the *Baptist Press* released a lengthy article by Dr. Robert L. Cate, pastor of First Baptist Church of Aiken, South Carolina. In this release, Cate said that the Bible clearly allows for the ordination of women. Golden Gate Seminary later appointed Cate Professor of Old Testament Interpretation and Dean of Academic Affairs. According to the 1984 SBC *Annual,* Cate continues in these positions of responsibility and authority (p. 408).

In the *Layman's Bible Book Commentary*, Broadman Press is now seeking to make Dr. Cate's views acceptable to Southern Baptist laymen. Such views include the historical-critical method of interpretation. In his commentary on Exodus in volume two of this series, Dr. Cate writes, "Traditionally [Exodus] has been called 'The Second Book of Moses,' but there is no ancient authority for that tradition" (p. 10). After admitting that some of the sources could have originated with Moses, he states, "Somewhere along the way, perhaps at a time of national crisis, these materials were combined and committed to writing" (p. 11). Liberals usually mean by this "national crisis" the time of the exile where they allege that the Pentateuch took most of its present form. This whole JEDP concept takes a subtle form from today's Liberals, who cannot be quite as brazen as they were years ago. Southern Baptist leadership, however, has committed itself to higher biblical criticism, and much of this leadership appears in the Southern Baptist Sunday School Board and in all six Southern Baptist seminaries.

Fred L. Fisher

The Executive Board of the Southern Baptist General Convention of California publishes the *California Southern Baptist*. The issue for January 21, 1965, carried an article entitled "Revelation and the Bible" by Dr. Fred L. Fisher, Professor of New Testament at Golden Gate Seminary. [2] Fisher clearly promulgates the liberal and neo-orthodox position. He says, "The Bible is not a revelation of God; it is a record of that revelation." Denouncing the doctrine of biblical inerrancy, Fisher adds, "Scientific and historical statements reflect the knowledge that men had of the world in that day; such statements may be in error." Fisher's Neo-orthodoxy determines his ideas concerning authority. "The Bible," to Fisher, "expresses God's authority, but . . . it is authoritative only when God actually speaks to us through it" (p. 14). This is typical Neo-orthodoxy, which teaches that the Bible is not absolutely the Word of God and only becomes subjectively the Word of God when it speaks to us.

In 1970 Broadman Press in Nashville published the book *Is the Bible a Human Book?*, edited by Wayne E. Ward and Joseph F. Green. Dr. Fred L. Fisher wrote chapter 8, entitled "How You Can Understand the Bible" (pp. 83-92), in which he expresses the view that the books of the Bible reflect only local ideas of Bible times and therefore could contain erroneous ideas. Carefully clothed in pious-sounding language, the discussion closes with this admonition: "We must remember that the Bible does not speak directly to our own situation in life. It was written to men of another age and time" (p. 91). Conservatives have always agreed and emphasized that proper biblical interpretation must include a careful consideration of the historical context of any book or passage, but Fisher seems almost oblivious to the timeless nature of God's Word, which transcends all time and space.

J. Kenneth Eakins

Dr. J. Kenneth Eakins is Professor of Archaeology and Old Testament Interpretation at Golden Gate Seminary. [3] In the *Southern Baptist Journal* for February 1981, Dr.

R. L. Hymers, Jr., a 1973 Golden Gate Seminary graduate, reported the following concerning his training at this Southern Baptist institution: "Dr. J. Kenneth Eakins, an Old Testament professor at Golden Gate, taught that the Genesis account was a myth, that a worldwide Flood never occurred, that Satan did not speak through the serpent. . . . Dr. J. Edward Humphrey taught Barthian neoorthodoxy [sic], actually liberalism, in his theology classes." Hymers adds, "Dr. J. Lynn Elder, who teaches pastoral counseling, said in a seminar that the Holy Spirit does not lead people. Dr. Fred Fisher, who smokes cigars up and down the halls of the seminary, laughed and mocked at Billy Graham's view of the Second Coming of Christ" (p. 1f.).

In the issue of the *Journal* for April/May 1981, Dr. Hymers made this offer: "I will give $500.00 to anyone who can get Dr. J. Kenneth Eakins to sign a notarized statement that reads, 'I love the teaching of biblical inerrancy as held by Dr. W. A. Criswell and Dr. Harold Lindsell, and I agree with it and teach it in my classes.'" Hymers then says:

> I offer $1,000.00 to anyone who can get Dr. Pinson or Dr. Eakins to answer the following items with a simple "yes" or "no." . . . 1. I believe that the Lord Jesus Christ was born of a virgin. YES or NO 2. I believe that God breathed every word of the original Bible and that there were no errors of any kind in the original Bible. Thus, I believe in the inerrancy of the original Bible. YES or NO 3. I believe that Adam and Eve were actually two human beings and that they gave birth to the first human babies. They were not "mythical representatives" but two actual people, from whom the human race sprang. YES or NO 4. I believe that the book of Jonah is literally true. Jonah was actually swallowed by some type of ocean creature. He actually lived and preached to the people of Nineveh. YES or NO 5. I believe that the Epistle of Second Peter was actually written by the Apostle Simon Peter, as Second Peter 1:1 states. YES or NO 6. I believe that Moses wrote all of the first five books of the Bible, with the possible exception of parts of the last chapter of Deuteronomy describing his death and burial. YES or NO 7. I agree

with what Jesus said after His resurrection (Luke 24:25)
that those who do not believe *all* that the prophets have
spoken are fools. YES or NO. [4]

Cooperative Program Support

On December 31, 1984, this writer telephoned both Dr.
Hymers and Dr. William A. Powell, the *Journal*'s editor,
and both confirmed that after almost four years no one
has persuaded the professors to answer the above
questions. Drs. Eakins, Fisher, and Cate continue to hold
their positions and to draw their salaries at Golden Gate,
which advertises itself as "conservative" and which
received $2,183,655 from the Southern Baptist Coopera-
tive Program in the fiscal year 1982-83. The amount
increases significantly in projected Cooperative Program
budgets. [5] Through their giving, every Southern Baptist
church member is involved directly or indirectly in making
common cause with the infidel enemies of Christ, the
Bible, and the Christian faith. The God of heaven instructs
His people to "have no fellowship with the unfruitful
works of darkness, but rather reprove them" (Ephesians
5:11).

Endnotes

1. *Church at Work.* January-March 1979; see also *The
People's Baptist Sentinel,* July 1979, p. 4.

2. The 1984 SBC *Annual* lists Dr. Fred L. Fisher as Professor
in Residence at the Southern California Center for Golden Gate
Theological Seminary (p. 408); see also *Catalogue,* Golden Gate
Baptist Theological Seminary, 1984-85, p. 83.

3. *Annual,* SBC, 1984, p. 408.

4. *Southern Baptist Journal,* April/May 1981, p. 10; see also
Southern Baptist Journal, July/August 1981, p. 1f.

5. *Annual,* SBC, 1984, p. 73.

Chapter Nine

Southeastern Baptist Theological Seminary

Southeastern Baptist Theological Seminary in Wake Forest, North Carolina, was founded in 1951 with a definite bent towards liberal theology.

John I. Durham

John I. Durham is Professor of Hebrew and Old Testament at Southeastern. [1] Durham contributed an article to volume one of the *Broadman Bible Commentary,* in which he advocates the JEDP historical-critical method. A discussion of this article appears in chapter 14.

Robert G. Bratcher and *Good News for Modern Man*

Southeastern Seminary recently added Dr. Robert G. Bratcher to its summer school faculty. [2] Bratcher, the translator of *Good News for Modern Man,* received two degrees from Southern Seminary in Louisville, where he has also taught. As a featured speaker at a SBC pastors' school, Bratcher once asserted, "The Bible is not a divine book. If it were, it would be irrelevant."[3]

In March 1981, the Southern Baptist Christian Life Commission invited Bratcher to speak to them. *Baptist Press* editor Dan Martin covered this meeting in an official press release. The following quotations from the press release reveal Bratcher's bold attack against the doctrine of inerrancy as he addressed the Christian Life Commission:

> The Scriptures are fine in their place, but that place isn't on the throne. . . . Only willful ignorance or intellectual dishonesty can account for the claim that the Bible is inerrant and infallible. To qualify this absurd claim by adding "with respect to the autographs (original manuscripts)" is a bit of sophistry, a specious attempt to justify a patent error.
>
> No truth-loving, God-respecting, Christ-honoring believer should be guilty of such heresy. To invest the Bible with the qualities of inerrancy and infallibility is to idolatrize it, to transform it into a false god. . . . Even words spoken by Jesus in Aramaic in the thirties of the first century and preserved in writing in Greek, thirty-five to fifty years later, do not necessarily wield compelling or authentic authority over us today. . . . As a biblical scholar, I view with dismay the misuse of scriptures by fundamentalists.
>
> We can never know in advance that we are doing the will of God. It is the height of presumption and arrogance to say, " 'I know this is God's will, and I am doing it."[4]

On the contrary, Bratcher seems to be the specialist in "presumption and arrogance."

Foy Valentine, the Executive Director of the Southern Baptist Christian Life Commission, later reported, "I have really caught the devil over Bratcher's statements, but in light of the reigning heresy I am glad he said them."[5] Of course, the "reigning heresy," as Valentine sees it, is the belief that the Bible is the infallible Word of God as it claims to be. The Christian Life Commission is an official, funded corporation of the SBC, and the Cooperative Program pays Foy Valentine's salary (and Bratcher's salary for lecturing at Southeastern Seminary). Bratcher's comments forced him to resign his position with the American Bible Society, [6] but Southern Baptists have distributed millions of copies of his liberal *Good News for Modern Man.*

W. W. Finlator and T. C. Smith

Others recently teaching at Southeastern Seminary include W. W. Finlator, who is a national vice president for the American Civil Liberties Union (a radical left-wing political organization), and T. C. Smith, who boasts that "there are at least 6,000 errors in the book of Luke alone." [7]

Southeastern Promotes Feminist Movement

A trend toward feminism is evident at Southeastern Seminary. The administration recently named an ordained Baptist female minister, Suzanne Martin Davis, as the new Associate Director of Student Field Ministries. The *Southern Baptist Journal* has reported that "part of every dollar given to the Cooperative Program goes to help pay the salary of a number of ordained women." [8]

Another example is the following published order of service which Southeastern Seminary used in its regular chapel service for March 17, 1983. It should be of interest to every reader.

Call to Worship	"All Praise to Thee"
	Hymn No. 43
Worship through Prayer	
Old Testament Lesson	Genesis 1:26-31
New Testament Lesson	2 Corinthians 5:17-21
Worship through Music	
Message	Nancy Unterzuber
Celebration of the New Humanity	

Female Liturgist: We as women are strong.
   We as women are powerful.
   We as women can do things.
Women: Liberation is ours for the claiming.
Female Liturgist: We need to be more in touch with our
   strength, our power, and our capabilities.

We need to be free to be ourselves.
We need not stifle our God-given talents.
Women: The gospel is liberation.
Female Liturgist: We don't have to stay in our place.
Women: The gospel frees us from the law.
Female Liturgist: Jesus broke law and tradition in his treatment of women.
Women: Jesus was a feminist!
Male Liturgist: When you are free, then we are freer.
We don't have to prove our manliness.
We don't have to prove our "natural superiority."
We don't have to claim anything.
Men: Liberation is ours for the claiming.
Male Liturgist: We need to be more in touch with our tears.
We need to be free to be ourselves.
We need to discard our "masculine role" and discover who we really are.
Men: The gospel is liberation.
Male Liturgist: We are free to share our responsibilities.
Men: The gospel frees us from the law.
Male Liturgist: Jesus challenged the status quo.
Men: Jesus calls us to full humanity.

All: We reject the notion that one sex should build bridges and the other keep the home.
We reject the idea of "proper roles," for roles belong to the realm of law, and freedom belongs to the gospel.
We believe the words of the New Testament that in God's time and place there is no male and female, no mankind or womankind, no manhood or womanhood, but simply humanhood, simply God's people.
We can and will be more human.
We will find ways of being men and women together.
Benediction [9]

Another recent "worship experience" at Southeastern included interpretive dance and many different instruments combining to form a "unique" service. [10]

President W. Randall Lolley Dedicates New Schlitz Brewery

W. Randall Lolley is Southeastern's third president. Sydnor L. Stealey[11] was the first, and Olin T. Brinkley was the second. Lolley received his graduate training at Southeastern and Southwestern Seminaries, his doctorate coming from the latter. As pastor of the First Baptist Church in Winston-Salem, North Carolina, and as president of Southeastern Baptist Theological Seminary, W. Randall Lolley prayed a dedicatory invocation for the formal opening of the Schlitz Brewing Company's new plant at Winston-Salem on May 8, 1970.[12] Here is Dr. Lolley's dedicatory prayer which he made in behalf of the largest brewery in the world:

> Dear Lord, we thank Thee today that Thou hast made us so that we can enjoy new beginnings and that Thou hast made us so we can participate in dedications and make commitments and enjoy new, fresh relationships. Our hearts tell us that industry is people, so we thank Thee, O Living God, for the persons who have been plunged into the life and fabric, the process of living and deciding and being in our community. We thank Thee for them and their families.
>
> We thank Thee, O God, for the influences that shall be engendered and the relationships that shall be enjoyed because of new friends from this plant and this industry moving into our community. Grant to them all the resources, wisdom and skill that shall be demanded of that industry and give them, O God, Thy Presence and Thy Peace and give us all the fruits, the joys of this day of dedication and the relationships and commitments that shall ensue to us all from it.
>
> In the strong Name of Our Lord we pray. Amen.[13]

Cooperative Program Support

The 1984 SBC *Annual* reported that Southeastern received $4,674,874 in Cooperative Program funds for the fiscal year 1982-83, and a much larger figure appears on their projected budget (p. 73).

Endnotes

1. *Annual,* SBC, 1984, p. 410; see also the valuable discussion of a Liberal's practice of "free expression" at Southeastern in the *Southern Baptist Advocate,* June 1984, p. 2.

2. *Southern Baptist Advocate,* February/March 1984, p. 4.

3. *The Baptist Courier,* July 21, 1977, p. 9. This is the South Carolina state paper for Southern Baptists.

4. *The Baptist Courier,* April 2, 1981, p. 6.

5. *Southern Baptist Advocate,* May/June 1981, p. 3.

6. *Lubbock Avalanche Journal,* June 17, 1981; *Christianity Today,* July 17, 1981, p. 81.

7. *Southern Baptist Advocate,* February/March 1984, p. 4. T. C. Smith has taught at Southern Seminary in Louisville and at Furman University in Greenville, South Carolina. He contributes frequently to Southern Baptist literature. For information on the American Civil Liberties Union, see *FAITH for the Family,* March 1985, pp. 3, 10-11.

8. *Southern Baptist Journal,* October 1978, p. 3.

9. According to this order of service, it was adapted from a reading included in *Sistercelebrations: Nine Worship Experiences* (Philadelphia: Fortress Press, 1974), pp. 41-42. See also the *Southern Baptist Advocate,* May 1983, p. 4.

10. *Advocate Update,* April 1984, p. 2.

11. Sydnor L. Stealey, Southeastern's first president, was long-remembered for his often-quoted statement that the virgin birth was not essential to the Christian faith. He regularly brought modernist speakers to the seminary and openly defended apostate Ralph H. Elliott of Midwestern Baptist Theological Seminary.

12. *Winston-Salem Journal,* May 9, 1970.

13. The text of the prayer appears also in William A. Powell's *SBC Issue & Question* (Buchanan, Georgia: Baptist Missionary Service, Inc., 1977), p. 132 and in the *Baptist Challenge,* July 1983, p. 18.

Chapter Ten

Midwestern Baptist Theological Seminary

Roy L. Honeycutt

Midwestern Baptist Theological Seminary was founded in Kansas City, Missouri, in 1957. Dr. Roy L. Honeycutt, who is now president of Southern Seminary in Louisville, was on the early Midwestern faculty. As the school's Professor of Old Testament, Honeycutt served on the editorial board of the *Broadman Bible Commentary* and wrote its commentary on Exodus in volume one. Embracing the historical-critical method of interpretation, Honeycutt taught the same liberal views that permeate the set. [1]

Charles A. Trentham at Midwestern

Midwestern Seminary hosted a number of liberal guest speakers in the early days of her history. In 1963 Midwestern brought Dr. Charles A. Trentham to deliver the H. I. Hester Lectures. That same year he expressed his opinion that the doctrine of the Bible as the infallible, authoritative Word of God is a "heresy." [2]

Bishop Gerald Kennedy at Midwestern

The 1967 H. I. Hester Lecturer was Bishop Gerald Kennedy, the unbelieving Methodist apostate who had openly denied the virgin birth, the deity of Christ, and the blood atonement. Using the typical approach of distinguishing between *deity* and *divinity*, Kennedy had said, "I believe the testimony of the New Testament taken as a whole is against the doctrine of the deity of Jesus, although I think it bears overwhelming witness to the divinity of Jesus."[3] When Dr. Millard J. Berquist, president of Midwestern, introduced the Methodist churchman to his Southern Baptist audience, he read some of the letters which protested the bishop's coming. This rocked his audience with laughter, and Berquist went on to introduce Gerald Kennedy as "a dear brother in Christ." Southern Baptist evangelist Billy Graham had already conditioned many leaders and laymen alike to accept Bishop Kennedy. It was Kennedy who had served as chairman of Mr. Graham's 1963 Los Angeles campaign.

The Ralph H. Elliott Controversy

Dr. Ralph H. Elliott received his training at Southern Seminary in Louisville and went on to become Chairman of the Old Testament Department at Midwestern. In 1961 the SBC Broadman Press published Elliott's book *The Message of Genesis.* Taking the Graf-Wellhausen position, Elliott teaches throughout that Genesis is not historically accurate, that Moses was not its writer (pp. 1-16) (though Jesus said he was), that the book was not written until the exile or later, and that early stories such as creation and Adam and Eve are not literal history (pp. 39-40). In fact, Elliott presents Genesis 1-11 as non-literal. He sees the Garden of Eden not as "an actual place but rather ... a setting for the message to be conveyed" (p. 43). Such is neo-orthodox thinking. To Elliott, Abraham only "thought he heard" a call from God to sacrifice his son (p. 145).

After heated conservative protest over this Broadman publication, the Midwestern trustees gave Ralph Elliott a fourteen-to-seven vote of confidence and regarded him as "a loyal servant of Southern Baptists" who should definitely stay on as head of the Department of Old Testament. The fifty-four-man Sunday School Board, representing Southern Baptists at every level, met January 29-31, 1962, and reapproved this controversial book which asserts that the ages of men in Genesis were exaggerated (pp. 58-59) and that Melchizedek was a priest of Baal (pp. 115-16). The Liberals even had sufficient power at the SBC meeting in San Francisco (June 1962) to vote down a motion to order the Southern Baptist Sunday School Board, which controls Broadman Press, to remove Elliott's book from circulation. The Liberals were able to block the motion with their continual plea for "Baptist freedom."

There was such widespread upheaval among conservative Southern Baptists over Elliott's heretical teaching, however, that Midwestern Seminary trustees finally asked Elliott to agree not to have a second edition published. The Sunday School Board had now agreed to withhold the book, at least for the present. Neither the Sunday School Board nor Midwestern expressed publicly any opposition to the book; they simply desired to let the waters settle. Elliott himself, however, insisted on having his book republished by another company, and Midwestern "reluctantly and regretfully" fired him. The seminary made it very clear that the dismissal was a matter of policy, not principle; they fired Elliott not for heresy but for his "insubordination" in insisting that another company publish his book. Midwestern never repudiated anything in the book, and they gave Ralph Elliott his salary and fringe benefits for a full year following his dismissal. Liberals have shown their willingness to "sacrifice" an occasional sacred cow like Elliott in order to quell the troubled waters of controversy.

Time magazine carried the Elliott story (November 9, 1962), quoting Southern Baptist Convention President Herschel Hobbs as insisting, "We are a people who grant to every individual the right to interpret the Scriptures as he is led by the Holy Spirit. We have no creed. The trustees thought the book was the center of the problem, and simply wanted it withheld until everything died down." So

Elliott's dismissal was not a repudiation of his Modernism; it was a means to stop the rocking of the ecclesiastical boat. They feared the loss of financial support, so they were eager to "let everything die down," according to the Convention president. *Time* quoted a Midwestern faculty member who said, "There is a very low morale as a result of what has happened. I would call it a sense of shame. This kind of thing gives another professor nowhere to stand." The article reported that 100 Midwestern students met in protest over Elliott's dismissal and that 70 percent of the student body had sent a resolution to the Board of Trustees calling for a return to "the Baptist position of freedom to interpret the Bible." The *Time* reporter quoted President Sydnor L. Stealey of Southeastern Seminary as saying that his own faculty and students were "deeply disturbed by the news and deeply sympathetic toward Dr. Elliott." The article cited a Southern Seminary professor who reported that the Louisville faculty was "almost one hundred per cent" in sympathy with Elliott's views. [4] *The Western Recorder,* the Kentucky Southern Baptist state paper, expressed the real problem: "They must know by now Elliott is not a glaring example of heresy among a host of safely orthodox teachers in our seminaries. If he is a heretic, then he is one of many and indeed is not at the head of the line. Professors in all our seminaries know Elliott is in the same stream of thinking with most of them and is more in the center of the stream than some of them." [5]

Dr. Millard J. Berquist, the Midwestern president who had just defended Ralph Elliott, would soon write an article in the *Baptist Training Union Magazine* attacking the doctrine of verbal inspiration in clear neo-orthodox terminology. [6] The Elliott crisis did lead Southern Baptists to adopt the *Baptist Faith and Message* statement of faith in 1963, but neither Liberals nor conservatives would ever consider this binding. They would simply let "Baptist freedom" ring!

William B. Coble

Dr. William B. Coble is Professor of New Testament

and Greek at Midwestern. In 1974 William A. Powell wrote to Dr. Coble asking the professor four simple questions: "1. Do you believe that there was a man by the name of Adam? 2. And that Adam was the first human being that God created? 3. Do you believe that God took a rib from Adam and made a wife for him? 4. Do you believe that Eve gave birth to the first human baby ever born?" Dr. Coble, however, could not give simple yes-or-no answers to these questions, because he is committed to the historical-critical method of interpretation and he denies the historicity of much of the Bible. Coble responded, "I determined never to give a written answer to anybody's yes or no questions on matters of faith." [7] Liberalism commits itself to no absolutes, however, and Coble moves in the stream of liberal thought. To Coble, *Adam* simply means "mankind." In the April 11, 1974, issue of *Word and Way,* the official Missouri state paper, Coble said this: "Genesis presents two forms of the story of mankind. In both stories, the most used Hebrew word for man is Adam with a little A. It means mankind, not the human, adult male." Coble ignores the great mass of scholarly literature which asserts that Adam was indeed a historical person and that the complete Genesis account is historical indeed. Dr. William B. Coble continues to teach at Midwestern. [8]

G. Temp Sparkman

Dr. G. Temp Sparkman, as Professor of Religious Education and Church Administration at Midwestern, espoused universalism, situation ethics, socialism, and rank modernism. In 1972 the Southern Baptist Sunday School Board in Nashville published Sparkman's book, *Being a Disciple.* In this work the author denies the doctrine of the depravity of man: "Man has been berated as a sinner and then told the good news that he can change," says Sparkman, "but the order is reversed. He is already good" (p. 17). To Sparkman, "it often appears that God Himself is fickle, punishing man and then changing His mind" (p. 20). Much of the book teaches universalism, that all will be saved and none are lost. [9]

Especially addressing young people, Sparkman advises them just to pretend that they agree with the old doctrines even when they do not. He tells them to wait patiently and try to change the old theology (pp. 31-32). This is situation ethics, and Larry Yarborough, Consultant for the Church Training Department of the Southern Baptist Sunday School Board, formally endorsed the book on its cover. Sparkman encourages socialistic goals for young grassroots Baptists: "If I had to state the major goals that a person might set for himself in being a disciple in our world, I would list these: 1. To work for peace wherever there is war 2. To work at distributing the wealth of the world 3. To work at assuring civil liberties to all people 4. To work at a healthy balance in the use of the environment 5. To work toward a moral climate that matches the dignity of man" (p. 72). Writing the book while serving on the staff of the Crescent Hill Baptist Church in Louisville, Kentucky, Sparkman expressed indebtedness to his liberal heritage: "This small book is a recycling of the thinking of my colleagues at Crescent Hill Baptist Church and my teachers at the Southern Baptist Theological Seminary, about three blocks from here" (p. 91). Broadman published this liberal book under the direction of Dr. James L. Sullivan, then president of the Southern Baptist Sunday School Board.

Judson Press published Temp Sparkman's *Salvation and Nurture of the Child of God: The Story of Emma* (1983). This book's central theme is the Bushnellian doctrine of Christian nurture, that is, that children must be progressively nurtured into Christianity; "salvation" is not instantaneous (pp. 16, 25, 30, 31, 33, 193, 194, 325). Sparkman describes the nineteenth-century Yale apostate Horace Bushnell as a "man whose thought came as a fresh spring rain over the Connecticut valley nurturing a budding view of humanity which the winters of stern Calvinism had stunted" (p. 91). "Salvation," whatever that is, comes through works (pp. 29, 76). Sparkman opposes having young children memorize Scripture (p. 65), and he opposes children's church (p. 66). He clearly teaches universalism; while he avoids the term *universal salvation,* he employs the phrase "universal status" (p. 233). His universalism appears throughout (pp. 41, 43-45, 72). Sparkman denies the reality of Christian absolutes (p. 91) and embraces the Graf-Wellhausen hypothesis (pp. 223, 228, 249). He thinks that God is both male and female (p. 99) and endorses the modern liberation movements (p. 152) and ecumenicity (p. 150). Two of Midwestern's trustees have just related to this writer that there is much speculation that Sparkman is now contemplating a move to another school. If fact, Sparkman may have other employment by the Spring of 1985. This professor is a popular speaker in Baptist circles. The Sunday School Board published his book, and he has indoctrinated students at Midwestern Seminary since 1973. The trustees observe that Sparkman's own students tend to rally to his defense whenever he is under criticism.

William H. Morton

Midwestern continues to harbor Liberals. No conservative purging has occurred. Even William H. Morton, who wrote the commentary on Joshua in volume two of the *Broadman Bible Commentary,* remains at Midwestern as Professor of Biblical Archaeology. [10] He denies in this Southern Baptist commentary that God supernaturally stopped the Jordan for the priests to cross, in Joshua 3 and 4 (p. 314).

Cooperative Program Support

The 1984 SBC *Annual* reports that Midwestern received $2,142,211 from the Southern Baptist Cooperative Program in the fiscal year 1982-83, with a significant increase projected for the coming year (p. 73).

Endnotes

1. See chapter 14; see also the *Baptist Challenge,* February 1966.

2. *Religious Herald,* November 1963. This is the Virginia state Southern Baptist paper. See also the *Maranatha Gospel*

Messenger, July 1968; and my discussion of Trentham in chapter 6 on Southwestern Seminary.

3. Gerald Kennedy, *God's Good News* (New York: Harper and Brothers, 1955), p. 125.

4. *Time,* November 9, 1962, p. 58.

5. *The Western Recorder,* September 27, 1962.

6. *Baptist Training Union Magazine,* September 1963.

7. *Southern Baptist Journal,* October 1974.

8. *Annual,* SBC, 1984, p. 408.

9. Temp Sparkman, *Being a Disciple* (Nashville: Broadman, 1972), pp. 11, 17, 18, 20-23, 25, 32, 34, 57, 59-61, 63, 65, 66, 91 and 92.

10. *Annual,* SBC, 1984, p. 409.

Chapter Eleven

Southern Baptist Responses to the Seminary Liberalism

Increased Financial Support

Since the inerrancy debate started, not one of the six Southern Baptist seminaries has committed itself to the use of the terms *infallible* or *inerrant*. Scores of Liberals indoctrinate more than 14,000 students annually [1] in these half dozen schools which received $24,311,832 from the Cooperative Program in the 1982-83 fiscal year. The amount rises significantly each year. The almost $24.5 million in that year was nearly $5 million more than the Home Mission Board received, and it was almost half the amount which went to the Foreign Mission Board. [2] Denominational responses to the seminary Liberalism have proved informative and significant; the following are typical from several levels of Southern Baptist life and work.

Grady C. Cothen

Grady C. Cothen, president of the Southern Baptist Sunday School Board from 1975 to 1984, announced,

"There is simply no evidence, in my judgment, indicating any trend toward theological liberalism in the SBC."[3] Such is the attitude of the highest level of leadership in the Sunday School Board, which operates Broadman Press and publishes all official Southern Baptist literature. It was Cothen who nominated Dr. Duke K. McCall for SBC president in 1982;[4] McCall was then resigning under controversy from the presidency of Southern Seminary in Louisville. Even back in 1969, as president of Oklahoma Baptist University, Cothen had the radical Quaker theologian Elton Trueblood speak at their opening convocation. Trueblood had widely published his views in twenty-seven books, including his *Philosophy of Religion,* in which he claims that the more a person is a sincere Christian, the more he will be a rationalist (one who believes that reason is the highest authority); and a good rationalist, added Trueblood, will be boldly pointing out the mythical and legendary elements in the Bible. Even W. A. Criswell twice quotes Trueblood favorably in his book *Look Up, Brother!* (pp. 37, 58), and as president of the SBC he had no objections to Trueblood's coming to address the Convention.

Billy Graham

Meanwhile, Evangelist Billy Graham, a member of Dr. Criswell's First Baptist Church in Dallas, was assuring grassroots Southern Baptists, "One of the great things about this denomination is that you are the most theologically sound of any of the major denominations."[5] This kind of supportive and undiscerning attitude more than any other thing has kept God's people from obeying the Word of God by separating themselves from all forms of apostasy. One does not have to wonder how the first-century apostles, or Christ Himself for that matter, handled false prophets and hypocrites. Liberalism, no matter how far it struts in the garb of Christianity, is not biblical Christianity; it is paganism, as Dr. J. Gresham Machen demonstrated many years ago in his classic, *Christianity and Liberalism.* Even the title suggests that Liberalism is not Christianity. They have "a form of godliness, but "deny "the power thereof." The apostle Paul says, "From such turn away" (II Timothy 3:5).

Southern Baptist State Papers

Most Southern Baptist state newspaper editors consistently editorialize against the conservative, inerrantist movement. One Southern Baptist writer counterattacked the liberal trend with his own editorial. He pinpoints the problem: "The most dangerous group are the editors of state papers who try to 'cover up' for the teachers in our seminaries and colleges who deny the Bible is without error. These editors build 'straw men,' 'smoke screens,' engage in the battle of semantics, become experts in camouflage and a variety of other cover up tactics. Thus, they have created a tragic Baptist Watergate."[6] These liberal editors are in control, however, and they consistently attempt to swing the "balance of power" to the Liberals by their votes on the Convention floor.

Judge Paul Pressler

Houston judge Paul Pressler is a prominent leader of the conservative, Bible-inerrancy advocates in the SBC. In Lynchburg, Virginia, in 1980 Pressler stated that conservatives are now seeking to have trustees appointed who "are not going to sit there like a bunch of dummies and rubber stamp everything that's presented to them." Immediately, the presidents of the Southern Baptist seminaries angrily responded to Pressler's charges that their Boards of Trustees consist of "dummies" and "rubber stamps." This was a brilliant public relations move. When thirty-four Southern Baptist state newspapers published the presidents' indignant responses, Judge Pressler backed off, saying that his comments in Lynchburg were really not intended as criticisms of the current trustees. [7] So the "battle" goes on; but there really is not much of a battle, because no one in the mainline conservative leadership appears committed to paying the price of true discipleship which Luke 14:25-35 describes.

Wallie Amos Criswell

Dr. Criswell served as president of the SBC from 1968 to 1970. At the press conference following his first election, a reporter asked about his attitude toward Liberalism in the SBC schools. This new conservative president's reply was that Liberalism was hard to find and that he would therefore devote his time and attention to promoting a great evangelistic missionary program. Dr. Criswell has been the patriarch of SBC conservatism.

In his book *These Issues We Must Face*, Dr. Criswell exposed the Modernism in the old Northern Baptist Convention but remained silent on the issue of Southern Baptist Liberalism (pp. 41-51). His church continues to contribute record sums each year to the Cooperative Program. In his book, *Look Up, Brother!,* Dr. Criswell admitted his basic toleration for liberal views: "Although the method of dissecting the Bible is carried to a sickening extent . . . I do not quarrel with a man confessing he believes in these sources [JEDP] if he honestly accepts the Bible as the Word of God." Dr. Criswell said that some of his "dearest friends" embraced the Graf-Wellhausen hypothesis and that they loved the Lord as much or more than he. Said Criswell, "If they believe the Bible to be the Word of God, even though they accept some of these higher critical conclusions, I have no word to say against them" (p. 80). Even the Liberals now speak freely of the fact that Dr. Criswell has "modified, if not muted, his criticisms."[8] Dr. Criswell, however, has molded the thinking of the major conservative Southern Baptist leaders of this generation. As patriarch of the whole conservative movement, he has instilled into the new leaders his own philosophies—toleration, peaceful coexistence, and loyalty to the Baptist program. He has publicly rebuked the most conservative element of the SBC.

In his *Look Up, Brother!* Dr. Criswell gave this exhortation: "For us to falter in our support of these fine schools because of the few [unbelieving professors] would be like burning down the barn to get rid of the rats or throwing out the baby with the bath water. Our forefathers who believed in the Holy Scriptures founded these institutions. It is for us to keep them growing" (p. 85). It is not a question of rats in a barn, however, and it is not a question of a baby and a bath. It is a question of whether Bible-believing Baptists are going to continue to support these seminaries whose professors are destroying what genuine faith is left in their students. As to these institutions being "founded by our forefathers," the Jewish nation too was founded by the forefathers—the Patriarchs and Moses. The Sanhedrin, which demanded the death of Christ as a malefactor and a blasphemer, was founded by forefathers. The fact is, the "rats" are now running the barn, and even the barnyard, and the "baby" has already been sacrificed to the polluted bath waters of heresy.

Southern Baptist conservatives like Dr. Criswell have turned their backs on their real heritage and made a god of the "latest scholarship." The whole thrust of Dr. Criswell's message in *Look Up, Brother!* is that he will not do one practical thing about the infidelity in Southern Baptist classrooms; he would rather strive to see them growing. Unchecked denominational loyalty has often led to a lack of real discernment. In obedience to a dream which he had while recuperating from a heart attack, Dr. Criswell has led his church to contribute over $1 million a year to the Cooperative Program—the largest pledge of any single church in the Convention. [9] It is no wonder that a news release on February 18, 1981, from the official *Baptist Press* in Nashville describes the Cooperative Program as "sacred." [10]

A Concerned Local Church

On April 9, 1981, the Executive Board of the Tennessee Baptist Convention, along with four disgruntled church members, filed a lawsuit against the pastor and deacons of the Bethel Baptist Church (formerly called Paynes Baptist Church) in Estill Springs, Tennessee. The suit petitioned the court to take all of the church property and assets from the "majority members" and transfer all of it to the "minority members," or to the Tennessee Baptist Convention's Executive Board. The basic complaints were these: the church supported independent missionaries; the church was not using Southern Baptist Sunday School literature, including the *Baptist Hymnal;* and the pastor had publicly criticized some SBC leaders as "Liberals."

When the congregation organized their church back in 1963, the Tennessee Baptist Convention had donated a $1,500 piece of land, the deed of which included a reversionary clause limiting the use of the property to work which is in accord with the "doctrines, faith, and practices of the members of the missionary Baptist Churches which cooperate with the . . . Tennessee Baptist Convention and the Southern Baptist Convention." Over the years the church had grown, and the property was now valued at $225,000 at the time of the lawsuit. The court heard the case on July 29-30, 1981; finally, on August 5, 1982, Judge Earl H. Henley announced his decision: all properties and assets would be transferred to the minority.

Interestingly, this pastor had reportedly never tried to encourage his people to withdraw from the SBC. Now, however, they had no choice. Their quarter of a million dollars worth of beautiful property had been stolen. Unable to afford any kind of legal appeal, the majority left and planted an independent Baptist work, and God has mightily blessed their endeavor.[11] Significantly, conservative Southern Baptist writer William A. Powell reports that "the SBC establishment has helped to develop the consensus that a church must buy its literature from the Nashville Board in order to demonstrate loyalty to the SBC."[12] Fundamental churches have discovered that loyalty to a denomination is not synonymous with loyalty to God.

Endnotes

1. *Annual,* SBC, 1984, pp. 170-83.

2. Ibid., p. 73f.

3. *Religious News Service,* November 26, 1980, p. 15.

4. *Annual,* SBC, 1982, p. 34.

5. *Baptist Record,* January 1, 1970; this is the official Southern Baptist state paper of Mississippi.

6. *Southern Baptist Journal,* October 1980, p. 2.

7. *Christian News,* October 20, 1980, p. 13.

8. *Review and Expositor,* Winter 1984, p. 115.

9. *The Dallas Morning News,* September 21, 1981; see also *The Lubbock Avalanche Journal,* September 21, 1981; *Plains Baptist Challenger,* November 1981, p. 1f.; and *Southern Baptist Advocate,* May 1983, p. 1f.

10. *Southern Baptist Journal,* March 1981, p. 4.

11. *Southern Baptist Journal,* January 1983, p. 12f.

12. William A. Powell, *The SBC Issue & Question* (Buchanan, Georgia: Baptist Missionary Service, Inc., 1977), p. 156.

Chapter Twelve

Southern Baptist Colleges

The Southern Baptist Convention controls and appoints the trustees only for the six seminaries. Each of the Southern Baptist colleges comes under its own state's jurisdiction. Many examples of apostasy continually present themselves—the Liberalism at Meredith[1] and Samford,[2] even the production of a sex movie at Stetson[3]—but this chapter attempts only to offer a few key samples—samples, however, which represent the extent to which theological and moral decay has secured itself even on the state level of Southern Baptist life and work.

Baylor University

Baylor University, in Waco, Texas, has harbored Liberals since J. Frank Norris and Dr. Samuel Grove Dow crossed theological swords back in the 1920s.

Ray Summers: Dr. Ray Summers, while on Baylor's religion faculty, wrote an article in volume eight of the *Broadman Bible Commentary* in which he uses and promotes "form criticism," which teaches that each book of the Bible is only a collection of various types of literature patched together by uninspired men. He specifically attacks the doctrine of biblical inerrancy on page 48. A discussion of this article appears in chapter 14. Summers had previously taught as Professor of New Testament at Southwestern Seminary.

Henry J. Flanders, Jr.: Baylor Professor of Religion, Dr. Henry J. Flanders, Jr., in *People of the Covenant,* attacks the Bible's inerrancy and refers to much of the Old Testament as myth. Flanders, who received his graduate training at Southern Seminary in Louisville, has been teaching at Baylor since 1969. [4] The University uses this and other liberal books in order to keep its accreditation and federal funds—so explained former Baylor president (now chancellor), Dr. Abner V. McCall. [5] McCall admitted that the Southern Association of Colleges and Schools was the determining factor in establishing Baylor's doctrinal position. [6] Flanders, who coauthored *People of the Covenant* and is Chairman of the Religion Department, apparently represents that "position." [7]

Bob E. Patterson: Baylor Professor of Religion, Dr. Bob E. Patterson, told a *Houston Chronicle* religious news editor, "I feel that creationism is poor (inadequate) theology. . . . Theistic evolution can make sense to both science and theology."[8] Patterson, who received his seminary training at Southern Seminary in Louisville, has been teaching at Baylor since 1961. [9] He is not the only evolutionist on Baylor's faculty.

Curtis Wallace Christian: Dr. Curtis W. Christian, Professor of Religion at Baylor, wrote a book called *Shaping Your Faith.* In 1973 Word Books in Waco, Texas, published this work which defends Darwinism. In Dr. Christian's opinion, "The disparity between Genesis and Darwin, if it comes down to it, has really been decided for all of us in Darwin's favor" (p. 67). Referring to the "clearly provable inadequacies of Scripture scientifically and historically," he accuses the Bible of falsehood (p. 70). These suppositions determine the professor's beliefs concerning authority. He says, "To the question, 'Are we bound by the Bible?' we must also answer no, for within the dialogue of faith are other sources of insights which we must hear. Our theology is not exclusively biblical theology" (p. 81). Dr. Christian, who has a degree from Southwestern Seminary, has been teaching at Baylor since 1958. [10]

President Herbert H. Reynolds Defends Mormon on Faculty and Attacks Conservatives: Baylor's president, Dr. Herbert H. Reynolds, not only defends Drs. Christian, Patterson, and Flanders; he also defends Dr. Phillip Johnson, a member of the Church of Latter-Day Saints (Mormon), who has been on Baylor's faculty since 1977. [11] In a 1984 preconvention sermon at Kansas City, Missouri, conservative Zig Ziglar protested Johnson's presence on Baylor's faculty. He remains, however, and a SBC Religious News Service release on October 19, 1984, cites President Reynolds as saying that the conservatives have set themselves up as "a little Baptist college of cardinals" who can no longer be tolerated. [12]

Playboy, Posters, and Booze: A resolution at the 1980 Southern Baptist Convention meeting in St. Louis, Missouri, praised Chancellor Abner V. McCall, who was then vice president of the SBC and president of Baylor, for his stand against Baylor's women students who had posed nude for *Playboy* magazine. [13] Even the *Southern Baptist Journal* praised McCall. [14] However, McCall later told the students that his ban on nude and semi-nude pictures of women and on beer posters in the men's dorms had been a mistake. He apologized, reversed the ban, and asked for "voluntary restraint." Incidentally each of the posing "ladies" received her degree. [15]

Beer posters have not been the only source of alcoholic problems at Baylor. Southern Baptists have complained that breweries sometimes sponsor Baylor's football team on television. President Reynolds defends the practice; after all, an estimated one-third of Baylor's students are regular drinkers, according to Dr. James Martin, dean for men's programs and housing. [16] So, as for the posters in the dorms, Dr. Reynolds simply declares that he will not "resort to any search, seize, and destroy mentality."

Students Present Manifesto to President Reynolds:
Conservative students at Baylor recently presented
President Reynolds with a six-page manifesto calling for
the dismissal of faculty members who refuse to provide
"a written account of their salvation experience," as well
as those who do not support the anti-abortion movement.
The manifesto's preamble states that its purpose is to call
attention to areas of university life that "are not subject
to the Lordship of Christ." It lists a number of areas,
including these: (1) "A personal relationship with Jesus
Christ is not necessary" before one can teach on Baylor's
faculty; (2) Phillip Johnson, a "cult"-member, is still on
the faculty; (3) The university's film society has presented
such R-rated films as *Body Heat* and *A Clockwork
Orange*, and the juke box in the student center includes
songs such as Marvin Gaye's "Sexual Healing" and
Prince's "Erotic City"; (4) A professor delivered a lecture
on "the advantages of being homosexual." The students
distributed copies of their manifesto to reporters and
invited them to the meeting in which they presented it to
the president. The administration banned the reporters. [17]

Southern Baptist Support: The Texas Baptist State
Convention has not publicly criticized Baylor University.
Of Baylor's 1983-84 budget of $7.58 million, $5.5 million
came from the Texas Baptist Convention.

Furman University

Furman University, established in 1826 in Greenville,
South Carolina, is now training more than 2000 students
in the "liberal tradition."

T. C. Smith: On February 23, 1970, Baptist Press, the
official news service arm of the SBC, issued a report on
the annual meeting of the Association of Baptist
Professors of Religion (ABPR), an organization of liberal
faculty members of Baptist schools. [18] In this news release,
Dr. T. C. Smith, president of the ABPR, attacked the
inerrancy of the Bible. "We need to come up with a concept
that is more suitable to ourselves, our students and our

conventions," asserted Smith, who was speaking as a Furman professor. Smith further insisted that modern Christians should have the liberty to determine their own canon of Scripture (i.e. which books belong in the Bible). He explained, "Modern scholarship has more valid criteria for selection of the canon than did religious leaders sixteen centuries ago." [19] Smith had taught at Southern Seminary in Louisville before coming to Furman. He has been a frequent contributor to Southern Baptist Sunday School Board literature.

L. D. Johnson: Another member of the ABPR was Dr. L. D. Johnson, who served as Chaplain and Professor of Religion at Furman from 1967 until his death in 1981. He received two graduate degrees from Southern Seminary. In 1969 the Southern Baptist Convention Press in Nashville published Johnson's *Introduction to the Bible,* in which he denied the inerrancy of the Bible (pp. 26-27). He said the first eleven chapters of Genesis are not historical, but simply contain "narratives" which serve as "vehicles" of truth. "The creation account is full of symbolic rather than scientific meaning" (p. 54). Dr. Johnson embraced the historical-critical method. "It is an oversimplification," he said, "to think of Moses as sitting down and writing the first five books of the Old Testament as they appear in the Bible" (p. 60). Apparently, to this professor the teaching of Jesus, who attributed the authorship of the Pentateuch to Moses, was an "oversimplification." Dr. Johnson described his book as "the text for course 3201 of subject area Biblical Revelation of the Christian Development Series, New Church Study Course . . . promoted by the Sunday School Board" (pp. ix, x).

Robert W. Crapps, Henry J. Flanders, and David A. Smith: In 1963 the Ronald Press in New York published a book entitled *The People of the Covenant* by three Furman University professors—Robert Wilson Crapps, Henry Jackson Flanders, Jr., and David Anthony Smith. This introduction to the Old Testament fully embraces the JEDP hypothesis (pp. 8, 11); teaches that the prophet Isaiah did not write Isaiah 40-66, which allegedly did not appear until the time of the exile (p. 306); and asserts that the prophet Daniel did not write the book which bears his name and which supposedly did not appear until about 168-165 B.C. (p. 417). Furthermore, the book presents Adam and Eve as non-historical "symbols" of humanity and the book of Jonah as a mere parable. Dr. Crapps, who received his seminary training at Southern in Louisville, has been teaching at Furman since 1957 and continues as Reuben B. Pitts Professor of Religion and Chairman of the Department of Religion. [20] Dr. Flanders taught at Furman from 1950 to 1962 and eventually went on to become Chairman of the Department of Religion at Baylor. Dr. Smith, a Southern Seminary graduate, has been teaching at Furman since 1960. [21] By 1980 at least twenty-four Southern Baptist schools were using *The People of the Covenant.*

When a *Greenville News* reporter recently asked Dr. Crapps for his views on the virgin birth, he tactfully avoided any direct answer. "The issue is not that a baby is born of a virgin," explained Crapps, "but that individuals can appreciate something is special about Jesus of Nazareth." He seemed relieved that contemporary students no longer talk "as much about the physiological virgin birth as they did fifteen or twenty years ago." [22]

Is Furman Really a Baptist Institution?: Some doubt that Furman is still a Baptist school. Furman University's chaplains are not only Baptist, but also Episcopal, Greek Orthodox, Roman Catholic, Lutheran, Methodist, Presbyterian, and even Jewish. These are all "available for pastoral care and counseling," and fourteen religious organizations, including an Episcopal Fellowship and a Jewish Student Association, "provide opportunities for service and fellowship, and seek to create an atmosphere conducive to spiritual growth." [23] Dr. Richard Roi Maag is a member of the Church of Christ, Scientist, cult and has been teaching at Furman since 1964. [24] Whether these chaplains and organizations can meet the spiritual needs of a born-again child of God is doubtful.

Southern Baptist Support: The South Carolina Baptist Convention gave $1,177,371 to Furman University in 1983. [25]

University of Richmond

Virginia Baptists established the University of Richmond in the 1830s, and Southern Baptists continue to contribute large financial amounts to the school. It is one of the largest and oldest of the Southern Baptist schools.

Frank E. Eakin, Jr.: Dr. Frank E. Eakin, Jr., is Bible Professor and Chairman of the Department of Religion at the University of Richmond. He holds a degree from Southern Seminary in Louisville. In *Review and Expositor,* Fall 1977, published by Southern Seminary, Eakin evaluates the plagues of Exodus. He concludes that the whole account is exaggerated and that no one can know what really occurred: "Perhaps some plagues are duplicate accounts of differently transmitted traditions. For example, the Yahwist's rendering of the plagues involving flies (8:20-32, number 4) and the cattle (9:1-7, number 5) is possibly duplicated by the Priestly account of the plagues involving the gnats (8:16-19, number 3 [KJV, "lice"]) and the boils (9:8-12, number 6). While dogmatism is inappropriate on the question of duplications, one can be assured that the present ten plague literary construction found in the text is an artificial one" (p. 476).

Eakin, in the same article, discusses the crossing of the Red Sea. He concludes that the Egyptians' chariots simply bogged down in a shallow body of water. No miracle occurred! Eakin explains: "When the J source and the Miriam couplet (Ex. 15:21) are juxtaposed, a probable event unfolds. The Hebrews fleeing Egypt were pursued by the Egyptians using chariots. When the Hebrews confronted a shallow body of water, a strong east wind blew back the water in a reedy, shallow area, permitting the Hebrews to cross. When the Egyptians sought to follow, their chariots were too heavy and bogged down.

As the horses attempted to pull free, some of the Egyptians were thrown into the shallow water and mud. In the confusion some Egyptians died" (p. 478).

For years, conservatives have been protesting Eakin's teachings in a Southern Baptist-supported institution, but he has been on Richmond's Bible faculty since 1966.

Robert S. Alley: Another Southern Seminary graduate, Dr. Robert S. Alley, has been on Richmond's faculty since 1963. In 1969 Alley told a reporter that the book of Jonah is a joke: "As for Jonah's ride in the whale," Alley railed, "if the author of that story were to step into the world today and discover that anybody was accepting him word for word, I have a feeling he'd just collapse from laughter."[26]

In 1970 the J. B. Lippincott Company published Robert Alley's book *Revolt Against the Faithful.* In this book the professor asserts that Adam and Eve are merely symbolic myth (pp. 13, 81, 142-43, 162). He shows contempt for the Bible: "The claim for the Bible as an objective authority is idolatry" (p. 68). He depicts Jesus as naive and uninformed: "Like his contemporaries, he [Jesus] envisioned the earth as flat. . . . The normal child of the modern generation possesses more accurate information about the planet earth and the universe than did Jesus" (pp. 85-86). Jonah and Noah were "fictitious persons" (p. 145). Alley argues that since Paul, Mark, John, and Peter do not mention Christ's miraculous virgin birth, the story is doubtful. He claims that some early, zealous Christians made up this legend to try to prove that Jesus was a real person; then later they used the story to claim His deity (pp. 147-51). He scorns belief in Christ's supernatural miracles (pp. 151-54) and bodily resurrection (pp. 154-58). Alley equates belief in an inerrant Bible with belief in a flat earth: "While some persons may continue to hold that 'the historic Christian belief in Biblical infallibility and inerrancy is the only valid starting point...,' such contentions should be heard with a smile and incorporated in the bylaws of the Flat Earth Society" (p. 167). The author's father, Dr. Reuben E. Alley, who was editor of the Virginia Baptist Convention's state newspaper, the *Religious Herald*, receives much credit from his son: "My father first gave rise to my understanding to genuine freedom.... He has provided great assistance in editing" (p. 8).

On December 6, 1977, Robert S. Alley gave a two-and-one-half-hour lecture to a group of self-proclaimed atheists in Richmond's First Unitarian Church. Speaking as Bible professor and chairman of the University of Richmond's Department of Religion, Alley said, "I don't imagine for a minute that he [Jesus] would have had the audacity to claim the deity for himself." Three days later, about sixty Southern Baptist pastors in the area met with University of Richmond's president, E. Bruce Heilman, who apologized for Alley's "bad judgment." Alley, however, admitted that he really "felt comfortable among the atheists," and he called the pastors "stupid." When he voluntarily transferred to another department in order to still the waters, his colleagues drew up a formal resolution demanding more academic freedom and protesting the conservative attacks on Alley. [27]

Robert S. Alley continues his theme. In a five-page article which appeared in *Free Inquiry,* Summer 1982, Alley said, "The phrase 'Word of God' is a hindrance.... It fails to take seriously the humanity and personality of the biblical writers. The phrase needs to be retired" (p. 7). The article is titled "The Word of God, a Phrase Whose Time Has Passed."

Southern Baptist Support: In 1982 Dr. W. A. Criswell told Southern Baptists that the University of Richmond "has ceased to be a Baptist school." [28] The Baptist General Association of Virginia budgeted $437,637 to the University of Richmond in 1984 and proposed $455,124 for 1985. [29] Robert S. Alley continues on the payroll as Professor of Humanities; Frank E. Eakin, Jr., continues as Professor of Bible and Chairman of the Religion Department. Other Southern Seminary graduates on Richmond's religion faculty include Philip R. Hart, Robison B. James, and O. William Rhodenhiser. [30] Robert S. Alley himself remains in good standing among Southern Baptists as an ordained minister of the denomination. Before coming to Richmond, Alley was at one time a Bible professor at William Jewell College.

William Jewell College

William Jewell College in Liberty, Missouri, was founded by Baptists in 1849 and named in honor of a great frontier statesman, physician, and benefactor. It claims to represent the finest of its Baptist heritage. However, Dr. David O. Moore, Professor of Religion and Chairman of the Department of Religion, openly denies the Bible's infallibility, Satan's existence, and even Christ's virgin birth. [31] Moore, who received his seminary training at Southern Seminary in Louisville, has been teaching Bible at William Jewell since 1956. Others on the religion faculty include J. Bradley Chance and David N. Duke from Southern Seminary, and Jerry B. Cain from Midwestern Seminary. [32] The Missouri Baptist Convention's projected 1985 budget provides $1,036,949 for William Jewell. [33]

Virginia Intermont College

Three months after becoming Virginia Intermont College's new president in July 1983, James E. Martin, Jr., curtailed visitation between sexes in the dorms, removed two nude sketches from a college art exhibit, and outlawed alcohol from college functions. Immediately, twenty-one faculty members (almost half the total faculty) signed a pledge criticizing Martin's actions. Martin had not actually eliminated visitation between sexes in the dormitories; he had only curtailed it. This was too strict, however, for these faculty members. [34] Martin resigned in July 1984. The school is located in Bristol, Virginia. The Baptist General Association of Virginia budgeted $237,022 to Virginia Intermont College in 1984 and proposed $247,897 for 1985. [35]

Conservatives Pose No Serious Threat

Southern Baptist colleges are among the most heavily endowed institutions of higher education in America. The

University of Richmond, for instance, enjoys a private endowment of over $130 million; Baylor has secured a nearly $121 million endowment. A few conservatives cannot seriously intimidate these schools. Since the North Carolina Baptist Convention made all support to Wake Forest voluntary in 1981, the school has not raised its fees beyond the national norm, and it continues to receive a very large percentage of its Southern Baptist support. Its private endowment is around $125 million.

Some Southern Baptists have privately expressed their feelings to me that as a matter of biblical principle they can no longer remain associated with a denomination so entrenched with those things which they abhor. No one can control these problems any longer. God's Word says that this is endorsement by association. "If there come any unto you, and bring not this doctrine, receive him not into your house, neither bid him God speed: For he that biddeth him God speed is partaker of his evil deeds" (II John 10-11).

Endnotes

1. Meredith, a women's college at Raleigh, North Carolina, has for many years hosted an array of apostate speakers. For example, in June 1954 Nels Ferré and E. McNeill Poteat appeared on one of their programs. Ferré was the featured speaker. Four years later, Modernists George Arthur Buttrick, Paul S. Minear, and F. Bredahl Petersen led a series of "Christian Studies" here. The list is long. The Virginia Baptist Convention contributed $814,557 to Meredith College in 1984, according to the Convention's financial statement.

2. *Southern Baptist Journal,* March/April 1979, p. 3.

3. *St. Petersburg Independent,* December 22, 1983; see also *Southern Baptist Journal,* March/April 1979, p. 1f.; *Southern Baptist Journal,* March 1977, p. 7; the Florida Baptist Convention's financial statement reports that Southern Baptists contributed $1,007,965 to Stetson University in 1984.

4. *Bulletin,* Baylor University, College of Arts and Sciences, 1984-85, p. 6.

5. *Baptist Challenge,* December 1980, p. 9.

6. *Southern Baptist Advocate,* October 1980, p. 3.

7. *Washington Post,* November 24, 1979.

8. *Houston Chronicle,* March 13, 1982; see also *Christian News,* August 2, 1982, p. 15.

9. *Bulletin,* Baylor University, College of Arts and Sciences, 1984-85, p. 10.

10. Ibid., p. 5.

11. Ibid. p. 7; see also the *Utah Evangel,* June 1982, p. 1 and December 1982, p. 3; *The Baptist Challenge,* September 1984, p. 11; *Southern Baptist Advocate,* January 1984, p. 4; and the *Christian News,* September 17, 1984, p. 19.

12. *Christian News,* October 29, 1984, p. 13.

13. *Annual,* SBC, 1980, pp. 31, 49.

14. *Southern Baptist Journal,* April 1980, p. 4.

15. *Biblical Evangelist,* March 16, 1984, p. 10.

16. *Southern Baptist Advocate,* May 1983, p. 6.

17. *Chronicle of Higher Education,* January 9, 1985, p. 3; *Dallas Morning News,* December 14, 1984.

18. The ABPR was founded in 1928 and publishes the journal *Perspectives in Religious Studies.*

19. *Christianity Today,* April 24, 1970, p. 5; T. C. Smith's Liberalism also appears clearly in his chapter, "The Canon and Authority of the Bible," in *Perspectives in Religious Studies,* Spring 1974, pp. 43-51 (esp. p. 50).

20. *Bulletin,* Furman University, 1984-85, pp. 76, 100.

21. Ibid., pp. 76, 103.

22. *Greenville News,* December 24, 1984.

23. *Bulletin,* Furman University, 1984-85, p. 17.

24. Ibid., pp. 69, 102; see also the *Greenville Piedmont,* November 17, 1982.

25. Financial statement from the South Carolina Baptist Convention.

26. *Newsweek,* May 5, 1969, p. 97.

27. *Richmond News Leader,* December 7, 1977; this was an official Baptist Press release; see also *Christianity Today,* February 10, 1978, p. 30; *Southern Baptist Journal,* April 1978, p. 3; *Southern Baptist Journal,* June 1978, p. 3; *Fundamentalist Journal,* February 1983, p. 20f.

28. *Fort Worth Star Telegram,* October 4, 1982; *Southern Baptist Advocate,* Fall 1982, p. 1f.

29. Mimeographed statement from the Budget Committee of the Baptist General Association of Virginia.

30. *Academic Catalog,* University of Richmond, 1984-86, pp. 105, 118f.

31. *Kansas City Star,* March 7, 1974; see also *Southern Baptist Journal,* October 1979, p. 1f.

32. *Catalog,* William Jewell College, 1984-85, pp. 99, 110-111.

33. Letter from the Missouri Baptist Convention's Department of Support Services.

34. *Christian News,* January 2, 1984, p. 2; *Southern Baptist Journal,* January/February 1984, p. 11.

35. Mimeographed statement from the Budget Committee of the Baptist General Association of Virginia.

Chapter Thirteen

The Matter of Creeds

In their opposition to "creedalism," Liberals continue their appeal to "individual liberty." The rallying cries of liberal inclusivism are pious-sounding clichés: "Baptists have no creed but the Bible"; "The New Testament is our creed." A sort of creedal paranoia prevails. Such clichés serve as smoke screens, however, intimidating conservative Southern Baptists from pressing the matter of real substance, such as biblical inerrancy and the virgin birth. Most Liberals do not wish to be pressed into stating specifically what they believe about some Bible doctrines.

Charles H. Spurgeon on Creeds

A century ago, Charles H. Spurgeon faced this same issue with the "latitudinarians" or Liberals in the Baptist Union of Great Britain and Ireland. The Baptist Union Liberals expressed a willingness to include any group which practiced immersion. They regarded the mode of baptism as more important than doctrine, and they abhorred any idea of a carefully worded doctrinal statement. It was in the midst of that great controversy, the "Downgrade Controversy," that Spurgeon made the following remarkable statement:

> I am unable to sympathize with a man who says he has no creed; because I believe him to be in the wrong by his own showing. He ought to have a creed. What is equally certain, he has a creed—he must have one, even though he repudiates the notion. His very unbelief is, in a sense, a creed.
>
> The objection to a creed is a very pleasant way of concealing objection to discipline, and a desire for latitudinarianism. What is wished for is a Union which will, like Noah's Ark, afford shelter both for the clean and for the unclean, for creeping things and winged fowls.
>
> Every Union, unless it is a mere fiction, must be based upon certain principles. How can we unite except upon some great common truths? And the doctrine of baptism by immersion is not sufficient for a groundwork. Surely, to be a Baptist is not everything. If I disagree with a man on ninety-nine points, but happen to be one with him in baptism, this can never furnish such ground of unity as I have with another with whom I believe in ninety-nine points, and only happen to differ upon one ordinance. To form a union with a single Scriptural ordinance as its sole distinctive reason for existence has been well likened to erecting a pyramid upon its apex: the whole edifice must sooner or later come down. I am not slow to avow my conviction that the immersion of believers is the baptism of Holy Scripture, but there are other truths beside this; and I cannot feel fellowship with a man because of this, if in other matters he is false to the teaching of Holy Scripture. [1]

James P. Boyce on Faculty Signing Creeds

Dr. James P. Boyce, a founding father of Southern Seminary, thought that every professor should sign a specific doctrinal statement. He said this: "It is with a single man that error usually commences; and when such a man has influence or position, it is impossible to estimate the evil that will attend it. Ecclesiastical history is full of warning upon this subject." Boyce continued with these

remarks: "The theological professor is to teach ministers
. . . in such a manner before his pupils that they shall arrive
at the truth without danger of any mixture of error
therewith. He cannot do this if he have any erroneous
tendencies, and hence his opinions must be expressly
affirmed to be, upon every point, in accordance with the
truth we believe to be taught in the Scriptures."[2]

Southern Baptists Do Have Confessions of Faith

In 1925 the SBC adopted the first statement of faith
in its long history. This statement, called the Baptist Faith
and Message, was based upon the New Hampshire
Confession of 1833. In 1963, following the Ralph Elliott
controversy at Midwestern Seminary, the SBC reaffirmed
and slightly revised its Baptist Faith and Message. The
following is the entire text of Article One of each of the
three statements:

The New Hampshire Confession (1833)
We believe [that] the Holy Bible was written by men
divinely inspired, and is a perfect treasure of heavenly
instruction; that it has God for its author, salvation for
its end, and truth, without any mixture of error, for its
matter; that it reveals the principles by which God will
judge us; and therefore is, and shall remain to the end
of the world, the true center of Christian union, and
the supreme standard by which all human conduct,
creeds, and opinions should be tried.

Baptist Faith and Message (1925)
We believe that the Holy Bible was written by men
divinely inspired, and is a perfect treasure of heavenly
instruction; that it has God for its author, salvation for
its end, and truth, without any mixture of error, for its
matter; that it reveals the principles by which God will
judge us; and therefore is, and will remain to the end
of the world, the true center of Christian union, and
the supreme standard by which all human conduct,
creeds, and religious opinions should be tried.

Baptist Faith and Message (1963)
The Holy Bible was written by men divinely inspired
and is the record of God's revelation of Himself to man.

It is a perfect treasure of divine instruction. It has God for its author, salvation for its end, and truth, without any mixture of error, for its matter. It reveals the principles by which God judges us; and therefore is, and will remain to the end of the world, the true center of Christian union, and the supreme standard by which all human conduct, creeds, and religious opinions should be tried. The criterion by which the Bible is to be interpreted is Jesus Christ.

Few Baptists Take Creeds Seriously

Conservatives have long noted that each of the three confessions describes the Bible as "truth, without any mixture of error." Conservative William A. Powell observes, however, that "there is a prevailing attitude within the SBC establishment that the 1963 Baptist Faith and Message *guidelines* is [*sic*] more of a 'window dressing' exercise than it is an effort to insure doctrinal purity in our denomination. It may be comparable to a published statement of the generals to appease the troops during an uprising in order to prevent a revolt."[3] Baptist Liberals never seem to take confessional statements seriously.

The Incredible Arkansas Policy

The following policy statement appears in the *Arkansas Baptist Newsmagazine,* an official state newspaper, on April 1, 1971:

All members of the staff of the Arkansas Baptist State Convention are not only allowed but encouraged to assume full liberty of academic and editorial freedom, to embrace their own beliefs, convictions, viewpoints, concepts and opinions on any and all matters pertaining to the Christian faith; to practice them, preach them, stand for them, defend them, and to live them. However, in the acceptance of full academic and editorial freedom, such must be accorded to all others. It is hereby agreed that every staff member shall have full access to freedom for himself as a person and may assume any theological stance he feels is right; he is not to promote, initiate, or become the part of any organization, conspiracy, movement or fellowship which would deny, impede, harass, disfranchise, or void any other child of God the same privilege. The staff of the Arkansas Baptist State Convention as a staff will assume no particular theological stance, nor will they promote such. Each staff member may enjoy the full privileges of religious freedom, freedom of press, and speech but is not at liberty to organize others or set in motion an organization or conspiracy to coerce, force or drive others to his particular position. The staff of the Arkansas Baptist State Convention will exercise no option to promote or discredit people with viewpoints at variance or in agreement with theirs. No person in a place of leadership in the convention will be prejudiced in the eyes of any staff person of the convention and shall not be persecuted or promoted because of the presence of or the absence of any particular opinion or viewpoint. [4]

Under much criticism, the Arkansas Baptist Convention has recently rescinded this statement as its "official" policy, but it is generally understood that it continues to represent the unofficial sentiment of the state's leaders. According to this statement, no person should be disenfranchised for any reason having to do with doctrine. He may be an agnostic, an atheist, a Buddhist, or a conservative; but "no person in a place of leadership in the convention will be . . . persecuted or promoted because of the presence or absence of any particular opinion or viewpoint."

The Case of Dallas Baptist College

Most Baptist institutions today are depending so much on government aid and accrediting associations that they would be unable to enforce any policy requiring faculty to sign a doctrinal statement. A few years ago, Dallas Baptist College moved its statement of faith to the personnel manual rather than having it remain a separate document. This was a last-ditch effort to avoid a court case, but most observers believe that this policy will be defeated if ever pressed in the courts of law. [5]

Endnotes

1. *Sword and Trowel,* February 1888; see also *Metropolitan Tabernacle Pulpit,* XXXIV (Pasadena, Texas: Pilgrim Publications, 1974), foreword.

2. James P. Boyce, *Three Changes in Theological Institutions,* cited in John A. Broadus, *Memoir of James Petigru Boyce* (New York: A. C. Armstrong and Son, 1893), p. 139.

3. William A. Powell, *The SBC Issue & Question* (Buchanan, Georgia: Baptist Missionary Service, Inc., 1977), p. 213. For a valuable discussion on how Southern Baptist Liberals interpret the Baptist Faith and Message, see the Kentucky Southern Baptist state paper, *Western Reporter,* June 5, 1984.

4. *Arkansas Baptist Newsmagazine,* April 1, 1971; this policy statement also appears in the minutes of the staff meetings of the executive board of the Arkansas Baptist State Convention, Charles H. Ashcraft, executive secretary.

5. *Moody Monthly,* June 1980, p. 93f.

PART III:
Southern Baptist Literature

The Sunday School Board—Past and Present

Headquartered in Nashville, Tennessee, the Southern Baptist Sunday School Board (BSSB) publishes the official SBC literature at every level. The earliest advocates of a Southern Baptist publishing arm were Southern Seminary founders Basil Manly, Jr., and John A. Broadus—hence, the name "Broadman," one of the Board's publishing trade names. With its modern network of facilities now spreading across the United States, the Sunday School Board employs more than 1,800 people, owns and operates two national conference centers and over sixty bookstores and mail order centers, and provides annually more than 162 million pieces of literature to over 36,000 churches. In a recent year, the Board spent $2.6 million for postage alone. In 1979 the Board, which is completely self-supporting, acquired the venerable Holman Bible Publishers—now identified as the Holman Division. This is a far cry from 1891 when the Board's founder, J. M. Frost, set up shop with one desk in a rent-free space in a friend's office. According to the 1984 SBC *Annual,* the Board's yearly budget is almost $150 million (p. 51). The three most recent Board presidents are James L. Sullivan (1953-75), Grady C. Cothen (1975-84), and Lloyd Elder (1984-   ).

More historical and statistical information is available in the *General Information Guide* (Sunday School Board of the SBC, 1984) and the *Sunday School Board Annual Report.*

Chapter Fourteen

Broadman Bible Commentary

Broadman Bible Commentary is a set of twelve large volumes covering the whole Bible. The Southern Baptist Sunday School Board (BSSB) produced it between 1969 and 1973 as its largest publishing venture. The set represents the thinking of a cross section of Southern Baptist leadership. There were fifty-nine contributors: eleven from Southern Seminary; four from Midwestern; seven from Southwestern; four from New Orleans Seminary; six from Southeastern; and one from Golden Gate. Others are from Baylor University, the University of Richmond, Wake Forest University, Campbell College, Carson-Newman College, Fuller Seminary, and the American Baptist Seminary of the West. Obviously, we cannot review the entire set in a work of this size, but the following should serve as key samples of the work's theology and philosophy.

The Volume-One Controversy

Volume one includes nine "General Articles" followed by commentaries on Genesis and Exodus. Clifton J. Allen, the set's general editor, contributed the opening article, called "The Book of the Christian Faith." Allen sets the tone of the entire set by advancing the suppositions of the historical-critical method. He says that the Old Testament laws "reflected the impact of Israel's cultural situation, the immaturity of the people in their spiritual and moral development" (p. 2). Allen denies the prophetical nature of books in both the Old and the New Testament. The book of Revelation, for example, was already history when the author penned it. It simply "points to persons and events and forces in the long distant past." This is also true, says Allen, of all apocalyptic literature, including the book of Daniel. Such literature was simply "the product of times of intense crisis" (p. 4). In line with the Graf-Wellhausen hypothesis, Allen asserts this about the Pentateuch: "There is a rather general consensus among scholars that editors collated written material, produced out of the sources described above [oral traditions and myths], and gave it permanent form. Trustworthy biblical study shows that the Pentateuch existed essentially in its present form by 400 B.C." (p. 10). He adds, "Its authority is not in inerrancy" (p. 11). Allen defends "dynamic inspiration," which he says "is not dependent on a mystical, inexplicable, and unverifiable inerrancy in every word of Scripture" (p. 7).

This man, Clifton J. Allen, who denied that the Bible is the infallible Word of God, served as a long-time Editorial Secretary of the Sunday School Board and as Recording Secretary of the SBC. On September 22, 1972, the Sunday School Board Trustees presented Allen with a certificate and a special plaque commending him for his work as General Editor of the *Broadman Bible Commentary*.

Another article in volume one is on "Archaeology and the Bible," by Joseph A. Callaway, who teaches that Adam was not a real person: "In the first place, Adam, like original man in other Near Eastern texts, is a representative man, all of mankind poured into one individual." This is one of several "guidelines for interpreting the Bible," says Callaway. "The guidance comes from literary texts outside the Bible that illuminate the meaning of the Biblical account" (p. 47). Callaway, however, who is still

Senior Professor of Old Testament at Southern Seminary in Louisville, expresses a higher esteem for pagan literature than for the Word of God.

Eric C. Rust, also from Southern Seminary, contributed an article entitled "The Theology of the Old Testament." Charging the Bible with false ideas which it never expresses, Rust makes a mockery of the Word of God. Describing what he considers a typical Old Testament writer, Rust says, "His world is a three-tiered universe. He pictures a flat earth, like a disc, with mountains at the edge on which the solid dome of heaven, the firmament, rests. Under the earth is the enlarged family grave, Sheol, where the shades of the departed go. Above the dome of heaven is God's palace. Genesis 1 and Psalm 104 alike illustrate this cosmology" (p. 73).

John I. Durham, who is still Professor of Hebrew and Old Testament at Southeastern Seminary, contributed an article on "Contemporary Approaches in Old Testament Study." Durham embraces the historical-critical method. "Current Pentateuchal study," Durham asserts, "recognizes in broad terms, the presence within the Pentateuch of three strata of sources: oral sources, written sources, and redactional or editorial sources" (p. 90).

G. Henton Davies, principal of Regent's Park College, Oxford, England, wrote the commentary on Genesis. In his introduction, Davies defends the JEDP hypothesis (pp. 109-116) and reduces the Genesis flood to the immoral act of an ancient god of pagan mythology. He explains: "The double account represents the Israelite transformation of a Canaanite account, that is, western version of flood stories originally circulating in the Babylonian or eastern area of the Fertile Crescent." Davies contends that the biblical account of a universal flood "calls for belief beyond reason. For many persons, the moral question is even more disturbing. Is God such a being that he would destroy the first mankind?" (p. 117). Davies obviously considers his own standards superior to the Bible's. Denying the Mosaic authorship of the Pentateuch, he says, "The biblical writer is almost certainly a priest and a learned man who writes . . . out of accumulated priestly knowledge" (p. 123). Concerning God's command to

Abraham to offer his son Isaac as a sacrifice, Davies asks, "What Christian or humane conscience could regard such a command as coming from God?" Davies, however, who was the president of the liberal Baptist Union of Great Britain, is blatantly denying the explicit statement of Holy Scripture in Genesis 21:1-2 (pp. 189-99).

Roy L. Honeycutt, Jr., then Professor of Old Testament at Midwestern Seminary, wrote the commentary on Exodus. Writing as one committed to the JEDP hypothesis (pp. 305-21), Honeycutt asserts, "The narrators have overlaid this historical nucleus with additional material" (p. 333). Commenting on Exodus 12, he denies that God smote the firstborn as verse 29 says. Honeycutt thinks that "a fatal pestilence struck the Egyptian children." He explains that through the years the whole story became just an exaggerated tale: "Through years of transmission within Israel the memory of the event was so shaped that . . . only the firstborn were involved" (p. 363). Discussing the crossing of the Red Sea, Honeycutt leaves it an open question as to whether or not one should take the biblical account literally at face value. He simply presents the various liberal views and ends the discussion (p. 386). Honeycutt is now president of Southern Seminary, from which he has announced his declaration of "holy war" against the conservative movement.

The above are only a few key examples of the rank Liberalism of Broadman's first volume. Modernism so permeates the entire volume that Southern Baptist conservatives arose in protest. Consequently, the messengers to the Denver SBC meeting in June 1970, with President W. A. Criswell presiding, instructed the Sunday School Board to withdraw the volume from further distribution and to rewrite it with "due consideration of the conservative viewpoint." The ballot count was 5,394 to 2,170.

While jubilant conservatives were hailing the resolution as a triumph for their cause, the more politically astute Liberals, including many state paper editors, were busy maneuvering. Soon, over half of the thirty-three state papers were criticizing the messengers' decision with such choice adjectives as "hostile," "unchristian," "bitter," "vitriolic," "arrogant," "unforgiving," and "militant." Meanwhile, when the Sunday School Board asked Davies and Honeycutt to rewrite their material, they insisted on "maintaining their integrity." In other words, at best these Liberals might be willing to make their interpretations a bit more palatable to the common man, but they would not present the historic Christian position. While Davies bowed out, Honeycutt "rewrote" his Exodus commentary.

The one who finally agreed to rewrite the Genesis section of volume one was Clyde T. Francisco, Professor of Old Testament at Southern Seminary. Admittedly sharing Davies's and Honeycutt's basic views, Francisco simply toned down a few of the most glaring liberal sections. [1] Even in the original first volume, he had contributed an article on the history of Israel in which he had denied the Mosaic authorship of the Pentateuch, placing its writing at about 500 B.C. (p. 57).

This whole "rewrite" is the "same song, second stanza." It continues to espouse the historical-critical method: "The materials used by the writer or writers were largely those received in their traditions, the accounts of their ancestors handed down among their forefathers. These sources belong primarily to two basic tradition groups, a priestly and a popular one" (p. 119). At best, Francisco teaches theistic evolution in his coverage of Genesis 1: "Creation is viewed as having occurred over an indefinite period of time, and having proceeded from the lower forms to the higher" (p. 120). [2]

Conservatives would hail this rewrite, which appeared in 1973, as "the greatest victory in our denomination thus far in the battle." [3] The Sunday School Board, however, made an agreement with Marshall, Morgan, and Scott Ltd., which gave the latter the exclusive right to reprint and publish the original volume one in most countries outside of the U.S.A. This volume has been most readily available from London book dealers.

Volume Two

Volume two covers Leviticus through Ruth. John Joseph Owens, who continues as Professor of Old

Testament Interpretation at Southern Seminary, wrote the commentary on Numbers. Accepting the Graf-Wellhausen hypothesis (p. 91), Owens speaks of "the priestly compiler" of Numbers (p. 85). Instead of Israel's army having 603,550 men as the Bible says, it probably had more like 5,500, according to Owens, who concludes, after all, "these figures are not to be taken as accurate" (p. 93). Furthermore, the manna which the Bible says fell from heaven was actually nothing more than the "juice" of the "tarfa tree" (p. 115).

William H. Morton, who continues as Senior Professor of Biblical Archaeology at Midwestern Seminary, wrote the commentary on Joshua. When he describes the stopping of the Jordan (Joshua 3:14f.), Morton uses the word "miracle," but, following the Graf-Wellhausen hypothesis, he goes to great lengths to explain away the supernatural with totally naturalistic causes. For example, Morton thinks that an earthquake occurred, upsetting some cliffs of clay above the water and thus damming up the river. Says Morton, "Verse 16 seems to be referring to just such an event" (p. 314). How fascinating the extent to which "scholarly" unbelievers will go in order to avoid acknowledging the supernatural. The Bible plainly says that God halted the Jordan as the priests bearing the ark entered and that He returned the water to its place, even overflowing all of its banks, when the soles of the priests' feet were lifted up on dry land (Joshua 3:15-16 and 4:15-18). Childlike faith has no difficulty believing this as it appears in the Scripture account. Admittedly, however, the story of the clay cliffs falling into the Jordan and stopping its waters also requires some degree of faith. Morton writes throughout like the typical modern, condescending "scholar," piously attempting to add a degree of erudition and respectability to exaggerated, ancient stories supposedly handed down orally by religious nationalists in their own bigoted styles.

Volume Three

Roy L. Honeycutt, Jr., wrote the commentary on II Kings in volume three. He denies that angels are created physical beings, and he reduces the Angel of the Lord to a figure of speech. Says Honeycutt, "Few people today would press the literal concept of physical beings who travel from heaven to earth and back again. . . . Most likely, the concept of the angel of the Lord was a profound but nonliteral means of speaking of God's presence." Any literal concept is too "ancient" and certainly not "obligatory for the contemporary reader" (p. 227).

Honeycutt heaps scorn upon the story of the floating ax head. To him, the whole affair is "a combination of saga and legend, inextricably interwoven." Such stories are examples of heathen magic: "The miracle story illustrates the ancient principle of imitative magic or contactual magic" (p. 242). After all, says this Modernist, "God works through history and the natural order, not apart from it" (p. 278). [4]

Volume Five

Page H. Kelley, who is still Professor of Old Testament Interpretation at Southern Seminary, wrote the commentary on Isaiah in volume five. He contends that the prophet Isaiah wrote only chapters 1-39 and that a "second Isaiah" wrote chapters 40-66 (p. 161). Kelley found support for this in Clyde T. Francisco's Th. D. thesis at Southern Seminary. Francisco had defended this "Deutero-Isaiah" view, refusing to acknowledge that the prophet actually foretold events which were beyond his own time. Liberals ignore the fact that the Lord Jesus cited Isaiah 53:1 and 6:10 and attributed both passages to the prophet Isaiah (John 12:38-41). *Broadman Bible Commentary* uses the Revised Standard Version throughout, and Page Kelley finds this especially helpful in Isaiah 7:14; he defends the RSV translation, "young woman" (p. 215), as opposed to "virgin."

Volume Eight

Volume eight begins the New Testament and opens with several "general articles" of introduction, beginning with "Contemporary Approaches in New Testament

Study," by Ray Summers of Baylor University. Summers applies the historical-critical approach to the Gospels. This is called form criticism (or *Formgeschichte,* which literally means "form history"). "Basic to all competent contemporary approaches in New Testament study," says Summers, "is the historicocritical method" (p. 48); as he explains, "It is a study of the history of how the materials of the Gospels came to be preserved and set in the form in which they appear in the written gospel" (p. 49). He adds, "Another feature of this method is the stress it places on the stage of oral traditions. . . . Its main concern is not with written sources. . . . It was by constant repetition during these years of oral use that the account received the 'form' which it possesses in the written account" (p. 50). So, according to the *Broadman Bible Commentary,* the Gospels were not written by the men whose names they bear; they are simply the product of a long "repetition" of "oral tradition," and they are not the verbally inspired Word of God. According to this view, John 14:26 could have little or no application to the writing of the Gospels: Jesus said, "But the Comforter, which is the Holy Ghost, whom the Father will send in my name, he shall teach you all things, and bring all things to your remembrance, whatsoever I have said unto you."

Frank Stagg, of Southern Seminary in Louisville, wrote the commentary on Matthew in volume eight, and he introduces this Gospel with a lengthy argument in favor of form criticism, a category of higher criticism (pp. 72-75). The commentary on Mark, in the same volume, condescendingly depicts Christ Himself as a poor, ignorant character who naively accepted the views of His own day and who should not be taken seriously: "Jesus accepted a world view of Satan and his kingdom that was contemporary with the years of his ministry." The "modern Christian," therefore, "is not bound to take the same view" (p. 293). The apostle Paul tells believers exactly how to respond to such teaching:

> If any man teach otherwise, and consent not to wholesome words, even the words of our Lord Jesus Christ, and to the doctrine which is according to

godliness; He is proud, knowing nothing, but doting about questions and strifes of words, whereof cometh envy, strife, railings, evil surmisings, Perverse disputings of men of corrupt minds, and destitute of the truth, supposing that gain is godliness: from such withdraw thyself (I Timothy 6:3-5).

Conclusion

No one who accepts the *Broadman Bible Commentary* completely, at face value, can really believe that the Bible "has truth for its matter, without any mixture of error," as the Baptist Faith and Message affirms. This massive set contains much good material, but subtle falsehood so permeates it throughout that it merits no general endorsement. Even a single bad apple ruins the whole basket. There are so many good, scholarly, conservative commentaries now available that no leader or layman needs to depend upon the *Broadman Bible Commentary.* Dr. W. Ross Edwards, editor of the Missouri Baptist newspaper, *The Word and Way,* once concluded, "If the interpretation of Genesis in the *Broadman Commentary* goes unchallenged, we owe an apology to Ralph Elliott."

Endnotes

1. Liberal church history professor, Leon McBeth of South-western Seminary, readily asserts that Francisco's rewrite was basically as liberal as Davies's original; see his article in *Review and Expositor,* Winter 1982, pp. 90-91.

2. Francisco's liberal bent appears much more restrained in an earlier work, perhaps because it was based upon John R. Sampey's *Syllabus* at Southern Seminary. Francisco's title is *Introducing the Old Testament* (Nashville: Broadman, 1950); see especially p. 47.

3. William A. Powell, *The SBC Issue & Question* (Buchanan, Georgia: Baptist Missionary Service, Inc., 1977), p. 48.

4. See other examples of Honeycutt's liberal bias on pp. 228, 232-33, 236, 238, and throughout his sections in the *Broadman Bible Commentary.*

Chapter Fifteen

Training Materials and Books

Conservative Southern Baptists have been expressing concern for years that the Sunday School Board uses liberal writers. Members of the characteristically liberal Association of Baptist Professors of Religion (ABPR) contribute regularly to Board material. Liberal spokesmen, such as George L. Ballentine, formerly of the First Baptist Church of Augusta, Georgia, and now president of Shorter College in Rome, Georgia, continue to write materials for the Sunday School Board's educational programs. [1] Since obviously no exhaustive compilation is possible in a survey of this nature and size, the following pages offer samples of the liberal thought which has appeared in Southern Baptist training materials over two decades.

Training Materials

Liberalism is not a new phenomenon in Southern Baptist training materials. In spite of constant conservative protests, it has appeared in Southern Baptist Sunday School Board literature for more than twenty years now.

The *Baptist Training Union Magazine* for September 1963 carried an article by Millard J. Berquist, the president of Midwestern Seminary who had just defended Ralph Elliott's liberal *Message of Genesis*. Falsely identifying verbal inspiration with the dictation theory (an often-used liberal tactic), Berquist concludes in his article that verbal inspiration is "unacceptable to most serious and thoughtful students of the Bible." Southern Baptist youth are constantly barraged with this kind of subtle attack on the verbally inspired and inerrant Word of God. Mainline Fundamentalism does not accept the dictation theory, which claims that the Scripture writers were completely passive and that they did not incorporate their own personalities and styles into the text. When Berquist says, "The Bible itself is not a revelation," he is expressing a liberal or neo-orthodox view. To him, "There is much evidence of different levels of inspiration in the Bible." So Berquist attacks the Bible by appealing to the latest liberal "scholarship." He insists that although the "verbal inspiration theory . . . assumes the Bible's complete accuracy in every detail, . . . archeological research and the science of biblical criticism have made this position unacceptable to most serious and thoughtful students of the Bible and Bible backgrounds." Such criticism leaves young people with the impression that conservatives are opposed to scholarly research and the science of textual studies. To the contrary, the greatest advances in the study of bibliography and textual research have come from such staunch conservative inerrantists as Benjamin B. Warfield, Edward J. Young, and A. T. Robertson.

The Training Union Quarterly, *Baptist Young People*, for April/May/June 1969 depicts the eighteenth-century Great Awakening as extreme and Horace Bushnell as the needed, balancing influence. Referring to the preaching of George Whitefield, Jonathan Edwards, and Gilbert Tennent, the lesson explains, "The revivalism movement emphasized moral depravity and radical conversion. Horace Bushnell came onto this scene in the middle of the nineteenth century to support needed correctives to the revivalistic emphasis" (p. 53). It is noteworthy that the lesson presents Bushnell as the hero who finally appears to supply the "needed correctives to the revivalistic emphasis." The Quarterly accurately describes Bushnell: "Bushnell introduced an entirely new Christian educational theory. The prevailing outlook emphasized a datable conversion experience. Christians were considered morally depraved until this radical change of heart became a part of their experience. The renunciation of sin and acceptance of Christ at a revival meeting was the central event in life for a young person. Bushnell was not comfortable with this point of view. . . . Bushnell thought children should be raised so that there should never be a time in their lives when they thought they were anything but Christians. They should always see themselves as members of the household of faith" (p. 54). This lesson left the impression that Bushnell's was the more acceptable view.

The lesson for June 29 promotes socialistic philosophy. This lesson, "Accepting God's Mission in the World," instructs young people that "the poor represent a living indictment against the society which perpetuates their poverty." Our American society, say these educators, should be ashamed for "failures in distribution of wealth" (p. 66). They add, "Our country cannot long endure a great divide between the *have's* and *have-not's*" (p. 67).

The young people's Training Union Quarterly for July/August/September 1969 falsely uses Dr. John Broadus as a model to encourage rebellion. The Quarterly is entitled *Good News through the Arts,* and in the July lessons, Unit I, the authors describe "Baptist Voices of Yesterday." Here Dr. Broadus appears as a "bearded man" who "was not narrow-minded—he had a broad view of life." As evidence of this, the lesson claims that Broadus "spoke of Charles Darwin with knowledge and appreciation." Broadus was allegedly "a pioneer in introducing Southern Baptists . . . to the historical methods of the continent." Such portrayal of Dr. Broadus as a Liberal and a rebel is false and wicked. This scholar never expressed any sympathy for Darwin's views or for higher biblical criticism. Because of his prolific erudition, however, the Liberals have always desired to claim Broadus, as they do in this lesson. Lesson Two (July 13) praises E. Y. Mullins as a "crusader for Rights" against "the wave of anti-evolutionist sentiment." The lesson for July 20 concerns "The Gospel and W. T. Conner." Here, Dr. Walter Thomas Conner of Southwestern Seminary appears as a pioneer hero attacking an "ultraconservative religious spirit" which "was not adequate for an educated minister" (pp. 16-18). The simple truth, however, is that Dr. Conner was himself a conservative who long defended the verbal inspiration and inerrancy of the Bible. Never did he identify with liberals or attack historic conservative positions. The Lesson for July 27 praises W. O. Carver of Southern Seminary for his willingness to be an innovator and a heretic. The Lesson attempts to make the term "heretic" an attractive label to inspire young people to dare to go against historic orthodoxy.

The October/November/December 1969 issue of *Context,* "a collegiate Bible study" in the Forefront series of the Sunday School curriculum, attacks the doctrine of biblical inerrancy as being outdated and unscholarly. "A college-age Christian" must be ready to acknowledge that "the scientifically trained mind will not permit one to accept literally such events as the creation of woman from the rib of Adam" (p. 5). This "Bible study" describes the Bible as having "inconsistencies" and "inconsequentials" (p. 55). "If by 'inerrant' it is meant that there are no errors of factual information in the Bible, then we cannot hold to the inerrancy of the Scriptures" (p. 59). After all, claims this lesson, "the discrepancies within the Bible are obvious" (p. 60). The October/November/December 1969 *Junior Teacher* propagates the liberal denial of the miracle at Jericho (p. 53, top left column, under the subhead "The Victory"). The falling of the walls appears here as simply a natural occurrence.

The January/February/March 1970 *Adult Teacher* depicts Jesus as being so hungry that he really did not know how long He had fasted, since the author assumes that He could not have fasted for forty days (p. 33, under left column—Verse 2). The January/February/March 1970 *Primary Teacher* attacks the book of Jonah: "To say the book of Jonah is actual history presents questions which are difficult to answer. . . . Jonah contains a 'thus saith the Lord' . . . truth just as a parable does" (pp. 56-61). Both the teacher's instructions and the children's own quarterly omit the great fish. The April/May/June 1970 *Junior Teacher* presents a subtle denial of the miracle of the water coming from the rock. Commenting on Exodus 17:4-6, the lesson piously explains, "Again they were ready to lose all faith when God, through Moses, provided a stream of water from a rock (perhaps a hollow limestone rock over an underground spring)" (p. 57). The Bible, however, offers no such idea of a natural phenomenon. To the contrary, it is clearly a miracle of which God reminds Israel in Deuteronomy 8:15 and Psalm 114:8. In the June 1970 issue of *Facts and Trends,* the Sunday School Board's own president, James Sullivan, confesses that the God he knows would not have asked Abraham to offer Isaac. Sullivan denies the Mosaic authorship of the Pentateuch and the inerrancy of the Bible. He was also on the Advisory Board of the *Broadman Bible Commentary.*

The February 1971 issue of *Outreach* carries an article by Howard P. Colson, who was editorial secretary of the Sunday School Board. In his article Colson discusses the phrase "truth without any mixture of error" from the Baptist Faith and Message statement of faith. Conservatives have always interpreted the phrase as a defense of the Bible's total inerrancy. The liberal Colson, however, discovered what he thinks is a loophole: "When we talk about truth without any mixture of error, we are talking about the kind of truth that has to do with man's relationship to God." Colson is desperately trying to limit inerrancy, and he uses this presupposition to remove himself from the Bible's authority: "If we try to make the Bible an authority on any and every subject, we not only miss the point and pervert its purpose, but we encounter difficulties which we cannot handle. . . . the Bible is not an authority on mathematics, science, and many other subjects." Colson is purposefully deceptive here. Inerrantists have always agreed that the Bible is not a *textbook* on mathematics, science, and many other subjects, but inerrantists do insist that whatever the Bible teaches on any subject is true. Whatever the Bible says about math, science, or history is the absolute, inerrant truth of God. Colson seeks to limit inerrancy to "religious truth." He asks, "What kind of truth, then, are we talking about when we affirm that the Bible has 'truth, without any mixture of error, for its matter'? We must be talking about religious or spiritual truth." A couple of paragraphs later, Colson explains, "For example, Galileo taught that the earth revolves around the sun, whereas the churchmen insisted that the Bible teaches otherwise. . . . Surely—they argued from Scripture" (pp. 2-3). Colson is completely dishonest here. He knows better. The "churchmen" of the Middle Ages did not "argue from Scripture" that the sun moves around the earth. These Roman Catholic scholastics argued from a church tradition that was based on Greek philosophy and reinforced by papal proclamation. Even scientists had for centuries taught that the sun moved around the earth. The Scriptures, however, do not anywhere teach this false view. Colson implies that they do, but he provides no chapter and verse. Colson even charges the Word of God with teaching that the earth is flat: "Some people still argue that the Bible is a perfect authority even in scientific matters. But if that were so, how does it happen that the conception of the earth's shape as found in Scripture has been shown not to be literal fact? The earth as the Bible writers speak of it is flat; yet we know that the earth is actually a sphere" (p. 4). However, not a single verse of Scripture teaches that the earth is flat; in fact, the Bible clearly asserts that the earth is round. Isaiah 40:22 refers to "the circle of the earth," and this literally means arch or globe shape. Job 26:7 says that God "hangeth the earth upon nothing." Therefore, according to the Bible the earth is both a circle (globe) and is out in space. Howard P. Colson, by the way, was also on the Advisory Board of the *Broadman Bible Commentary.*

The July/August/September 1979 *Convention Uniform Series* (Young Adult Sunday School Quarterly, Vol. 21, No. 4), suggests that the book of Exodus (specifically 15:1-18) did not appear until later than Solomon's day and that Moses could not, therefore, have written it. Speaking of Exodus 15, the lesson explains: "A careful reading of the hymn in its entirety (vv. 1-18) leads us to believe that its final composition may have belonged to later times. Its verses or lines may have grown with the years. For instance, while the hymn was given soon after the crossing of the Red Sea, verses 13-16 recount how God protected Israel during the days of her sojourn in the wilderness." To the contrary, a careful reading of the hymn in its entirety reveals that there is no mention of the wilderness. The reference is to Egypt, not the wilderness. (See Keil and Delitzsch's *Commentary on the Old Testament,* Volume One, p. 53f.)

The Sunday School Quarterly continues, "In verse 17, the worshiper remembers the Temple and the worship of God in Jerusalem during the time of Solomon. Much like a ballad, the song would have covered many years. In its entirety, the song praises God for his goodness to Israel (p. 51)." There is not a single conservative commentary which would agree with that analysis. If there is any reference at all to the temple, it is at best only an allusion to the future sanctuary.

The quarterly suggests that the prophet Daniel did not write the book which bears his name. They explain, "Although there are some who think Daniel was the actual author," Daniel "may be an assumed name" (p. 61).

In the April/May/June 1984 *Senior Adult Bible Study* book in the *Life and Work* curriculum, the authors attempt to lead readers along with sentimental questions to conclude that Southern Baptist churches ought to ordain women as deacons and preachers:

> How do you feel about the status given to women in the Southern Baptist Convention? Many Southern Baptist churches will not elect women as deacons, and an even greater number will not accept ordained women as pastors. When the Bible is used to justify this kind of thing, does it become an instrument of oppression rather than the book of liberation it really is? How would Jesus feel about this? Did not Christ liberate women as fully as he did men? Does God withhold from women gifts he makes to men?

The May 1984 issue of *Light,* a publication of the SBC Christian Life Commission, contained an article by Harvey Cox, the notoriously radical author of *The Secular*

City. Helen Caldicott, the left-wing, anti-nuclear propagandist, contributed an article in the same issue. Caldicott had been a speaker at the World Council of Churches Assembly in 1983.

Broadman Press Books

The Sunday School Board's *General Information Guide* carries the following promise to Southern Baptists: "The biblical premise for all material published by the Sunday School Board is the Baptist Faith and Message, a statement adopted by the Southern Baptist Convention in 1963. Careful and prudent consideration is given to all manuscripts and information submitted." Careful perusals of some of these Board "materials," however, make one question how the Board leaders really interpret the 1963 statement. Since 1963 the Board has continued producing such liberal works as Humphreys' *Death of Christ* (1978) and Sparkman's *Being a Disciple* (1972). Discussions of these appear earlier in this book. The following are samples of other key materials which have received the Board's "careful and prudent consideration."

Is the Bible a Human Book?: In 1970 Broadman published a book entitled *Is the Bible a Human Book?*, edited by Wayne E. Ward, who continues as Professor of Christian Theology at Southern Seminary in Louisville, and Joseph F. Green, who has been editing Bible-study books for the Sunday School Board for twenty-five years. James Flamming, pastor of First Baptist Church of Abilene, Texas, contributed a chapter called "Could God Trust Human Hands?" He argues that since God did choose and use human hands to write the Bible, then the Bible is a mixture of truth and error. To Flamming, "If God could use Mark with sixth-grade grammar, and an occasional misquote from the Old Testament, maybe he can use me too!" (p. 11). He concludes that "if God is obsessed with perfection as we are, God could hardly trust man to write the Bible, for nothing man touches ever comes close to perfection (Romans 3:23)." (p. 18). The writer's conclusion then is that the Bible does not come "close to perfection." He claims to see a contradiction in the creation accounts of Genesis 1 and 2. Denying that Moses wrote this, Flamming places the writing during David's and Solomon's time (p. 9).

John R. Claypool, former pastor of Crescent Hill Baptist Church in Louisville, wrote a chapter on "The Humanity of God." He attacks the infallibility and authority of the Scriptures. "It borders on the heretical," asserts Claypool, "to speak of the Bible as the final authority in all matters religious" (p. 28). The writer employs neo-orthodox arguments to attack the Bible. To Claypool, the Bible sometimes "becomes his word to us in an intensely personal way." Because of this "the mistakes and errors and conflicting opinions of the biblical record do not invalidate it for me" (p. 29). In Claypool's own doctoral dissertation, which Southern Seminary had accepted in 1959, he attacks the doctrine of "everlasting punishment" and argues for the "annihilation of the wicked."[2] Surely, the Sunday School Board knew this man's positions. He was pastor of one of the most notoriously liberal churches in the nation—the church where many of the Southern Seminary faculty and students attend.

Wayne E. Ward, the Southern Seminary theologian and coeditor of *Is the Bible a Human Book?*, contributed a chapter called "Stories That Teach." He goes to great lengths to attack the historicity of the biblical accounts of creation and of the fall of man: "Misguided is the attempt of very literalistic minds to make every detail of these stories literal fact. . . . Some people are determined to make the 'serpent' in Genesis 3 a literal snake. . . . People who insist on making him a literal snake are denying the Bible itself" (p. 78).

John M. Lewis, pastor of the First Baptist Church of Raleigh, North Carolina, wrote a chapter entitled "The Bible and Human Science." Committed to the historical-critical method, Lewis attempts to make the biblical account of creation seem ridiculous, but he demonstrates his own ignorance of the basic Bible stories themselves: "Many Bible students recognize," says Lewis, "that there are two accounts of creation in Genesis. . . . the older account in Genesis 2 is more primitive and childlike in its concepts and picturizations of God. Here man is created before any other living creatures." The "later story . . . marks a tremendous advance in the 'scientific understanding' of ancient man. . . . If one tries to take these [creation] accounts as literal scientific truth he does violence to the real intent of the Bible itself" (p. 98).

The chapter written by Brooks Hays, a former SBC president and U. S. Congressman from Arkansas, is titled "What the Bible Means to Me." Hays, a layman, has learned a popular liberal tactic and employed it well in his attack against conservatives. He equates belief in an inerrant Bible with the belief that every word of the Bible must be interpreted literally. Liberals do this constantly. They simply make *inerrantist* synonymous with *literalist*. Conservative scholars, however, have always recognized that there are symbolical and allegorical portions of Scripture. This has nothing to do, however, with the belief that the whole Bible is the infallible Word of God. Hays, like other Liberals, has set up a straw man. "I must say at the outset," confesses Hays, "that I do not accept all of the Bible as literally true" (p. 131). "Inerrancy," Hays falsely charges, is an "irrational and unhistoric position of a few literalists" who are guilty of "bibliolatry" (p. 134). [3]

It is noteworthy that on the jacket of *Is the Bible a Human Book?* the editors describe the book this way: "For the first time, a cross section of recognized Baptist leaders spells out what they really believe about the Bible." In other words, this book represents the thinking of today's leading Southern Baptists, and the Sunday School Board published it after "careful and prudent consideration." One of the book's editors, Joseph F. Green, was on the Advisory Board of the *Broadman Bible Commentary*.

The Heart of the Gospel: Joseph F. Green has also authored a few books himself, one of which is *The Heart of the Gospel*. In this book, which Broadman published in 1968, Green claims that humans do not have immortal souls (p. 37), that the Bible does not teach that Christ will return to set up a kingdom on earth (pp. 65-66), and that the phrase "blood of Christ" is only a figure of speech (pp. 68-69).

The Bible's Secret of Full Happiness: In 1970 Broadman published another work by Joseph F. Green; this one is titled *The Bible's Secret of Full Happiness.* In his chapter called "Sex—Sin or Sacred?" Green explains, "In this chapter, we'll look at what the Bible really teaches about sex" (p. 95). One section of this chapter is called "Sex Before Marriage." Here Green encourages young people that "sex is a powerful drive, and some kind of sexual expression before marriage seems almost inevitable. Psychologists have long agreed that self-stimulation is almost universal among boys and frequent among girls. . . . Students of the Bible, also, agree that the Bible does not condemn the practice" (p. 98).

Green served for twenty-five years as the editor of Bible study books for the Southern Baptist Sunday School Board—a Board which promises customers that it gives "careful and prudent consideration" to all manuscripts submitted, a Board which advertises that "the biblical premise for all materials published . . . is the Baptist Faith and Message." Now, however, the Sunday School Board has even endorsed abortion in this official Broadman publication. In it Joseph Green says, "It seems to me that the growing acceptance of abortion is consistent with Christian faith and moral values." Furthermore, says Green, "no woman has a moral right to bear more than two children" (p. 100). As for divorce, Green counsels, "If your marriage is merely a legal fiction and you have done everything you can to make it more, I believe that you have the moral freedom to end it" (p. 102).

It would perhaps be redundant to offer analyses of any more of the liberal Broadman publications such as Harold Wahking's *Being Christlike,* which denies the substitutionary atonement,[4] or the new *Layman's Bible Book Commentary,* which promotes the historical-critical method (Volume I, p. 9; Volume II, pp. 10-11). The Southern Baptist Sunday School Board wields enormous power in the lives and ministries of over 36,000 churches with more than fourteen million members; its promotional materials are attractive, impressive, and very expensive. Some of these materials are good and helpful, produced by well-qualified, godly individuals. The Board, however, has broken its published promises to grassroots Southern Baptists. Dangerous, poisonous publications appear without warning on the same bookstore shelves with good books. Wicked attacks upon the Bible receive at least as much publicity as do the more conservative materials. All of this is true, even though the Sunday School Board is only a corporation under the legal jurisdiction of the Southern Baptist Convention. Obviously, Liberalism has permeated and gained control of far more than the seminaries and colleges.

Endnotes

1. *Christian News,* May 19, 1980, p. 13.

2. John R. Claypool, "The Problem of Hell in Contemporary Theology" (Ph. D. dissertation, Southern Baptist Theological Seminary, 1959), pp. 262-69.

3. See also the article by Robert M. Tenery in the *Southern Baptist Journal,* April 1980, p. 5.

4. Harold L. Wahking, *Being Christlike* (Nashville: Broadman, 1970), pp. 40-42.

PART IV:
Southern Baptists and Contemporary World Issues

Chapter Sixteen
Issues of Morality

Abortion

Many Southern Baptist leaders are supporting the pro-abortion cause. For example, Foy Valentine, head of the SBC Christian Life Commission, appeared as a sponsor of the Religious Coalition for Abortion's Rights. Dr. Paul D. Simmons, who continues as Professor of Christian Ethics at Southern Seminary in Louisville, addressed a forum which the Religious Coalition for Abortion's Rights sponsored. A Religious News Service release from Washington, D. C., on May 19, 1981, reported that Simmons delivered a popular lecture to this forum in which he asserted that the Bible refutes the anti-abortionists' position. [1] In a testimony before the Senate Judiciary Subcommittee on Separation of Powers, Dr. Simmons, the "ethicist" of Southern Seminary, debated against a proposed anti-abortion bill. [2]

Southern Baptist hospitals perform "therapeutic" abortions, and the South Carolina Convention even defeated a motion that would have limited abortions to "extreme emergency" situations in which the mother's life is "clearly in jeopardy." The Trustees of the South Carolina Baptist hospitals have now issued an open-ended policy allowing abortion when "in the professional judgment of the attending physician, they are medically necessary and comply with the staff regulations of the hospitals."[3] In some states, undesignated financial support to the Cooperative Program has been the sole basis for voting rights. In Virginia, for example, all Southern Baptist pastors have had to support the Baptist Hospital in Lynchburg in order to be able to vote. This hospital's policy has been to perform abortions on the signature of any two doctors.

Conservative leader Dr. W. A. Criswell has expressed publicly his belief that abortion should be permitted in the case of rape or the expected birth of a retarded child.[4] Following the 1973 pro-abortion ruling by the U. S. Supreme Court, Dr. Criswell publicly expressed satisfaction. A Religious News Service release in Dallas quoted his remarks: "I have always felt that it was only after a child was born and had life separate from its mother, that it became an individual person, and it has always, therefore, seemed to me that what is best for the mother and for the future should be allowed." Criswell has not changed his views on the matter since he made this statement, a fact which this writer verified by calling his office.[5]

Sin's Smorgasbord on Southern Baptist Campuses

Just prior to the annual SBC meeting in St. Louis in 1980, Dr. Don Touchton, the Convention's second vice president, openly admitted that "some of our Baptist colleges and seminaries allow drugs, sex, drinking, and dancing to be a daily fare of sin's smorgasbord on campus. Other things could be named which are equally as decadent, both in churches and denominational institutions." That statement appeared on SBC stationery in an eight-page "Cry of Concern," which Dr. Touchton mailed to 8,500 SBC pastors, editors, and other officials. Touchton is pastor of the Central Baptist Church in Brandon, Florida. [6]

Such is hardly surprising to most conservatives, however, because a spirit of permissiveness and toleration has infiltrated the SBC at every level for many years now. The *Christian Index*, which is the Georgia Southern Baptist state paper, reported on December 25, 1969, that three speakers for an upcoming "morality seminar" would be Anson Mount, Joseph Fletcher, and Julian Bond. The SBC Christian Life Commission sponsored this seminar, which was held March 16-18, 1970. [7] Anson Mount was public affairs manager for *Playboy* magazine; Joseph Fletcher was the apostate Episcopalian who wrote *Situation Ethics*; and Julian Bond was the radical, pro-socialist legislator from Atlanta.

In more recent years, some Southern Baptist homosexuals have united as "Passionists." Their expressed purpose is to change the Convention's attitudes towards lesbian and gay concerns. [8]

Sex Scandal and Financial Misconduct in the Southern Baptist Sunday School Board

When an employee, Donald Sloan Burnett, exposed a sex scandal and financial misconduct in the Southern Baptist Sunday School Board, the BSSB president, Dr. Grady C. Cothen, and several other Board personnel attempted to have Burnett committed to a mental institution against his will. Burnett consulted psychiatrist Dr. James Cheatham of Dalton, Georgia, who declared him sane. The Board refused to reinstate him.

Mr. Burnett brought a suit against the Sunday School Board for assault and battery, outrageous conduct, wrongful discharge, gross negligence, false arrest, imprisonment, and defamation. When all the evidence was in, after two weeks of testimony in Judge Joe Loser's Third Circuit Court in Nashville, Mr. Burnett won his case. The jury awarded him a $400,000 judgment against the Board.

Judge Loser reduced the judgment to $60,000, and Mr. Burnett accepted it because he could not afford a new trial; nor could he endure the additional anguish of more hearings. Most of the events relating to the Burnett story occurred in July and August 1976, when scores of Board personnel were named in allegations of sexual and financial misconduct and neglect of duties. [9]

When the Board's president, Grady C. Cothen, retired in 1984, James W. Clark, the executive vice president, released the figures of Cothen's retirement package. Cothen was to receive the following:

1. All expenses paid to the SBC meetings for Dr. and Mrs. Cothen as long as he lives.
2. All expenses paid to the Baptist World Alliance Commission meetings in Berlin in 1984 and in Los Angeles in 1985. (He is Chairman of the Commission on Education and Evangelism.)
3. An automobile of his choice valued up to $15,883.
4. A Tel Net satellite receiving system valued at $2,730.
5. A matching gift for his wife.
6. $4,901 a month ($58,812 a year), excluding the Annuity Board and Social Security money.

According to the *Southern Baptist Advocate*, this handsome retirement package guarantees an annual income which exceeds 95 percent of that which all other SBC employees receive. [10] At the annual 1984 SBC meeting in Kansas City, the Convention passed a lengthy resolution of appreciation for Grady C. Cothen and presented him with a beautiful plaque. [11] Some conservatives seemed baffled as they thought back through Cothen's record and his assertion that "there is simply no evidence, in my judgment, indicating any trend toward theological liberalism in the SBC." [12]

Christian Life Commission Reports on Drug and Alcohol Abuse

At the Glorieta Baptist Conference Center, Ronald D. Sisk of the SBC Christian Life Commission recently outlined the scope of drug and alcohol abuse among Southern Baptists. According to Sisk, "Recent surveys indicate 48 percent of all Southern Baptists drink. An estimated 16 percent of those persons become alcoholics— a higher percentage than virtually any other religious group in the nation." Sisk said that the "surveys also reveal that one-fourth of active Southern Baptist church youth have used alcohol and nine percent have used some kind of hard drugs in the past twelve months." Sisk was addressing a week-long 1984 conference. [13]

Endnotes

1. *Christian News,* June 1, 1981, p. 2.

2. *Greenville* (S. C.) *News,* May 30, 1981; *Review of the News,* June 24, 1981, p. 21.

3. *Greenville News,* November 14, 1984; *Greenville* (S. C.) *News-Piedmont,* November 25, 1984; *Greenville* (S. C.) *Piedmont,* November 17, 1982; *Southern Baptist Advocate,* December 1984, p. 15.

4. Billy Keith, *W. A. Criswell: The Authorized Biography* (Old Tappan, New Jersey: Fleming H. Revell Company, 1973), p. 193.

5. Religious News Service release in Dallas—cited in *Baptist Bible Tribune,* February 16, 1973, p. 1. This writer telephoned Criswell's office on February 12, 1985, and spoke with his secretary, since he was out of the office. She asked him for me if his position on abortion which appeared in his biography and in the above Religious News Service release had changed. His words were, "Quote me."

6. *St. Petersburg Times,* June 7, 1980; *Greenville News,* June 7, 1980; *Plains Baptist Challenger,* September 1980, p. 4; Don Touchton, "A Cry of Concern," paper of April 4, 1980.

7. *Christian Index,* December 25, 1969.

8. *Christian News,* August 1, 1983, p. 3.

9. *Southern Baptist Journal,* December 1981, p. 1f.; *Christianity Today,* October 2, 1981, p. 46f.; *The Christian News,* August 2, 1982, p. 15f.

10. *Southern Baptist Advocate,* June 1984, p. 1f.; July/August 1984, p. 11f.

11. *Annual,* SBC, 1984, p. 51.

12. Religious News Service, November 26, 1980, p. 15.

13. *Charisma,* September 1984, pp. 131-32.

Chapter Seventeen

Southern Baptist Involvement in One-World Movements

Baptist World Alliance

The Baptist World Alliance membership includes 127 Baptist conventions or unions in ninety-three countries, but the Southern Baptist Convention contributes almost one-half of the Alliance's operating budget. The Alliance is an inclusivistic organization supporting Baptist groups that work hand-in-hand with Communist governments worldwide; its leadership includes spokesmen for both the National and World Councils of Churches. In the fiscal year 1983-84, the SBC—the Alliance's single largest member—contributed $325,900 of the $764,000 budget. Dr. Duke K. McCall, chancellor of Southern Baptist Theological Seminary, has been on the Alliance's General Council since 1947 and in 1980 became president for a five-year term. [1]

Left-Wing Sentiments

A large and vocal segment of the SBC represents a wide range of left-wing causes around the world. In the Texas

138

state Convention, for example, the "new left" succeeded a few years ago in appropriating $5,000 for Americans United for Separation of Church and State, an organization with outspoken atheists and humanists in leadership positions. The main spokesmen for the SBC "new left" movement in Texas included Kenneth L. Chafin, pastor of South Main Baptist Church in Houston, and Steve Lyons, pastor of University Baptist Church in Abilene. Chafin is a Southwestern Seminary trustee and Southern Seminary professor. [2]

In an editorial in *USA Today,* January 3, 1984, Foy Valentine—Executive Director of the SBC Christian Life Commission—expressed his glee that conservatives had so few victories in the 1983 Congressional elections. He also commended the Roman Catholic bishops for their condemnation of nuclear arms. The Christian Life Commission is under the jurisdiction of the SBC, whose Cooperative Program provides its funds. David Matthews, pastor of First Baptist Church in Greenville, South Carolina, has been an outspoken liberal Board member of the Commission. [3]

In 1979 a convocation on "Peacemaking and the Nuclear Arms Race" drew even W. A. Criswell's support. Calling for a shift from nuclear weapons to "basic human needs," Dr. Criswell spoke out against the "waste" of military spending, which could be "useful for the poor and the lost of the world." [4]

At the SBC meeting in Kansas City, Missouri, in June 1984, Liberals succeeded in defeating a conservative attempt to cut off funding for the controversial Baptist Joint Committee on Public Affairs. Although eight other Baptist denominations belong to this Joint Committee, the SBC provides about 82 percent of its funding and has only one-third of the vote. The outspoken liberal Southern Baptist, James Dunn—Executive Director of the Joint Committee—has voted against and lobbied aggressively against anti-abortion resolutions; he likewise exerted equal energy opposing President Reagan's School Prayer Amendment. In 1984 the SBC appropriated $411,000 for the Baptist Joint Committee on Public Affairs. [5]

Southern Baptist Leaders and the Ecumenical Movement

For decades many Southern Baptist leaders at every level have promoted the ecumenical movement. When Herbert C. Jackson was teaching at Southern Seminary in Louisville in 1961, he delivered an address calling for Christianity to conform to the more "respectable" religions of the world. His speech later appeared in published form: "Christianity, if it hopes to 'stand' with the resurgent non-Christian religions, must ecumenicize its theology by drawing from the whole world and creating something entirely new, a system . . . that will be intellectually respectable . . . to the upper classes."[6] A number of SBC churches are also members of the American Baptist (Convention) Churches in the U.S.A., which is a member of the National Council of Churches. There are also Southern Baptist leaders such as Donald J. Burke, E. Glenn Hinson (Professor of Church History at Southern Seminary), and G. A. Iglehart, who are or have been active members of various NCC agencies and Commissions, such as the Commission of Faith and Order, the Stewardship Commission, and the Commission on Justice, Liberation and Human Fulfillment.[7] Several Southern Baptist state newspapers reported that C. A. Roberts, pastor of the First Baptist Church in Tallahassee, Florida, had a Roman Catholic priest fill his pulpit on Sunday, October 16, 1966. Roberts, who was also the president of the SBC Pastors' Conference, was speaking to the Southern Baptist Student Union Convention in Fort Worth, Texas, while "Father Cunningham," of the Blessed Sacrament Catholic Church "preached" to his 4,400-member Southern Baptist church.[8] *Time* magazine reported on December 12, 1969, that Dr. Dale Moody, the prominent Southern Seminary (Louisville) professor, was lecturing at Rome's Pontifical Gregorian University. The *Christian Index,* Georgia's Southern Baptist state paper, reported on December 25, 1969, that Brooks Hays, former SBC president, was director of "ecumenical studies" at Wake Forest and one of twenty vice presidents at large of the National Council of Churches. Wake Forest itself is a Southern Baptist-supported institution. In May 1969, however, Wake Forest hosted an "Ecumenical Institute"—the first jointly organized "Baptist-Catholic dialogue." From the initiative of former SBC president Brooks Hays, these fifty-eight participants (thirty-nine Southern Baptists and nineteen Roman Catholics, including two bishops) adopted a pro-ecumenical resolution: "The principle focus of our interest is the unchallenged and overwhelming fact that we are brothers in Christ."[9]

Another former SBC president, Dr. Herschel H. Hobbs, pastor of First Baptist Church in Oklahoma City, hosted an ecumenical gathering in his church. Roman Catholics, Nazarenes, Episcopalians, Presbyterians, Methodists, and Southern Baptists were "eating, laughing, praying, and singing together" at what Hobbs called a "rally for the Agency for Christian Cooperative Ministry." Hobbs, the host pastor and a member of the steering committee of the proposed agency, explained, "I feel that by being here, I'm no less a Baptist, but much more a Christian."[10] Apparently, Hobbs's ecumenical enthusiasm was contagious; a few months later, a Roman Catholic priest led a "revival meeting" in a Southern Baptist church in Birmingham, Alabama, according to *Christianity Today,* April 10, 1970. The article reports that Franciscan Duane Stenzel of Louisville preached during a revival series in Vestavia Hills Baptist church and led "renewal discussions" with the congregation. The *Greenville* (S.C.) *News-Piedmont,* on April 18, 1970, carried a lengthy article on Father Michael Kaney, the Roman Catholic priest serving as a chaplain at Furman University, a Southern Baptist-supported institution. The *Atlanta Journal*, on February 27, 1971, carried an article entitled "Nun Becomes 'Fellow' at Baptist School." The story revealed that Southern Seminary in Louisville had chosen Sister Mary Catherine Vukmanie, a staff member of Ursuline College, as one of its thirty-eight "Garrett Fellows." Ursuline is a Catholic school about two blocks from the Seminary, and "Sister Mary" was in her last year of doctoral studies at Southern. Such Catholic-Baptist cooperation continues into the 1980s. In August 1980 twenty-five Baptist ministers from the Alabama state convention met with twenty-five Roman Catholic clergymen at Shocco Springs Baptist Assembly for the purpose "of helping leaders of the two denominations build bridges that may help them work together more often than they have in the past."[11] In 1984 the SBC Executive Committee showed liberal leanings by voting 32-22 in favor of a joint sponsorship of the National Council of Churches' Conference on Governmental Intervention. The Committee cast their votes after Ed Drake voiced strong opposition to such a joint endeavor. "I would not like to see Southern Baptists associated with the World Council of Churches, the National Council of Churches, or the American Civil Liberties Union in any way, shape, or form—now or in the future," said Drake. He lost.

W. A. Criswell on the Ecumenical Movement

The *Dallas Morning News*, on December 7, 1972, reported an interview with Dr. W. A. Criswell. Reporters asked the prominent Southern Baptist if he would engage in dialogue with the National Council of Churches. Dr. Criswell responded, "I would not be opposed to it." The interview appeared in newspapers throughout the religious world. Although this long-time pastor of the First Baptist Church in Dallas stopped short of endorsing SBC membership in the NCC, he emphasized his feeling that "there are more common grounds than we realize, more things that bind us together than separate us."[12] In 1971 Pope Paul VI had received Criswell and some 400 members of his church in a papal audience, and even his official biographer noted that Criswell was never the same again. Criswell describes his feelings: "What I came to see was, there are great cities in this world, that were it not for the Catholic witness there would be no Christian witness at all. . . . I'm not a Catholic . . . and I couldn't be, but I thank God for what they have done to name the name of Christ in the world and what they represent in . . . our large cities."[13] The *Dallas Morning News*, on August 19, 1978, quoted Criswell as saying, "I don't know anyone more dedicated to the great fundamental doctrines of Christianity than the Catholics."

This pastor of the world's largest Southern Baptist Church has also expressed affinity with other non-Christian groups. In 1982 Dr. Criswell invited Israeli Prime Minister Menachem Begin to Dallas for what he called a "Christian rally in support of Israel and its people."[14] On another occasion, Criswell accepted an invitation to participate in a Jewish Sabbath Day synagogue service. Evangelicals United for Zion published his personal account of this "experience." Criswell testified that "every moment of the course of ritual blessed my heart." There was no word of criticism from Criswell. In fact, he expressed his belief that a Jewish rabbi can be doing the Lord's work apart from faith in Christ as Saviour. In the same article he speaks in glowing terms of his friend, Rabbi Saul Besser, who had extended the invitation to him: "We help each other in the work of the Lord." Criswell described the synagogue service as "a doubly meaningful service ... a holy and worshipful hour."[15]

Criswell endorses not only Romanists and Judaizers but also some of the most notorious apostates of the century. In *Eternity* magazine, April 1980, Dr. Criswell endorsed modernist Norman Vincent Peale's book, *The Power of Jesus Christ.* "Just reading this book," says Criswell, "commends new life in Christ through every experience of new-found power in Him."[16] Peale publishes *Guideposts* magazine, which endeavors "to promote amity & [sic] understanding among ... the three major faiths in this country: our staff is made up of Protestants, Catholics and Jews."[17] In *Leadership* magazine, Spring 1983, Criswell publicly endorses the ministry of Robert Schuller of Garden Grove, California. Criswell said, "Sharing Jesus as Lord and Saviour with the hurting lost people in our communities is at the very heart of our Lord's Great Commission. This is what Robert H. Schuller and the magnificent Crystal Cathedral are all about." Schuller had already widely published his anti-Christian views. His book *Self-Esteem* is a repudiation of the principles of the sixteenth-century Reformation

(p. 36). The book's subtitle is "The New Reformation." Says Schuller, "I offer theology of self-esteem as a starting position" (p. 37). To him, "sin is any act or thought that robs myself or another human being of his or her self-esteem" (p. 14). Furthermore, "to be born again means that we must be changed from a negative to a positive self-image" (p. 68) and "Jesus never called a *person* a sinner" (p. 126). Based upon the authoritative teachings of Scripture, Robert H. Schuller's "new theology" is an anthropological, hamartiological, and soteriological heresy—long condemned by both the Bible and historic Christian affirmations. Dr. Criswell's endorsement in *Leadership* continues: "I know Dr. Schuller personally. He's my good friend. I've spoken on his platform. I'm well acquainted with his ministry. If you want to develop fruitful evangelism in your church, if you want your laity to experience positive motivation and ministry fulfilling training, then I know, without a doubt, that you will greatly benefit from the Robert Schuller Film Workshop."[18] Of course, other prominent Southern Baptists have endorsed Schuller. Billy Graham used him as a leader of his 1972 Anaheim Crusade—the same year that Schuller himself invited Romanist Bishop Fulton J. Sheen to his pulpit and joined with Catholic bishops at their mass at the Annual Mary's Hour at the Los Angeles Sports Arena. Graham said, "There is no one in all the world I love in Christ more than I do Bob Schuller. I have known him for many years. . . . He has done some of the greatest things for the Kingdom of God of any man in our generation."[19] Graham invited Schuller to be a speaker at the 1983 Conference for Itinerant Evangelists in Amsterdam, the Netherlands, and Dr. Kenneth L. Chafin of Southern Seminary in Louisville wrote an endorsement for the book jacket of *Self-Esteem*. Convention leaders at the highest level have officially endorsed this man's ministry, and sixty Southern Baptist Bookstores across the country enthusiastically promote both Schuller's and Peale's literature. Dr. W. A. Criswell, "conservative" former president of the SBC, represents the strongest conservative leadership within the Convention. Members of his church include such major conservative leaders as Zig

Ziglar and Paige Patterson. Patterson serves as head of Criswell's own school. Just how effective can these conservatives ever be in purging all heresy from the Convention? Some are beginning to realize that no complete purging is really possible or even in the plans of conservative leaders. Said one Southern Baptist pastor, "Maybe it's all just power politics after all, just like the Liberals are saying."

The New Evangelical movement has forsaken the biblical principle of purity. The Bible says, "Be ye not unequally yoked together with unbelievers: for what fellowship hath righteousness with unrighteousness? And what communion hath light with darkness? . . . Wherefore come out from among them, and be ye separate, saith the Lord, and touch not the unclean thing; and I will receive you" (II Corinthians 6:14f.).

Endnotes

1. *Annual,* SBC, 1984, pp. 226-27; *Annual,* SBC, 1982, p. 41.

2. *Southern Baptist Advocate,* November 1980, p. 15; *Annual,* SBC, 1984.

3. *USA Today,* January 3, 1984; *Annual,* SBC, 1984, pp. 26, 373. David Matthews's term expires in 1985.

4. *Dallas Times Herald,* January 8, 1979; *The Christian Citizen,* February 2, 1979, p. 11.

5. *Annual,* SBC, 1984; *Christian News,* June 25, 1984, p. 1f.; *Christianity Today,* July 13, 1984, pp. 32-33.

6. *Occasional Bulletin,* March 15, 1961.

7. *Plains Baptist Challenger,* March 1982, p. 5.

8. *Baptist and Reflector,* November 3, 1966. This is the Tennessee Southern Baptist state paper.

9. *FAITH for the Family,* November 1981, pp. 26-27.

10. *Voice of the Nazarene,* January 1970.

11. *Birmingham News,* August 22, 1980.

12. See also the *Tarrant County Baptist* (Fort Worth, Texas), December 12, 1972.

13. Billy Keith, *W. A. Criswell: The Authorized Biography* (Old Tappan, NJ: Fleming H. Revell Co., 1973), p. 213.

14. *The Dallas Morning News,* November 16, 1982.

15. Cited in *FAITH for the Family,* July/August 1979, p. 6.

16. *Eternity,* April 1980, p. 52.

17. *Guideposts,* March 1980, p. 22.

18. *Leadership,* Spring 1983; Robert H. Schuller, *Self-Esteem* (Waco, Texas: Word Books, 1982); for sample reviews of *Self-Esteem* and of Schuller's ministry, see *Foundation,* Vol. V, Issue 5, p. 17f.; *The Reformed Journal,* May 5, 1981, p. 8f.; *Sword of the Lord,* December 31, 1982, p. 1f.; *FAITH for the Family,* November 1980, p. 5f.; *Christianity Today,* January 21, 1983, p. 22f.; *Evangelical Newsletter,* September 4, 1981; *Australian Beacon,* November 1980, p. 9. On Sunday, August 13, 1978, Schuller had Oral Roberts on his "Hour of Power" broadcast.

19. *Foundation,* Vol. V, Issue 5, p. 17f.

PART V:

The Contemporary Conservative Movement Within the Southern Baptist Convention

Chapter Eighteen

Prelude to War

The Baptist Watergate

While the official news agency for the SBC is the Baptist Press, thirty-five of the thirty-seven organized Southern Baptist state conventions publish their own official newspapers. Most of these papers have both a full-time editor and an editorial staff. Conservatives have for a long time viewed with great concern what they see as a "Baptist Watergate"[1] kind of coverup in many of these papers—a coverup of the liberal takeover of the Convention's institutions.

Jack U. Harwell, for example, is editor of the Georgia Baptist Convention's *Christian Index.* Harwell attacks the Bible's inerrancy and denies the historicity of Adam and Eve. Referring to the comment in the Baptist Faith and Message doctrinal statement that the Bible is "truth without any mixture of error," Harwell said this: "The statement says that truth is not mixed with error but it does not say that the Bible is not mixed with error. . . . I do not believe in the plenary verbal inspiration of the Bible. . . . I do not believe that Adam and Eve were one man and one woman. I believe that the terms Adam and Eve represented mankind and womankind. One of the most simple and basic answers to refute the belief that Adam and Eve were one man and one woman is the simple question 'Where did Cain get his wife?' "[2] However, the genealogical tables in Genesis, Chronicles, and Luke depict a historical, literal Adam, and even Paul refers to the first and to the second Adam. "Holy men of God" who spoke as they were "moved by the Holy Ghost" seem a bit more convincing than Mr. Harwell does to conservative Southern Baptists.

The Dodge County (Georgia) Baptist Association voted on October 25, 1979, to request that the Executive Committee of the Georgia Baptist Convention dismiss Harwell as editor of the state's paper, whose circulation is now 100,000. The Georgia Convention, however, voted four to one approving Jack Harwell and extending to him a vote of confidence. [3]

Unofficial Conservative Southern Baptist Papers

The Southern Baptist Journal: Concerned Southern Baptist conservatives had met at the First Baptist Church of Atlanta, Georgia, in March 1973 to form "the Baptist Faith and Message Fellowship," whose main purpose is to publish the *Southern Baptist Journal.* The *Journal,* whose editor is William A. Powell, Sr., attempts to counteract the liberal SBC publications.

Dr. William A. Powell, Sr., is an active Southern Baptist. He graduated from New Orleans Seminary and went on to pastor the First Southern Baptist Church of Chicago. He served as moderator and superintendent of the Chicago Southern Baptist Association. He was on the national leadership staff of the SBC Home Mission Board for eleven years. The *Southern Baptist Journal*, however, is an "unofficial" publication, and its address is P. O. Box 468, Buchanan, Georgia 30113.

In 1978 the Baptist Faith and Message Fellowship elected Dr. Harold Lindsell as its president; his *Battle for the Bible* had appeared two years earlier, and his *Bible in the Balance* would appear in 1979. Today the president is Benton E. Card of Stone Mountain, Georgia. The Baptist Faith and Message Fellowship is almost an exact parallel to the Fundamentalist Fellowship, which conservatives established within the Northern Baptist Convention in 1920. Eventually, these Northern Baptist Fundamentalists concluded that the only effective way to deal with apostasy was to withdraw the Fundamentalist Fellowship completely from the denomination. [4]

The Southern Baptist Advocate: The *Southern Baptist Advocate* is another "unofficial" conservative paper within the SBC. Edited by Russell Kaemmerling, the *Advocate* is actually a break-off from the *Southern Baptist Journal*. Dr. Kaemmerling left the *Journal* and founded the *Advocate;* it first appeared in August 1980, and its address is P. O. Box 214268, Dallas, Texas 75221. [5]

The Atlanta Convention—1978

The 1978 SBC meeting in Atlanta, Georgia, hosted special speakers Coretta Scott King, Mrs. Billy Graham, radical Quaker theologian Elton Trueblood, [6] and Jimmy Carter. This Convention also received a video-taped message from Malcolm Muggeridge. The messengers reelected liberal Jimmy R. Allen as SBC president, and they chose Douglas Watterson over Anita Bryant as their first vice president. [7]

With such philosophical and doctrinal diversity present within the SBC, could conservatives actually "rescue" the organization? Carl Carter, religion editor of the *Birmingham* (Alabama) *News,* later interviewed President Allen for the "Religion Today" section of his paper. In this interview Allen openly favored ERA and the practice of ordaining women preachers. [8] Liberalism had the upper hand in the SBC.

The Pressler-Patterson Strategy

Paul Pressler, a deacon and Sunday School teacher (in his fifties) in Houston's Second Baptist Church, is a Texas Appeals Court judge. When five young people who had trusted the Lord through one of his Bible study classes went off to Baylor University and nearly lost their faith, Judge Pressler joined with Paige Patterson to establish a conservative "strategy" to combat Southern Baptist Liberalism. Patterson, the associate pastor of W. A. Criswell's First Baptist Church in Dallas and president of the Criswell Center for Biblical Studies, had long expressed his concern over the "creeping Liberalism" in Convention schools. [9] Also supporting the "Pressler-Patterson Coalition" has been Edward E. McAteer, a lay deacon in Bellevue Baptist Church in Memphis and founder of "The Roundtable," a conservative Christian caucus group. [10] McAteer's pastor is Adrian P. Rogers.

The politically astute Pressler and the equally concerned Patterson devised a plan which they believed would completely turn the tide and place all SBC agencies and institutions under conservative control within one decade—beginning in 1979. The key to the plan was for conservatives to succeed in getting their own men consecutively elected to the SBC presidency over a whole decade. It was supposed to work as follows. The SBC president is empowered to name the Convention's Committee on Committees, [11] which in turn nominates the Committee on Boards, which in turn nominates the trustees of the SBC agencies and institutions. Any nomination by the Committee on Boards is usually tantamount to election. The elected trustees in turn hire administrators and make policies for the SBC agencies and institutions, including the six seminaries. These trustees are the general overseers of the institutions; they employ the various seminary presidents, faculties, and staffs. Each year a percentage of trustees rotate off; [12] so, ultimately, the SBC president possesses a large amount of potential power. Pressler and Patterson predicted that the election of several successive conservative presidents would bring about a complete turnover of trustees on the various boards and consequently turn the tide of Liberalism. Now, after six elections and four consecutive conservative presidents, the Liberals are still in the seminaries, and they remain in control of the various agencies, such as the Sunday School Board and the Christian Life Commission. Not one of the four presidents has expressed any desire to purge the denomination; in fact, each has publicly expressed his own abhorrence to any such idea.

Endnotes

1. *Southern Baptist Journal,* October 1980, p. 2.

2. Letter to Joe Dunaway, December 31, 1974, cited in Harold Lindsell, *The Battle for the Bible* (Grand Rapids: Zondervan, 1976), p. 97.

3. *Baptist Challenge,* January 1980, p. 1f.

4. Some Southern Baptist conservatives have recognized the liberal control in the official schools and consequently have established their own unofficial institutions: Robert Witty founded Luther Rice Seminary; B. Gray Allison and others established the Mid-America Baptist Theological Seminary in Memphis (Allison formerly taught at New Orleans Seminary); W. A. Criswell established the Criswell Center for Biblical Studies in Dallas, with Paige Patterson as its president. These leaders, however, continue to help to pay the salaries of the Liberals in the official schools through the Cooperative Program, thus diminishing their own effectiveness.

5. *Christian News,* November 3, 1980, p. 16; *Review and Expositor,* Winter 1982, pp. 92-95.

6. For example, see Elton Trueblood, *Essence of Spiritual Religion* (New York: Harper and Row, 1975), p. 61; and *Future of the Christian* (New York: Harper and Row, 1971), p. 69.

7. *Annual,* SBC, 1978, pp. 24-27, 45, 46, 51-53, 56, 59, 62, 70; see also *The Atlanta Journal and Constitution,* April 29, 1978.

8. Cited in *Biblical Evangelist,* January 1979, p. 3.

9. *Texas Monthly,* November 1981; *Christianity Today,* August 5, 1983, p. 38f. For a Liberal's view of Paige Patterson, see *Review and Expositor,* Winter 1982, pp. 105-20.

10. *Western Recorder,* June 28, 1982. This is the Kentucky Southern Baptist state paper. McAteer ran for a seat in the U. S. Senate in 1984.

11. The president appoints from each qualifying state two representatives to be on the Committee on Committees. The president also appoints the Resolutions Committee for the annual Southern Baptist Convention meetings.

12. Most of the trustees are elected to a four-year term, then reelected to a second four-year term; then they rotate off.

Chapter Nineteen

Adrian P. Rogers (1979)

Speakers for the 1979 SBC meeting in Houston, Texas, included such a variety of people as Billy Graham, Jerry Clower, and Georgi Vins. Clower is a Southern Baptist entertainer, and Vins is a Baptist pastor from the Soviet Union who was formerly imprisoned for his faith. Cliff Barrows led the congregational singing. Conservatives had conducted an extensive campaign to get their man elected to the Convention's presidency, and it worked. The messengers elected Adrian P. Rogers, pastor of the Bellevue Baptist Church in Memphis, Tennessee, as the new president. Rogers was the second successor to Dr. R. G. Lee as pastor of Bellevue Baptist. Although conservatives were jubilant, there was not much that really went their way in Houston.

Although Rogers won the presidency on the first ballot, the messengers elected the liberal Baylor University president Abner McCall to the office of first vice president. One messenger presented a resolution to ask future nominees to the offices of president and vice president to sign voluntarily a simple and basic doctrinal statement. The messenger was finally compelled to withdraw his motion. [1] Another messenger moved to amend the SBC

Constitution (Article IX) by adding that the SBC "will not recognize the ordination of women as being scriptural." The resolution failed. [2] On the other hand, the messengers adopted a resolution (#16) which expressed special appreciation to the six seminaries' faculties and openly rebuked the conservative movement. [3] Another resolution (#21) disavowed "political activity" in selecting Convention officers. This was such an overt attack against the conservatives that Paul Pressler immediately asked for permission to respond, but the resolution had already passed. [4] Some conservatives would soon receive other unwelcome news—Adrian Rogers did not plan to do a single thing to purge Liberalism from Southern Baptist institutions.

Conservatives knew that their president believed in biblical inerrancy, but immediately following his election, Adrian Rogers informed a packed news conference, "I don't want any witch hunt to purge the seminaries." [5] The following May, Rogers unexpectedly announced that he would not seek the customary second one-year term as president. Two days later, conservatives were shocked by a Religious News Service release (May 9, 1980) in which W. A. Criswell announced that his associate, Paige Patterson, *would* withdraw his leadership from the coalition which had pledged to cleanse the SBC of Liberalism. [6] Criswell publicly repudiated what he called the conservatives' precinct-like organizations and their modern communications systems on the Convention floor. [7] Most observers saw Criswell's edict as tantamount to a public humiliation of Paige Patterson.

It now seemed strange to many that in his book, *These Issues We Must Face*, Dr. Criswell had discussed "the curse of Modernism" this way: "Modernism must be kept out. We have no other choice if we are to live as Christians but to purge Modernism out, keep it out, root it out.... Even though it grieves us to part company in our institutions with the affable, personable, scholarly modernistic preacher or teacher—we ought to purge out corrupting leaven wherever it appears." [8]

When conservatives thought that they had a chance to do some purging, however, Dr. Criswell refused to follow his own scriptural advice.

Endnotes

1. *Annual*, SBC, 1979, pp. 33, 34, 45, 58.

2. Ibid., pp. 31, 34.

3. Ibid., pp. 34, 55.

4. Ibid., p. 58; see also the *Birmingham News*, June 17, 1979; and the *Southern Baptist Journal*, September 1979, p. 1f.

5. *Greenville* (S. C.) *News*, June 14, 1979; *Enquirer* (Columbus, Georgia), June 14, 1979; *Washington Post*, June 15, 1979; *Eternity*, August 1979, p. 8; *Baptist Bulletin*, September 1979, pp. 11-12; *Annual*, SBC, 1979, p. 60.

6. *Christian News*, May 19, 1980, p. 13; *Christian News*, May 26, 1980, p. 2.

7. *Review and Expositor*, Winter 1982, p. 99.

8. W. A. Criswell, *These Issues We Must Face* (Grand Rapids: Zondervan, 1953), p. 50.

Chapter Twenty

Bailey E. Smith (1980-81)

The St. Louis Convention—1980

The 1980 SBC meeting in St. Louis, Missouri, elected conservative Bailey E. Smith to the presidency. The forty-one-year-old Smith, pastor of the First Southern Baptist Church in Del City, Oklahoma, had long voiced a strong belief in the Bible's inerrancy. His church is the second largest in the SBC. Thinking that they now had a president with clout who was also willing to begin a purge of Liberalism from the Convention, conservatives rejoiced. For many, however, the celebration was shortlived; President Smith was unwilling to have Liberals ousted.

In the news conference following his election, Smith told reporters that he was "not out to ax anybody" and that he "would serve every segment of the denomination," including "friends who disagree with me on the Bible."[1] Smith added, "The liberals we have are few compared to the great majority of our people."[2] Many conservatives believe that this is exactly the reason that they could never expect to win any real victory in the Convention—"A little leaven leaventh the whole lump." When leaders are willing to tolerate a little Liberalism, they have already lost the battle. Some conservatives are now saying that there are far more Liberals in the SBC than most of the leaders and even some grassroots Baptists are willing to admit. Even more significant is the fact that these Liberals occupy key educational positions which shape the future of the Convention. Following Smith's news conference, one reporter concluded, "It is sad, indeed, to see a great group of delegates who are able to vote on a president who is a believer in inerrancy but are totally powerless to eradicate the malignancy that is obviously in their schools."[3]

Here Comes the Judge: Liberals Organize

Although Paige Patterson was now on the sidelines, Judge Paul Pressler decided to press on with the battle. In September 1980, he told an audience at the Old Forest Road Baptist Church in Lynchburg, Virginia, that "the lifeblood of institutions are trustees. We need to go for the jugular and get to the root of the problem."[4] Liberals picked up on his intended metaphorical expression, "going for the jugular" and began portraying Pressler as an evil and bloodthirsty witch-hunter. Alarmed over the possibility that conservatives might gain back some control in the Convention, liberal leaders Cecil Sherman and Kenneth L. Chafin rallied fellow "moderates" to a special meeting in Gatlinburg, Tennessee, to organize a plan to counter the conservative strategy. The makeup of the liberal party is informative.

Cecil Sherman, pastor of the First Baptist Church of Asheville, North Carolina, was president of his state's Convention. Speaking to the annual meeting of the Theron Rankin Association in Conover, North Carolina, Sherman once asserted that he does not believe in the Bible's inerrancy and that he could not "pretend" something he does not believe. Inerrancy, said Sherman, "leads you into a swamp you can't get out of."[5] Sherman's brother Bill, pastor of Woodmount Baptist Church in Nashville—where many Southern Baptist Sunday School Board employees attend—also went to Gatlinburg to join the new liberal coalition. Then there was Kenneth L.

Chafin of the South Main Baptist Church of Houston and member of the Board at Southwestern Seminary. He assured the "Gatlinburg gang" that the whole conservative movement was nothing less than "a naked grab for power." Chafin was then dean of the Schools of Evangelism for the Billy Graham Evangelistic Association, a position which he finally quit in 1983 in order to give more attention to his own church's financial problems. Many remember Chafin for his ordaining the well-known Baptist preacher, Mrs. Rosemary Crenshaw, [6] a divorcee, as a deaconess to join her daughter, Mrs. Sherry Melton, who was already on his board of deacons. An American Baptist church had ordained Mrs. Melton. Chafin, by the way, has recently become Professor of Christian Preaching at Southern Seminary in Louisville. [7] Other liberal leaders joining the new coalition included Larry Coleman of Long Island, New York; Earl Davis of Memphis, Tennessee; Bill Self of Atlanta, Georgia; James Slatton of Richmond, Virginia; C. Weldon Gaddy; and Ralph Langely, the pastor of First Baptist Church of Huntsville, Alabama, who would nominate the liberal Abner McCall of Baylor for SBC president at the next Convention meeting.

The Liberals' strategy would be a basic formula: (1) to deny vociferously that there are Liberals in the SBC schools; (2) to label the conservative crusade as "a naked, ruthless reach for personal power" that says "any means are justified"; (3) to sell the idea that any attempt to defend the doctrine of inerrancy is a diversion of precious time from the all-important mission of soulwinning (One may question just how much these Liberals really know or care about soulwinning); and (4) to sell themselves as the denomination's true "loyalists" who are striving to keep peace in this "great family." [8] So now the Liberals had a better organized strategy than did the conservatives; the Liberals, moreover, were uniting, while conservatives were going their separate ways. Most conservatives took comfort in the fact that at least their man Bailey Smith was now president of this largest Protestant denomination in America. Smith would soon stir some ecclesiastical waters himself, but he would do it in a very unexpected manner.

Does God Hear the Prayers of Jews?

In August 1980, Bailey E. Smith publicly stated that God did not hear the prayers of the Jews. The worldwide negative response was so overwhelming that Dr. and Mrs. Smith decided to demonstrate that they were not anti-Semitic. They went to Dallas to observe and to partake of the Passover Supper with some Jewish leaders.[9] That, however, offended many conservative friends, who believed that since Christ is our Passover (I Corinthians 5:7-8), the Smiths had violated passages such as Galatians 4:9-11. Smith, however, would offend many other conservatives by inviting Theodore Freedman, director of the Anti-Defamation League of B'nai B'rith, to speak at a Wednesday night service in his Del City, Oklahoma, church.

The Los Angeles Convention—1981

The 1981 SBC meeting in Los Angeles reelected Bailey Smith as president, but it was not without some chagrin for the conservatives. Traditionally, the SBC has reelected incumbent presidents by acclamation, without opposition. This year, however, the Liberals registered their protest to the conservatives by providing a 39.30 percent vote to Abner V. McCall, the high-ranking, liberal chancellor of Baylor who had been president there for twenty years. Smith received 60.24 percent of the vote.[10] The Liberals had sent their message: only about 10 percent of the vote made the difference at that meeting; almost half of the messengers had openly favored an avowed Liberal as president. The conservatives, therefore, would have no *carte blanche* with which to purge out the Liberals.

McCall told reporters that he had really only expected to win 10 to 20 percent of the vote and that he was thrilled to be "standard-bearer" for "the people who were unhappy with the trend toward narrow credalism." McCall added, "We Baptists have agreed upon programs, not upon creeds. It is our programs that hold us together."[11] The messengers then elected Mrs. A. Harrison Gregory of Virginia as first vice president. This was the first time in SBC history that a woman had received this honor.

The Liberals also succeeded in derailing several conservative nominees to agency boards; they then voted to reinstate several pro-liberal trustees whom the Committee on Boards had dropped. Two of these Liberals were Home Mission Board Trustees; one was a Southwestern Seminary trustee.[12] The official SBC Baptist Press release declared that, all in all, the 1981 meeting had "modified a two-year turn to the right."

Even William E. Hull, former dean and provost at Southern Seminary, won the honor of delivering the Convention sermon for the following year. Messengers remembered Hull for "Shall We Call the Bible Infallible?," his infamous sermon in which he had preached a blistering attack against the inerrantist position.[13] Jess Moody, who had recently brought his First Baptist Church of Van Nuys, California, into the SBC, addressed the Los Angeles meeting. Telling his audience, "the only difference between Liberals and Fundamentalists is that they deny different verses," Moody received a standing ovation.[14] Not all Convention announcements are so well-planned, however.

On Wednesday evening (June 10),[15] the whole L.A. convention was stunned by the announcement that Dr. Duke K. McCall, after three decades as president of Southern Seminary, had abruptly resigned. Allegations had it that McCall had been observed drinking alcoholic beverages while on a trip to China and that he had simply resigned in order to avert an investigation. The Trustees had then elected him as the school's Chancellor, a position which they supposedly considered a bit more aloof from such personal scrutiny.

Reporters began asking President Bailey Smith about any future conservative plans to purify the Convention. He had none! One reporter asked Smith, "What does your reelection today mean in terms of the battle between conservatives and the moderates?" Smith replied, "Well, you know I really don't believe we have any sides in our denomination."[16] Faced with the 40 percent opposition vote, an unprecedented vote against any incumbent, Smith continued his conciliatory stance, calling for all elements to "come together in a spirit of unity." He insisted that he was not "pushing a conservative . . . demand for stricter doctrinal conformity" and that he was opposed to firing teachers who would not teach biblical inerrancy.[17] Smith had repeatedly called for more support to the Cooperative Program, which is the hand that pays the teachers' salaries. Both Liberals and conservatives went home from L.A. claiming victory, because the emphasis was on peace; many saw it, however, as peace above purity and noted that the issue of infidelity in the SBC schools had never come up on the Convention floor.

More Conservatives Give Up

In November 1981, a reporter for the *Texas Monthly* interviewed Paige Patterson to learn his feelings about the "ongoing battle." Patterson again "denied supporting the removal of any professors, even those who have publicly doubted the authority of certain Scriptures." He added, "There is really no way to eliminate liberalism without becoming some kind of gestapo."[18] Conservatives were now expressing publicly their feeling that once Liberalism takes control, it will never let go. Clinging to a dead organization, apostasy refuses to allow anyone to bury the corpse.

Endnotes

1. *Greenville* (S. C.) *News,* June 12, 1980.

2. *Foundation,* July/August 1980, p. 5f.; *Christianity Today,* July 18, 1980, p. 50f.

3. *Baptist Bulletin,* September 1980, p. 13.

4. *Christianity Today,* August 5, 1983, p. 38f.; *Southern Baptist Advocate,* September/October 1984, pp. 10-11.

5. *Southern Baptist Advocate,* November 1980, p. 8.

6. *Southern Baptist Advocate,* May 1983, p. 12.

7. *The Tie,* November/December 1984, p. 2. This is a Southern Seminary publication.

8. *Christianity Today,* August 5, 1983, p. 38f.; see also the *Christian Century,* October 22, 1980, p. 1000.

9. *The Dallas Morning News,* October 17, 1980.

10. *Annual,* SBC, 1981, p. 42.

11. *Foundation,* July/August 1981, p. 9f.; see also the *Southern Baptist Advocate,* May/June 1981, p. 1f.; *Newsweek,* June 22, 1981, p. 88.

12. *Annual,* SBC, 1981, p. 44f.; *Christianity Today,* July 17, 1981, pp. 80-81. This Convention also rejected a conservative nominee to the SBC's Executive Committee.

13. William E. Hull, *The Integrity of the Theological Curriculum* (Louisville: The Southern Baptist Theological Seminary, 1969), p. 5; *The Baptist Program,* December 1970, p. 17.

14. *Foundation,* op. cit., p. 9f.

15. *Annual,* SBC, 1981, p. 49.

16. *Foundation,* op. cit., p. 9f.

17. *Greenville* (S. C.) *News,* June 11, 1981 *Moody Monthly,* September 1981, p. 114f.

18. *Texas Monthly,* November 1981, pp. 178, 304.

Chapter Twenty-One

James T. Draper, Jr. (1982-83)

The New Orleans Convention—1982

The 1982 SBC meeting in New Orleans, Louisiana, elected conservative James T. Draper, Jr., to the presidency. Draper, pastor of the First Baptist Church of Euless, Texas (a Dallas-Fort Worth suburb), did not win easily, however. Grady C. Cothen, president of the Southern Baptist Sunday School Board, nominated Duke K. McCall, who, as we have noted, had resigned from his long presidency at Southern Seminary and had subsequently become the school's chancellor. Reports were still circulating that McCall's resignation had resulted from the charge of an alleged drinking problem. [1] In his nomination, Cothen characterized McCall as "a man who has been vilified but never impeached." On the first ballot, Draper received 46.03 percent of the vote and McCall received 34.88 percent; two other candidates received the rest. On the runoff ballot Draper received 56.97 percent of the vote, and McCall received 43.03 percent. Observers saw this as a very strong liberal showing of strength. Convention messengers even passed a resolution (#14) expressing special "appreciation for Duke Kimbrough

McCall." They presented McCall with a beautiful plaque containing the entire lengthy resolution. [2]

Liberals were to receive consolation in other ways as well. The vice-presidential offices both went to the Liberals: John Sullivan of Shreveport, Louisiana, became first vice president, and Gene Garrison of First Baptist Church in Oklahoma City became second vice president. James L. Pleitz, the liberal pastor of Park Cities Baptist Church in Dallas, received the honor to preach the next annual Convention sermon. When outgoing President Bailey Smith assumed the chair on Wednesday morning (June 16), he ruled that messengers were not to speak negatively concerning any nominees to committees. [3]

Kenneth L. Chafin then led a successful attempt to block some conservative trustee nominations: Liberals replaced two nominees to the Sunday School Board and one for Southeastern Seminary's board. The Convention dropped one conservative nominee when Liberals pointed out that this man did not use Sunday School Board literature in his church. This well-meaning conservative had simply desired to become a trustee so that he could be a good influence on a SBC institution. He discovered, however, that in order to be a purifying influence, he must first feed his flock on a good diet of Sunday School Board literature. To one observer, it would have been "doing wrong in order to get a chance to do right." The Liberals were wielding their power.

One reporter wrote that he sat in full view of all of the state newspaper editors and that, without exception, they voted against the resolution which supported voluntary prayer in public schools. All but three voted against an anti-abortion and anti-infanticide resolution, and they unanimously voted against the resolution supporting the teaching of scientific creationism in public schools. [4] The reporter expressed surprise that these editors were so much "out-of-step" with the rank and file of Southern Baptist people. [5] Another reporter, sitting near the table reserved for SBC agency heads, observed that they voted "by a ten-to-one margin" with the Liberals and against the conservatives. [6] It was no surprise to many when Georgia reported a large number of churches no longer on SBC rolls. [7] Conservatives did, however, have their man as Convention president, and many had specific questions for him.

Immediately after his election, Draper held a press conference. The first question asked him was, "Would you disavow any attempt by Patterson and other fundamentalists to stack the denominational boards and take over?" Draper responded, "I have never embraced that philosophy. . . . I'm not part of any orchestration. . . . I will appoint those who have a deep commitment to the Word of God and who have proven their loyalty to the Convention. . . . They do not have to use the word 'inerrancy.'" When asked, "What do you mean by 'those who have demonstrated loyalty to the Southern Baptist Convention'?", Draper replied, "Those who have participated on committees, boards, etc., and have led their churches to become involved in participation in cooperating missions [the Cooperative Program] both through their finances and their efforts." Then came the clincher: "Would you support the appointment of those who had not led their people to contribute to the Cooperative Program?" The answer was a quick "No!" Concerning the seminaries, Draper, who himself is a former associate of W. A. Criswell at Dallas, informed reporters, "I can accept a man who says, 'I believe Adam and Eve are allegorized, but here's what others believe.' But I wouldn't want a new one like him [appointed]. . . . I don't want anybody fired. . . . I have great confidence in our schools." [8]

The newly elected president had sent his message to all trustees: he had calmly informed his constituents that he had confidence in the schools, that he wanted no one fired, and that in his opinion loyalty to the "program" is the most important goal. [9] Some conservatives noticed the similarity of these remarks with those of Dr. McCall only a year earlier: "We Baptists have agreed upon programs, not creeds. It is our programs that hold us together." Liberals are not concerned when conservatives "take a stand," so long as conservatives continue to pay the bills—including the Liberals' salaries.

The Pittsburgh Convention—1983

The 1983 SBC meeting in Pittsburgh, Pennsylvania, reelected "conservative" James T. Draper, Jr., as president; conservatives, however, were not in command, and they took home few if any real prizes. During the annual Pre-Convention Pastors' Conference, on Monday, June 14, the Liberals held an "alternative meeting" on the top floor of the U. S. Steel Building. Here Cecil Sherman explained that, because the traditional Pastors' Conference is too heavily stacked with conservative speakers, "moderates" simply desired this time to get together, make new friends, and discuss strategy. This year the strategy was simple. There was no need at all to oppose Draper's election because, as the Liberals saw it, there were very few differences between them. [10]

Even in a Pre-Convention news release, Paige Patterson promised that there would be "no witch hunt," that conservatives did not intend to take over the seminaries, and that the conservatives' goal was simply to achieve "parity," in which their views could just receive fair recognition in classrooms and publications. It seemed astounding to some that the conservatives were actually willing to accept error on an equal basis with truth in classroom situations and in the publications which mold young people's lives as well as the Convention's future.

At the press conference following his reelection, Jimmy Draper admitted that he had met Southern Baptists "in the academic community who would not give you a straight answer if you asked them if Jesus were virgin born." Draper quickly explained, however, "I have no accusations to make and I haven't asked that anybody be fired." Posing as a "peacemaker," Draper urged "coexistence between the warring groups." Draper later explained that even in his presidential address he had purposefully avoided using the terms *inerrancy* and *infallible* in reference to the Scriptures. Said Draper, even the term *authority* "needs a better definition." Authority, however, is the real issue in the battle. What will be the ultimate authority for concerned Baptists who desire to do right? It was easy to see why even liberal leaders Cecil

Sherman and Kenneth Chafin heaped praises upon Jimmy Draper. Even the Southern Seminary Liberal E. Glenn Hinson, writing in the *Christian Century*, would express relief that the SBC had veered to the left at Pittsburgh. [11]

Many conservatives expressed perplexity after Draper's reelection when Paige Patterson, president of the Criswell Center for Biblical Studies in Dallas, claimed "victory" for the conservative movement. Announcing that the conservatives had now achieved the goals proclaimed in 1979, Patterson said, "We are grateful that the entire awakening came two years quicker than anticipated." [12]

This Convention, however, reelected Liberal John Sullivan as first vice president. Liberal Gene Garrison, pastor of First Baptist Church in Oklahoma City, had chosen not to run for reelection as second vice president because of the boiling controversy surrounding his church's changing its bylaws to permit ordaining women as deaconesses. So the Convention elected a retired liberal businessman, C. Edward Price, as second vice president. [13] Garrison's church was causing a real stir in Oklahoma; it had already ordained three women. The Capital Baptist Association in Oklahoma voted in 1983 to refuse the seating of representatives from Garrison's church. One year later, however, the Association would reverse its decision, when none other than Bailey Smith himself would move to seat these messengers "in the spirit of harmony." [14] Conservative SBC presidents have proved themselves quite conciliatory.

Looking to 1984

Three months following his 1983 reelection, Jimmy Draper, addressing more than 400 Southern Baptist leaders of the Northeast, was still insisting, "We should never fend for the faith when it alienates a brother." [15] Suddenly, however, a Religious News Service release of December 6, 1983, reported that Draper was appealing for five doctrinal "guidelines" in the Convention's institutions. These included a statement on the Bible as the authoritative Word of God, belief in the full humanity and deity of Christ, the substitutionary atonement by Christ for the sins of mankind, justification by God's grace through faith, and the bodily resurrection of Christ. These are simple and basic "bedrock doctrines" which should not offend any true Christian. Immediately, however, Liberals bombarded Draper with negative response to his simple proposal. Draper retreated: "I in no way implied," the conservative explained, "that I wanted to bind anybody, or require anyone to do anything. I am not starting a witchhunt." Draper further insisted that he would certainly "not make inerrancy an issue." [16]

Since Jimmy Draper had expressed his own doubts about the Christian's proper concept of the term *authority*, he decided to write a book. In *Authority: The Critical Issue for Southern Baptists,* [17] Draper still demonstrates a blind loyalty to his denomination. He uses some good strong language, but Jimmy Draper is committed to peace above purity. He uses the word *inerrancy* in his book to prove that he believes in it, but he prefers normally to avoid the term since it causes alarm. Harold Lindsell reviewed Draper's book, finding both strong and weak features. [18]

Some staunch conservatives entered 1984 expressing privately to this writer their feeling that they were still looking for a real leader, one who would not only recognize the problem of Liberalism but who would commit himself to purging it from the camp. Some were wondering if they could ever purge out the Liberals, even if a conservative president were wholeheartedly committed to it. Time had really been on the Liberals' side after all, and even now the Liberals were boldly announcing their own "Rebel Pastors' Conference" for the coming year. [19] That "rebel" conference would become known as the Forum. Meanwhile, however, the mainline Pastors' Conference had elected Dr. Charles Stanley as its president, and conservatives hoped that this would be the steppingstone to the SBC presidency for this popular spokesman.

Endnotes

1. Several papers reported this charge. One editor noted that McCall seemed rather surprised at all the fuss and insisted that for years now he had drunk nothing stronger than beer and wine! See the *Southern Baptist Journal,* December 1981, p. 7 and *Plains Baptist Challenger,* August 1981, p. 1.

2. *Annual,* SBC, 1982, pp. 40, 41, 46-48.

3. Ibid., p. 49.

4. James Dunn, of the Baptist Joint Committee on Public Affairs, bitterly opposed each of these resolutions.

5. *Southern Baptist Journal,* June 1983, p. 14.

6. *Christianity Today,* July 16, 1982, p. 36f.

7. Ibid., The article states that Georgia reported 144 churches no longer on the SBC rolls.

8. *Christianity Today,* July 16, 1982, p. 36f.; *St. Louis Post Dispatch,* June 16, 1982; *Christian News,* June 21, 1982, p. 16; *Sword of the Lord,* July 16, 1982, p. 1f.; *Christianity Today,* August 5, 1983, p. 38f.; *Presbyterian Journal,* June 30, 1982, p. 2f.

9. *The Houston Chronicle,* November 20, 1982; *Southern Baptist Journal,* January 1983, p. 5f.

10. *Christian News,* July 11, 1983, p. 2; *Fundamentalist Journal,* September 1983, p. 54 and February 1983, p. 14f.

11. *Christian Century,* July 6-13, 1983, p. 639f.; see also *Christianity Today,* August 5, 1983, p. 38f.

12. *Fundamentalist Journal,* September 1983, p. 54.

13. *Annual,* SBC, 1983, pp. 39, 50.

14. *Christian News,* November 5, 1984, p. 10; see also *Christianity Today,* June 15, 1984, pp. 68-69. Even the SBC Home Mission Board has now hired an ordained woman.

15. Religious News Service, September 28, 1983; *Christian News,* October 10, 1983, p. 2.

16. *Christian News,* December 19, 1983, p. 23.

17. James T. Draper, *Authority: The Critical Issue for Southern Baptists* (Old Tappan, N.J.: Revell, 1984).

18. *Southern Baptist Journal,* January/February 1984, p. 1f.; see also *Southern Baptist Advocate,* January 1984, p. 6f.

19. *Southern Baptist Advocate,* February/March 1984, p. 1f.

Chapter Twenty-Two

Charles F. Stanley (1984-   )

The Kansas City Convention—1984

The 1984 SBC meeting in Kansas City, Missouri, elected conservative Charles F. Stanley to the presidency. Stanley, pastor of the First Baptist Church of Atlanta, Georgia, had drawn enthusiastic applause at the annual Pastors' Conference when he exhorted conservatives to "stand up, become strong, courageous and bold, and stop 'pussyfooting' around." Stanley won the presidency on the first ballot, receiving 52.18 percent of the vote. Both of the vice-presidential offices went to conservatives. Zig Ziglar, a nationally known, motivational lay speaker, became first vice president. He teaches a televised Sunday school class in W. A. Criswell's First Baptist Church in Dallas, and he has authored motivational-type literature. Donald V. Wideman of Missouri became second vice president. The messengers selected conservative Judge Paul Pressler to fill an unexpired vacant seat on the SBC Executive Committee. [1]

This was the sixth straight year that conservatives had succeeded in putting their man into the president's chair. Liberals protested when they discovered that only 2.1

percent of the missions budget in Stanley's church had gone to the Cooperative Program the preceding year. The church's total missions budget had been $644,000. [2] For such a man with relatively little past involvement in Convention activities to become president that suddenly was indeed unprecedented. Many have asked how this could have happened. The answer is quite simple: Charles Stanley is a "media minister." Sixty-six television stations nationwide broadcast his Sunday worship services, called "In Touch." One hundred and fifty radio stations carry his program, and he mails out 40,000 sermon tapes each month. He was a founding director of the Moral Majority, Inc. Stanley is a director of the Religious Roundtable and serves on the board of directors of the National Religious Broadcasters. The point is this: Charles Stanley did not even need to candidate for the high office of president; the messengers knew him, and they liked what they saw. Most simply assumed that he was more involved in Convention matters than he actually was. Stanley, however, has now committed himself to greater loyalty to his Convention. He has degrees from the University of Richmond, Southwestern Baptist Theological Seminary, and Luther Rice Seminary, and he had served as pastor of Southern Baptist churches in North Carolina, Ohio, and Florida before coming to his Atlanta pastorate in 1971.

Stanley's Expressed Concern Over Liberalism Within the Southern Baptist Convention

Atlanta's First Baptist Church publishes a weekly paper called *The Witness*. Soon after Dr. Stanley became the church's pastor, he made the following statement of concern in the paper's "pastor's column":

> But there is an aspect of this problem that troubles me equally, if not more so. When fine young men and women who know Christ in the fullness of the spirit go away to college and have to sit and listen to unbelieving professors, some whose salaries are paid by their home church, criticize and hammer away at their faith in the Bible as the Word of God, is it any wonder that they begin to drift in their faith? This should never be

allowed, but it goes on and on. I'm almost convinced that a Christian student is better off on a secular, heathen campus where he doesn't expect any sympathy, than on a so-called church related campus where cunningly by degrees his faith is shattered by a "Baptist professor."

At every Southern Baptist Convention the problem with unbelief in our schools rises to the surface. We talk about it, but somehow the convention closes and we return to the same evil.

It seems the only language that attracts the attention of our colleges and universities is "dollar." I have a strong conviction that if the supply diminished to a certain critical low, they would begin to give serious consideration to our questions of why they allow their professors to destroy the faith of our children under the cloak of academic freedom. Academic freedom is one thing but doctrinal freedom is something else. Doctrinal freedom within a denomination will destroy its very foundation. The problem with many of these men is that they have a warped idea of the real meaning of freedom. Freedom is not the right to do as you please, but the power to do what is right. Is it ever right to destroy someone else's faith in the Bible?

We must pray and work for God to remove those who use their positions either in ignorance or deliberately to confuse, shatter, and destroy the faith of their students rather than to build them up in the knowledge of Christ and in their commitment to Him.

Stanley's Opposition to a Pro-Inerrancy Statement in Georgia

At the 1975 annual meeting of the Georgia Baptist Convention, LeRoy Cooper (pastor of the Mt. Olive Baptist Church in East Point) made a motion that the messengers affirm their faith in the verbal inspiration of the Bible as the Word of God. Cooper had hardly finished presenting his motion when Pastor W. Henry Fields, a Southern Seminary graduate, rose in protest and presented a counter-motion. Confusion came upon the Georgia gathering. [3] The next morning, Ken E. Edwards, Jr., a conservative layman from Dr. Stanley's church, presented a motion that the messengers simply affirm a strong stand on the verbal inspiration and total inerrancy of the original manuscripts of Scripture. When this matter first came up, one of Dr. Stanley's staff members had telephoned to inform him. Stanley responded negatively; he stood opposed to the Ken Edwards motion. Stanley even telephoned the president of the Georgia Convention to inform him that Ken Edwards was acting alone and that Edwards's convictions were not the convictions of his "whole church body." The president responded, "I understand fully." On the Convention floor, J. Howard Cobble, a liberal pastor, offered a counter-motion to the Edwards proposal. The Cobble motion carried, and Ken Edwards stood publicly humiliated because his own conservative pastor had refused to stand with him on a simple motion to affirm belief in the Bible's verbal inspiration and infallibility.

At the following business meeting at First Baptist Church in Atlanta (Wednesday, November 19, 1975), some of Stanley's more conservative membership questioned the pastor's actions. Stanley attempted to answer his critics. The following story taken from the cassette tape of this entire business meeting clearly reveals Dr. Stanley's expressed feelings. Before the messengers from Stanley's church had left for the Convention, the pastor had urged them, "Please do not do anything that would hurt the image of this fellowship . . . I do not want my influence hindered when I go to Virginia at the Southern Baptist Convention." Stanley explained to his members, "If this church . . . or this pastor gets tagged as being uncooperative, non-Conventional, . . . we have lost half our impact." He confessed frankly, "That is not politics. That is carnality." In other words, that is just the way it is in this old world; in order to achieve standing, one must practice a little compromising. Fundamentalists have viewed this as a classic illustration of the New Evangelical philosophy. New Evangelicals appear constantly concerned with their "image." Dr. Stanley explained to his people that he personally believes in biblical inerrancy, and most observers feel that he is sincere in his statements.

Dr. Stanley argued to his church that conservatives cannot effectively take a strong stand on the Bible on the local and state levels. The SBC itself is the only level on which to wage an effective war against the Liberals, he explained: "If you are going to fight a war, do not fight over a little skirmish. Fight in a big battlefield; and when you win, be sure you have a total victory."[4]

Stanley's Public Statements Since His Election

In Kansas City in 1984, conservatives elevated Dr. Stanley himself to that "big battlefield." When the ballot count had come in, conservatives had been so elated that some literally shouted up and down the Convention halls. Many now waited eagerly for the coming press conference to hear their new leader's firm words of wisdom and conviction.

At the business meeting in 1975, Stanley had told his people that he was fully aware of the liberal professors in Southern Baptist schools but that "the right president for a period of three terms can clean house." When Stanley assumed the office of Convention president, the conservatives had elected "the right president" for six consecutive years, and the Liberals were still waxing eloquent in the seminaries and gladly receiving their Cooperative Program salaries. To the conservatives' chagrin Stanley proved no different from the other conservatives. He announced to the press conference that he is "not committed to anyone."[5] Said the new president, "I think we have to learn to live together and love each other, whether we agree or not." Asked what his emphases would be during his administration, Stanley repeated the now-familiar theme of newly elected conservative presidents: he would "seek to unify the fractured denomination" and pledge himself "to work with all Southern Baptists." With no intention of "cleaning house," Stanley simply wanted to direct his efforts toward holding conservatives and Liberals together. When a reporter asked him about the biblical inerrancy controversy, Stanley explained that he personally believes that the Bible is without error but that he does not want to see any division over this issue. "You are not going to ever get all Baptists to agree," he said, "and I think we have to accept that. . . . I think we have to learn to live together and love each other, whether we agree or not."[6] Even though conservative SBC presidents have refused to clarify the differences between their own camp and the Liberals' camp, the Liberals themselves have not been so reserved. Cecil Sherman, the liberal pastor of First Baptist Church in Asheville, North Carolina, said recently, "Let's face it: their Gospel is one thing, and our Gospel is largely another thing altogether." The statement appeared in an Associated Press release.[7]

The Liberals, however, continued to examine Dr. Stanley's past contributions to "the program" and began hurling charges of "disloyalty" toward him and his church. The pressure was overwhelming. Dr. Stanley announced to the Baptist Press Association on September 17, 1984, that he had now challenged his church to more than double its Cooperative Program giving for the coming year and to "rethink" its entire missions program. His election to the presidency had forced him to change his outlook on the Cooperative Program. So instead of announcing plans to put liberal professors out of the Southern Baptist institutions, Dr. Stanley instead announced his intention to encourage greater financial support for the Program which pays the salaries. Some of Dr. Stanley's church members still remember his words to them in that emotional business meeting back in 1975: "Nobody from Nashville tells this church what to do. . . . There is no organization above us, below us, beside us, who can dictate to us how we spend one single penny of our money. No one! Now, a church that listens to someone else tell them what to do, they are out of fellowship with God."[8] However, as president of the SBC, Dr. Stanley led his church to increase its funding quickly and steadily in order to demonstrate loyalty to "the Program." This agrees with Dr. Russell Dilday's advice to the 1984 SBC. Dilday, the president of Southwestern Seminary, preached the annual Convention Sermon, in which he called for toleration in doctrinal matters. He exhorted Southern Baptists to "turn from forced uniformity to the higher ground of autonomous individualism." Dr. Dilday's "autonomous individualism," however, applied to seminary professors, not to local Baptist churches.

The 1984 Resolutions

The 1984 SBC meeting in Kansas City adopted some impressive conservative resolutions. These resolutions opposed the following: women's ordination; the appointment of a U. S. Ambassador to the Vatican; gambling; alcohol and all other mind-altering drugs; abortion; growing and smoking tobacco; and secular humanism. Other resolutions urged these actions: greater efforts toward world-wide evangelism; approving "Equal Access Legislation"; and changes in the Civil Rights Act of 1984 to protect religious schools and institutions. Most offensive to Liberals was Resolution #3, which encourages participation of women "in all aspects of church life and work other than pastoral functions and leadership roles entailing ordination."[9]

Many observers saw such resolutions as "symbolic victories" at best, however, because in the wave of liberal protest even conservatives felt compelled to emphasize that resolutions are not binding on any church—they simply express the sentiment of the majority of the messengers gathered at the particular meeting. Moreover, President Jimmy Draper's proposed "five doctrinal guidelines" had never even merited a discussion on the floor, and the Liberals had defeated a motion to cut funds for the controversial Baptist Joint Committee on Public Affairs. The Liberals, however, were upset, especially over the resolution opposing women's ordination, and they were not about to lie down and play dead.

Women in Ministry

Southern Baptist churches have ordained an estimated 250 women, at least thirteen of whom serve as pastors.[10] These figures will rise significantly in the wake of liberal protest over the 1984 Resolution #3. Women now account for about 21 percent of the students in the six Southern Baptist seminaries.

During the 1983 Convention, some 75 women met in a Pittsburgh hotel and created an official organization called "Women in Ministry" to promote women's ordination. [11] Reba Cobb and Betty Pierce edit *Folio,* the group's newsletter. For their second annual meeting at the 1984 SBC meeting in Kansas City, the group enjoyed the use of SBC Woman's Missionary Union facilities, and the WMU even announced that its 1985 budget would include support to the organization. [12] Women in Ministry conducted a Sunday morning worship service in which Susan Lockwood Wright, pastor of Cornell Avenue Baptist Church in Chicago, preached. This controversy over women's ordination has divided the Convention in more ways than the inerrancy debate ever did.

Martha Gilmore, an ordained Baptist preacher, recently left Cliff Temple Baptist Church in Dallas to become a pastor in a United Methodist Church, while her husband remained at Cliff Temple and served as Chairman of the Board of Trustees of the SBC Home Mission Board. Cliff Temple Baptist had ordained her in 1977. Mrs. Gilmore had graduated from Baylor University and gone on to receive a graduate degree at Southern Methodist University, where she serves as a professor of religion in their Perkins School of Theology. [13] The SBC Home Mission Board is not the only agency experiencing problems, however. The SBC Foreign Mission Board has at least eight ordained women serving overseas, and many expect this number to increase almost immediately. Less than 18 percent of Cooperative Program money ever gets to the Foreign Mission Board, and even that amount supports compromise and disobedience. Liberals are not about to capitulate to the conservatives' new resolutions or even to their presidents.

In Dr. Stanley's own city, a Baptist Press release on July 11, 1984, reported that the executive committee of the Atlanta Baptist Association had in protest adopted a motion opposing the SBC resolution against women's ordination. Women in Ministry will continue to promote its cause. Debra Woodbury, an associate minister in Ridge

Road Baptist Church in Raleigh, North Carolina, has declared, "I have sermons I want to preach and pastoral skills I want to develop. I have a dream of walking through the door of a Southern Baptist Church as its pastor."[14] Diane Wisemiller, a pastor at the National Baptist Memorial Church in Washington, D. C., led an emotional and successful appeal in behalf of women's ordination on the SBC floor in Pittsburgh in 1983. This issue will simply not go away.

The Forum

While most of the messengers to the annual SBC meetings attend the Pastors' Conference which precedes the Convention, the Liberals have started holding their own "SBC Forum." In 1984 an estimated 2000 attended—an impressive showing. While these 2000 messengers were indeed a minority, one should not assume that the 10,000 who attended the Pastors' Conference were all conservatives. The Liberals know that if they attend the Forum, they will be labeled as "Liberals," and most of them would rather avoid that. Until now the Forum has represented only the most outspoken Liberals, but their numbers are expected to increase significantly with the widespread opposition to the 1984 resolution against women's ordination.

Gene Garrison, pastor of the First Baptist Church of Oklahoma City, served as the 1984 Forum moderator. Garrison's church has drunk deeply into the wells of liberal thought since former pastor Herschel Hobbs led them down that road years ago. David Matthews, pastor of First Baptist Church of Greenville, South Carolina, spoke to the Forum, warning the group against the conservative movement. He said conservatives are "leaning toward an idolatry of the Bible." This was Matthews's attack against biblical inerrancy. The Bible "is not God," he insisted, and "should not be elevated to the sovereignty which belongs only to God."[15] Matthews told the story of a young seminary student who grew so fond of his fiancée's letters that he remained at school during the holidays to cherish her letters rather than going to be with her. "Healthy people never confuse the letter with the lover," said Matthews. Conservatives, according to this Liberal, are not "healthy people"; they are sick people who worship the Bible. Other Liberals on the Forum's program for 1984 included these: Kenneth Chafin, the Southern Seminary professor; Sarah Ann Hobbs, director of the Missions Division of the North Carolina Baptist Convention; Kirby Godsey, president of Mercer University in Macon, Georgia, who upbraided Southern Baptists for "allowing themselves to become trapped in a theological mudslide"; and Duke K. McCall, Southern Seminary's chancellor. [16]

The Holy War

On August 28, 1984, Dr. Roy L. Honeycutt, president of Southern Seminary, spoke to an overflow audience at the opening convocation. He called for a "holy war" against the "unholy forces now at work." The Seminary printed this message and made it available in booklet form under the title *To Your Tents O Israel! A Biblical Call to Duty, Unity and Honor.* "We shall not submit again to slavery's yoke," declared Honeycutt (p. 5). His audience punctuated the message with frequent "amens", cheering, and even a lengthy standing ovation. "As Israel raised the war-cry to rebel against the oppressive rule of Rehoboam, so every person who is responsive to duty . . . should raise a denominational battle-cry against injustice and oppression" (p. 5). Liberals must now rise up against the conservatives' "unscrupulous use of power and manipulation" (p. 12). Said Honeycutt, "Our problem is that *independent-fundamentalist revisionists* are rewriting Southern Baptist history to suit their agenda" (p. 11). Of course, Honeycutt claims that he and his faculty are teaching precisely those things which Southern Baptists have always believed and that the conservatives are the ones who have shifted from the "historic Baptist position" on the Bible. If the 1979 Pressler-Patterson Coalition was "Pearl Harbor," then Honeycutt's 1984 declaration was the "Day of Infamy," to which Paige Patterson responded, "The only other person in recent decades who has declared a holy war is in fact the Ayatollah Khomeini." [17]

Honeycutt answered conservatives on the women's issue by formally installing Dr. D. Anne Davis as dean of the Seminary's new Carver School of Social Work; this was the school's first woman dean of an academic department. The president also inducted Dr. Molly Marshall-Green as an assistant professor of theology—the school's first woman theology professor. [18] Calling for a public debate, Paige Patterson asked Honeycutt to allow all classroom lectures to be taped for the next two years and to make those tapes available to all. Honeycutt rejected both the call for debate and the request for taping. Homer G. Lindsay, Jr., a Southern Baptist pastor in Florida, called for Honeycutt's ouster. [19]

If conservatives oust Honeycutt, however, they will also have to contend with the other five seminary presidents. Only seventy-two hours following Charles Stanley's election to the SBC presidency, Russell Dilday, president of Southwestern Seminary, was pledging himself publicly to work to unseat Stanley in 1985. W. Randall Lolley, Southeastern Seminary's president, began an organized effort in North Carolina to promote the liberal cause. Lolley answered the conservatives' 1984 resolution against ordaining women by hiring Donna Myra Forrester as the school's new chaplain. Knollwood Baptist Church in Winston-Salem had ordained Forrester in 1976; she holds degrees from Southern and Southeastern Seminaries. Lolley had already employed women on his seminary faculty. [20]

The Nationwide Liberal Coalition

There emerged a grassroots Southern Baptist liberal movement—a kind of confederation, as yet without a clear national leader. In the *Richmond Times-Dispatch,* on August 10, 1984, 130 Liberals sponsored a full-page ad attacking the 1984 SBC resolution against women's ordination. On September 29, 1984, 50 liberal Southern Baptist leaders conducted a special seminar at the First Baptist Church of Chattanooga, Tennessee. [21] In the same month, 40 liberal North Carolina pastors and church leaders met at the First Baptist Church in High Point, where Lamar King is pastor. They organized themselves into "Friends of Missions" and castigated the whole conservative movement. [22]

Liberal grassroots organizations also sprang up in many other states. In 1984-85 the Liberals began using Baylor University's computers to help build and coordinate a national coalition. Baylor's president, Herbert Reynolds, went on the offensive against the conservatives, saying that they can no longer be tolerated because they are "a priestly and self-anointed group," out to make "clones" by controlling Southern Baptist education. [23] In Georgia, hundreds of Southern Baptist Liberals organized under the direction of Bill Self, pastor of Wieuca Baptist Church in Atlanta. They established statewide coordinators, regional coordinators, and state consultants working at every level for the liberal cause. In South Carolina, the liberal organizers included David Matthews and Harold Cole. In Mississippi, Ray Lloyd, pastor of First Baptist Church of Starkville, divided his state into eight regions, each with its own coordinator. In Louisiana, coalition leaders included pastors Joe Blair, Pat Harrison, and John Harris. Liberal leaders are instructing their seminary and college students to get to the SBC meetings and vote for liberal causes. Professor Kenneth Chafin at Southern Seminary urged the students in a recent chapel service to "start saving your nickels and dimes. Get on as a messenger from some church. Get ... those ... ballots in your hands and vote." [24] Both Liberals and conservatives were predicting that twice the usual number of messengers would attend future Southern Baptist Convention meetings. In Alabama, Virginia, Missouri, and many other states the Liberals were regrouping, and the lamps were going out all over Nashville.

Last-Ditch Effort to Revive a Corpse

While the messengers to the SBC annual meetings enjoy their Pastors' Conferences and liberal Forums, few reporters seem to notice the small "satellite conferences" which the more conservative pastors and church leaders conduct to discuss their own concerns about the Convention's future. In 1984, for example, the Red Bridge Baptist Church in Kansas City sponsored such a conference prior to the SBC meeting and featured strong speakers representing the Baptist Faith and Message Fellowship—William A. Powell, Sr., who edits and publishes the *Southern Baptist Journal;* Malone Cochran, pastor of Mt. Zion Baptist Church in Jonesboro, Georgia; and W. D. Martin of Shreveport, Louisiana. Red Bridge's pastor is Bud Long. [25]

The handful of surviving founders of the General Association of Regular Baptist Churches (GARBC) movement views the present struggle within the SBC as a replay of the old Fundamentalist-Modernistic battle within the Northern Baptist Convention (NBC) back in the 1920s. [26] The Liberals won that battle. Perhaps such comparison is an oversimplification. There are more differences than similarities between the two battles. The SBC is largely conservative, but it is a conservatism rooted in loyalty to the denomination. Millions of lay people in the SBC generally think of loyalty to Christ and to the Bible in terms of loyalty to denominational leaders and to the Baptist name and program. This is the reason that the Liberals' Forum still constitutes a minority; relatively few have been willing to identify outwardly with a "rebel cause." The Pastors' Conference is a mixed multitude of conservatives and Liberals—Liberals who are determined to stay in the mainstream, work quietly to change the Convention's basic philosophy, and to avoid the "Liberal" label. This situation is rapidly changing as more and more Liberals are rallying publicly to defend their causes. At this time a definite polarization appears to be developing. Rumors abound about legal searches into deeds and constitutions of churches, schools, and agencies to see who could win court battles over property in case of a split.

Endnotes

1. *Annual,* SBC, 1984, pp. 44f.

2. *Greenville* (S. C.) *Piedmont,* June 13, 1984; see also *Christian Century,* July 18-25, 1984, p. 701f. Dr. Stanley's

church designated 2.6 percent of its missions budget to the Cooperative Program in 1984 and 5.2 percent in 1985. A recent Baptist Press release stated that this church's total 1985 missions budget was $600,000.

3. William A. Powell, *The SBC Issue & Question* (Buchanan, Georgia: Baptist Missionary Service, Inc., 1977), p. 244.

4. Charles F. Stanley, *Wednesday Business Meeting,* cassette tape (Atlanta: First Baptist Church, November 19, 1975).

5. *Greenville* (S. C.) *Piedmont,* June 13, 1984.

6. *Christian News,* June 25, 1984, p. 1f.; *Christian News,* October 29, 1984, p. 13; see also *Moody Monthly,* September 1984, p. 80.

7. Cited in *Southern Baptist Journal,* October 1984, p. 13. Cecil Sherman has recently moved from Asheville to Broadway Baptist Church of Fort Worth, Texas.

8. Stanley cassette tape, op. cit.

9. *Annual,* SBC, 1984, pp. 58-66.

10. *Christianity Today,* July 13, 1984, pp. 32-33; *Christian News,* June 25, 1984, p. 1f.; see also *Christian Century,* July 18-25, 1984, p. 701f.

11. *Christian News,* July 11, 1983, p. 2; *Fundamentalist Journal,* September 1983, p. 54.

12. *Advocate Update,* June 1984, p. 1.

13. *Charisma,* September 1984, p. 132f.

14. *Greenville* (S. C.) *News,* November 27, 1980.

15. *Greenville* (S. C.) *Piedmont,* June 12, 1984.

16. *Christianity Today,* July 13, 1984, pp. 32-33; *Fundamentalist Journal,* September 1984, p. 63.

17. *Baptist Challenge,* November 1984, p. 1.

18. *The Courier-Journal,* August 29, 1984; *Southern Baptist Journal,* October 1984, p. 1f.

19. *Houston Chronicle,* October 13, 1984; *Christian News,* September 24, 1984, p. 1f.; *Christian News,* October 22, 1984, p. 6.

20. *Christian News,* September 17, 1984, p. 1; *Southern Baptist Advocate,* September/October 1984, p. 1f.

21. *The Tennessean,* August 29, 1984; *Christian News,* September 24, 1984, p. 20.

22. *Greenville* (S. C.) *News,* September 18, 1984, p. 3A.

23. Religious News Service release on October 19, 1984, cited in *Christian News,* October 29, 1984, p. 13; *Southern Baptist Advocate,* December 1984, p. 1f.

24. *Christianity Today,* November 9, 1984, p. 42f.

25. *Southern Baptist Journal,* October 1984, p. 5.

26. *Baptist Bulletin,* February 1983, p. 7.

Part VI:
Conclusion

Chapter Twenty-Three

Will the Convention Change or Split?

Early in 1983, according to a Dallas news release in the *Fort Worth Star,* Dr. Criswell told reporters in a special interview that he predicts no split: "I don't think we will ever split. I think we will erode. . . . I think we will gradually acquiesce." Criswell said that he sees the Convention as following the path of the United Methodist, Presbyterian, and other mainline denominations: "The death that I see in these old-line denominations is coming to our Southern Baptist Convention." In this special interview, the pastor laments the fact that the denomination as a whole is dead: "I don't know when I've seen a great revival among Baptists. By revival I mean people . . . moved Godward. . . . It is not the main thrust of preachers in our churches any more." Even Southern Baptist newspapers cited the pastor's remarks. [1]

It is not revival but rather loyalty to the Convention's program which seems to be intensifying, however. One Southern Baptist paper recently even referred to the

Cooperative Program itself as "sacred."[2] How can such a statement be made regarding a system which, as we have seen, provides the funds for apostate teachers and authors to propagate their heresies? It reminds one of the Hindus who refer to the Ganges as their "sacred river." There is a report that a stranger once tried to show them through a microscope the bacteria in these foul waters where they bathed and from which they drank. Their response was to break the microscope and to continue using the contaminated waters. They refused to heed the warning because their river was "sacred." The result of drinking from these tainted waters continues to be physical death, and the result of drinking from the Convention's tainted wells will continue to be spiritual death. This is what the Word of God says.

> These are wells without water, clouds that are carried with a tempest; to whom the mist of darkness is reserved for ever (II Peter 2:17).

> But whosoever drinketh of the water that I shall give him shall never thirst; but the water that I shall give him shall be in him a well of water springing up into everlasting life (John 4:14).

Outwardly, the SBC appears to be continuing its Baptist tradition, with conservatism gaining in strength. Inwardly, however, the deadly diseases of apostasy and compromise run rampant and unchecked. No longer is it a matter of "creeping Liberalism"; now it is "controlling Liberalism." Although Southern Baptist conservatives have discovered the presence of the malignant cancer of apostasy in the body, they have refused a complete diagnosis and removal of that cancer until it is now terminal. Conservative voices within the SBC are not expressing, nor have they expressed since J. Frank Norris's day, any real commitment to removing the cancer completely. At best, contemporary conservatives are officially expressing only a desire that truth receive a hearing alongside error. Time, therefore, is on the Liberals' side.

It appears that the "program" will continue to hold Liberals and conservatives together. Those "conservative trustees"—usually lay businessmen—will never be able, even if enough of them wished, to perform the "miracle surgery" on the hideous cancer of unbelief. The Liberals may allow a few concessions to avoid offending the silent majority, but philosophies which have dominated institutions for thirty years will not disappear. At best, they will appear in more subtle forms in printed materials until the battle subsides. While time may still be on the Liberals' side, eternity is not. The Lord Jesus said:

> Beware of false prophets which come to you in sheep's clothing, but inwardly they are ravening wolves. Ye shall know them by their fruits. Do men gather grapes of thorns, or figs of thistles? Even so every good tree bringeth forth good fruit; but a corrupt tree bringeth forth evil fruit. A good tree cannot bring forth evil fruit, neither can a corrupt tree bring forth good fruit. Every tree that bringeth not forth good fruit is hewn down, and cast into the fire. Wherefore by their fruits ye shall know them. Not every one that saith unto me, Lord, Lord, shall enter into the kingdom of heaven; but he that doeth the will of my Father which is in heaven. Many will say to me in that day, Lord, Lord, have we not prophesied in thy name? and in thy name have cast out devils? and in thy name done many wonderful works? And then will I profess unto them, I never knew you: depart from me, ye that work iniquity (Matthew 7:15-23).

By its own admission, as seen in these pages, the SBC has shifted from its solid historic position of belief in and obedience to the Word of God, and the time has come to acknowledge the fact that the house is on the sinking sand.

> Therefore whosoever heareth these sayings of mine, and doeth them, I will liken him unto a wise man, which built his house upon a rock: And the rain descended, and the floods came, and winds blew, and beat upon that house; and it fell not: for it was founded upon a rock. And every one that heareth these sayings of mine, and doeth them not, shall be likened unto a foolish man, which built his house upon the sand: And the rain descended, and the floods came, and the winds blew, and beat upon that house; and it fell: and great was the fall of it (Matthew 7:24-27).

The reader should consider seriously these words, especially since they follow directly upon the strong warning about false teachers that we saw above in verses 15 through 23.

While many conservative Southern Baptist churches will continue to withdraw from the Convention and become fundamental and unaffiliated, it would not seem likely that there will be a major split within the Convention itself, given the strong denominational loyalty and the retirement pensions vested in the Annuity Board. There is a perennial "joke" which pastors tell at each annual meeting: "If the Convention splits, I'm going with the Annuity Board!" The Board does appear to be the "cement of the empire."

What Should Bible-Believing Southern Baptists Do Now?

"Can two walk together, except they be agreed?" (Amos 3:3). There is a great need for honesty and sincerity in this matter of being true to Christ and His Word. A person who speaks out against liquor but who votes to have licensed bars is not straightforward and sincere. The person who sympathizes with his neighbor and tries to console him when a snake bites his child is not completely honest if he is protecting and feeding rattlesnakes. The man who preaches the fundamentals of the faith and then supports infidels by his associations is not an honest man. "Blessed is the man that walketh not in the counsel of the ungodly, nor standeth in the way of sinners, nor sittest in the seat of the scornful" (Psalm 1:1).

Will the reader of this book accept the blessing offered in this psalm? In many cases in order to have this blessing the layman will have to leave his church or the pastor will have to leave his pastorate. The cost is great. In other cases it will mean the loss of friends; it will mean misunderstanding; it will mean cross-bearing (Luke 14:25-35). Martin Luther knew the feeling, as did C. H. Spurgeon and John Bunyan and scores of others who counted the cost and considered it all joy that they might please Christ and stand before Him unashamed. Such a move will also open doors of fellowship with scores of other believers in churches which already know the joy of serving Christ in complete freedom from a denominational connection that identifies God's people with the very things which the Bible condems. My mother and father left the Convention with me more than twenty years ago, and we will always cherish the memories of those days when God transformed our anxieties into sweet and lasting fellowship with Fundamental, missionary-minded Christians from all over the world. Several years ago, a Southern Baptist survey revealed that two or three churches leave the Convention each week and become unaffiliated. [3] The official SBC literature simply does not report this fact.

Someone argues, "But shall we turn the SBC colleges, seminaries and other institutions over to the liberal unbelievers?" The truth is that you have already done that. These institutions have been a theological melting pot since the 1950s. The cancer has permeated every area of the body, and no Bible believer should continue to feed it. As previously stated, some conservative Southern Baptist leaders are secretly fearful of obeying the Lord in biblical separation because of the inevitable loss of their accumulated annuities. They have paid money into the retirement fund for years, and they are afraid to forsake it. Dear friend, if the Lord Jesus bought you and redeemed you with His own blood, can you not trust Him to care for His own as He has done through many centuries? "O ye of little faith . . . seek ye first the kingdom of God, and his righteousness; and all these things shall be added unto you" (Matthew 6:30, 33f.). "Blessed are ye, when men shall revile you, and persecute you, and shall say all manner of evil against you falsely, for my sake. Rejoice, and be exceeding glad: for great is your reward in heaven" (Matthew 5:11-12a).

Another may argue, "I will stay in the SBC and fight from within. At least I will be an inside voice." The simple truth is that you only stay in because you feel more loyalty to a denomination than to Christ and the Bible. As long as you are "within"—associated directly or indirectly with apostasy—you are in no position to "contend for the faith" (Jude 3). Few people would listen to one posing as a

190

spiritual leader but who is continuing to support and identify with disobedience. The Good Shepherd "goeth before" His sheep (John 10:4); He has set the example of obedience; by His own obedience and example through the shedding of His blood for the remission of sin, He has earned the right to be heard.

> That he might sanctify the people with his own blood, [He] suffered without the gate. Let us go forth therefore unto him without the camp, bearing his reproach (Hebrews 13:12-13).

> Wherefore come out from among them, and be ye separate, saith the Lord, and touch not the unclean thing; and I will receive you, And will be a Father unto you, and ye shall be my sons and daughters, saith the Lord Almighty (II Corinthians 6:17-18).

Endnotes

1. *Southern Baptist Journal,* March/April 1983, p. 8.

2. William A. Powell cites and criticizes the article in his *Southern Baptist Journal,* March 1981, p. 4.

3. *Southern Baptist Journal,* May 1974, p. 1.

Appendixes

Appendix One
New Evangelicalism

Origin and Definition

The New Evangelical movement constitutes a major segment of the Southern Baptist Convention. New Evangelicalism is the religious mood or attitude which advocates dialogue with apostates and infiltration into apostate institutions. Harold J. Ockenga (1905-1985) coined the term in his 1948 presidential convocation speech for Fuller Theological Seminary. On that occasion, Dr. Ockenga stated that the New Evangelicals are a "new breed." He expressed three areas of dissatisfaction with Fundamentalism. The first area was Fundamentalism's "wrong attitude" of suspicion toward those who do not hold to every doctrine of orthodoxy. The second area of dissatisfaction was Fundamentalism's "wrong strategy" of separating from religious liberalism. He proposed, as a "correct strategy," infiltration; that is, forgetting doctrinal differences and looking for areas of agreement and cooperation. Now, after almost forty years, the clear evidence is that Dr. Ockenga's "right strategy" has not and will not succeed, because it violates the biblical principle of separation from apostasy. The Word of God is crystal clear on this point. When a church, institution, or denomination becomes theologically unclean, we are to shun it: "Touch not the unclean thing" (II Corinthians 6:17). Dr. Ockenga's third area of dissatisfaction was Fundamentalism's "wrong results" of having lost nearly every battle with Liberalism. Liberalism had taken over virtually all of the schools of the mainline denominations, including the SBC, and the New Evangelicals aimed to "recapture denominational leadership" *(Christianity Today,* October 10, 1960, p. 11f.; *Park Street Spire,* February 1958; "Dr. Ockenga Release"—mimeographed sheet dated December 8, 1957).

In the Foreword to *The Battle for the Bible,* a book by conservative Southern Baptist spokesman Harold Linsell which was published in 1976, Dr. Ockenga offers a first-hand, definitive reminiscence of New Evangelicalism's origins:

> New-evangelicalism was born in 1948 in connection with a convocation address which I gave in the Civic Auditorium in Pasadena. While reaffirming the theological view of fundamentalism, this address repudiated its ecclesiology and its social theory. The ringing call for a repudiation of separatism and the summons to social involvement received a hearty response from . . . spokesmen such as Drs. Harold Lindsell, Carl F. H. Henry, Edward Carnell, and Gleason Archer. . . . It differed from fundamentalism in its repudiation of separatism and its determination to engage itself in the theological dialogue of the day (Foreword).

Therefore, according to Dr. Ockenga's own definition, New Evangelicalism differs from Fundamentalism in three major areas: (1) a repudiation of the doctrine of separation; (2) a summons to greater social involvement; and (3) a determination to engage in theological dialogue with Modernism.

Dr. Ockenga listed four major agencies of the New Evangelical movement: (1) the National Association of Evangelicals, which conservative SBC leaders at every level enthusiastically support, (2) Fuller Theological Seminary, (3) the journal *Christianity Today,* and (4) Billy Graham's ecumenical evangelism (*Battle for the Bible* [Foreword]; also *Christianity Today,* October 10, 1960, p. 11f.).

Billy Graham: New Evangelicalism's Evangelist

Billy Graham, a member of the First Baptist Church in Dallas, Texas, has given great impetus to New Evangelicalism's infiltration and accommodation to Liberalism. For example, he had liberal spokesman Henry P. Van Dusen on his New York crusade committee in 1957 and Bishop Gerald Kennedy in his Los Angeles crusade in 1963. Mr. Graham has spoken at Belmont Abbey, a Roman Catholic school which awarded him an honorary doctorate. In 1966 Mr. Graham addressed the National Council of Churches meeting in Miami and likened it to a "second Pentecost." Recently, Mr. Graham described Pope John Paul II as the "Builder of Bridges"—"the greatest religious leader of the modern world, and one of the greatest moral and spiritual leaders of this century" (*Saturday Evening Post,* January/February, 1980, p. 72).

Appendix Two

Fundamentalism

The Origin of Fundamentalism

Mainline Fundamentalism originated in the northern states. The editor of the Baptist periodical *Watchman-Examiner* coined the term *Fundamentalist* in 1920 to describe a group of concerned Baptists who had just met at the Delaware Avenue Baptist Church in Buffalo, New York, to discuss the problem of Modernism in the Northern Baptist Convention. The American roots of Fundamentalism, however, go back to the interdenominational Bible conference which met at Swampscott, Massachusetts, in 1876. This was the beginning of the American Bible conference movement; it gave birth to American Fundamentalism.

One of the most significant of the early Fundamentalist conferences was held from October 30 to November 1, 1878, at the Church of the Holy Trinity (Episcopal) in New York City, where Stephen H. Tyng, Jr., was the minister. Equally important was the conference which met in Farwell Hall in Chicago, November 16-21, 1886. The leaders of these pioneer conferences included spiritual giants of several denominations: Baptists included George C. Needham, A. J. Gordon, G. C. Lorimer, F. C. Chapell, and A. J. Frost; Methodists included L. W. Munhall, W. E. Blackstone, Henry Lummis, J. S. Kennedy, and

E. T. Stroeter (Wesleyan); Presbyterians included Albert Erdman, W. J. Erdman, James H. Brooks, H. M. Parsons, W. G. Moorehead, John Wanamaker, John T. Duffield, S. H. Kellogg, C. K. Imbrie, J. T. Cooper, Nathaniel West, A. T. Pierson, and D. C. Marquis; Congregationalists included E. P. Goodwin and D. W. Whittle; Episcopalians included Stephen Tyng, Jr., and Maurice Baldwin; Lutherans included Bishop Joseph A. Seiss and G. N. H. Peters; Reformed Episcopalians included Bishop W. R. Nicholson; and even the Dutch Reformed were represented by George S. Bishop.

The Definition of Fundamentalism

Many definitions have surfaced throughout Fundamentalism's history. In June 1976—exactly a century after the first gathering at Swampscott, Massachusetts—another faithful group of Fundamentalists held a World Congress of Fundamentalists at Ulster Hall, Edinburgh, Scotland. These Fundamentalists, who gathered from many nations of the world for a week of fellowship, instruction, and inspirational preaching, defined the term *Fundamentalist* as a born-again believer in the Lord Jesus Christ who

1. Maintains an immovable allegiance to the inerrant, infallible, and verbally inspired Bible; 2. Believes that whatever the Bible says is so; 3. Judges all things by the Bible and is judged only by the Bible; 4. Affirms the foundational truths of the historic Christian Faith: the doctrine of the Trinity; the incarnation, virgin birth, substitutionary atonement, bodily resurrection, ascension into heaven and second coming of the Lord Jesus Christ; the new birth through regeneration of the Holy Spirit; the resurrection of the saints to life eternal; the resurrection of the ungodly to final judgment and eternal death; the fellowship of the saints, who are the body of Christ; 5. Practices fidelity to that Faith and endeavors to preach it to every creature; 6. Exposes and separates from all ecclesiastical denial of that Faith, compromise with error, and apostasy from the Truth; and 7. Earnestly contends for the Faith once delivered.

Therefore, Fundamentalism is militant orthodoxy set on fire with soulwinning zeal. While Fundamentalists may differ on certain *interpretations* of Scripture, we join in unity of heart and common purpose for the defense of the Faith and the preaching of the Gospel, without compromise or division (*Faith for the Family*, September/October 1976, p. 9).

A true Fundamentalist, of course, believes far more than this simple listing; but he desires to go on record as affirming those timeless truths or principles which have come under religious attack. The list may need more refining and even expanding as Satan changes his focus of attack. Issues today are far more complex than they were a hundred or even twenty years ago.

That Fundamentalism can be reduced to the "five points published at the Niagara Bible Conference of 1895" is an often-repeated myth. Actually, the Niagara Bible Conference published a fourteen-point creed. The one five-point declaration which did influence Fundamentalists was the one which the General Assembly of the Presbyterian Church adopted in 1910 and reaffirmed in 1916 and 1923. Fundamentalism, however, has never been and never could be limited to the affirmations of any particular denomination. The *Fundamentals of Fellowship transcend denominational distinctives*, and they do so without weakening or compromising such distinctives. For example, Fundamentalists have always been good Presbyterians or good Baptists and still able to fellowship with Fundamentalists of other groups. While Fundmentalists certainly do differ among themselves on certain interpretations of Scripture, they unite in fellowship and "common purpose for the defense of the Faith and the preaching of the Gospel," accepting the Bible alone, without question, as the divinely and verbally inspired, inerrant, and authoritative Word of God.

Before Fundamentalists lost the mainline denominations, including the SBC, to the Liberals' control, the terms *conservative* and *Fundamentalist* were basically synonymous. This is no longer the case. Many conservatives today are New Evangelicals who have remained in membership or in working cooperation with the Liberals, while the Fundamentalists have come out of the mainline denominations and formed their own churches, schools, and other institutions. Even though an increasing number of New Evangelical leaders today are calling themselves "Fundamentalists," they are not identifying with old mainline Fundamentalism which began by leaving the apostate denominations thirty to sixty years ago.

Appendix Three

What Fundamentalists Mean by the Term *Separation* or *Holiness*

The term *biblical fellowship* is the positive side of the separation coin. Fundamentalists believe that the Scriptures clearly teach certain criteria for true Christian fellowship.

The Scriptural Criteria For Fellowship

Fundamentalists believe that the scriptural bases for fellowship are genuine belief in and consistent obedience to Christ and the Bible. They regard the doctrine of biblical fellowship as fundamental. It is inherently part of the scriptural doctrine of God's absolute holiness—separation (sanctification) from the world, from false religion, and from every practice of disobedience to God's Word. Key Bible passages teaching separation from the world include I John 2:15-17, II Corinthians 6:15-7:1, and James 4:4. Key passages teaching separation from false teachers include Galatians 1:8-9, II John 9-11, and I Timothy 6:20-21. Key passages teaching separation from disobedient Christians include I Corinthians 5:1-13, II Thessalonians 3:6, 14-15, and Matthew 18:15-18.

The Scriptural Attitude Toward Disobedient Brethren

There is a basic difference between separation from religious apostates and separation from erring Christian brethren: separation from a brother is not irrevocable. Separation from a Christian brother should never be a total rejection which allows no place for repentance. Allowance should be made for ignorance, errors of judgment, and momentary weakness. Nevertheless, when Christian leaders begin to steer God's people into disobedience and compromise they must be scripturally rebuked and their error exposed. This principle of rebuke and correction is often illustrated in the Bible: Leviticus 19:17; Joshua 22:11-20; Proverbs 25:12; Ezra 9-10; Nehemiah 13:13-29; Matthew 18:15-18; I Corinthians 5:1-13; II Thessalonians 3:6, 14-15; Titus 3:9-10; and in many other passages.

Appendix Four

Liberalism

Varieties of Liberalism

Liberalism, the modern revolt against God which masquerades as Christianity, has gone through an astonishing number of changes since it developed in the 1800s. Since it is governed by the whims of human reason and is no longer restrained by the authority of Scripture, Liberalism has produced numerous schools of thought, most of which enjoyed only a brief popularity. There are, however, three main movements which have dominated the twentieth century: old-line Liberalism or Modernism, Neo-liberalism, and Neo-orthodoxy. The older Liberalism or Modernism has as its starting point that the Bible cannot be the inerrant Word of God and the absolute authority in matters of theology, because the advances man has made in history, science, philosophy, and other disciplines prove that it is a fallible, human book. Characteristically, Modernism tends to discount the supernatural elements of the Bible, explaining away the miraculous wherever possible. The three doctrines which the older Liberalism emphasized the most were the universal fatherhood of God, the universal brotherhood of man, and the social gospel as the answer to man's needs. Some of the most influential liberal theologians were F. D. E. Schleiermacher (1768-1834), Albrecht Ritschl (1822-1889), and Adolf Harnack (1851-1930).

Perhaps the best refutation ever written of the older Liberalism was the book *Christianity and Liberalism*, written by J. Gresham Machen in 1923. He points out that Liberalism attempted to remove the "temporary symbols" of Christianity, such as the creation, the fall of man, the substitutionary atonement, heaven and hell, and, in short, everything that is distinctive about Christianity. Their purpose was to "rescue certain of the general principles of religion," but the result was a totally non-Christian religion posing as Christianity (*Christianity and Liberalism*, rpt. Grand Rapids: Eerdmans, 1977, p. 6).

Neo-liberalism, which emerged about 1935, is an attempt to preserve the basic tenets of Liberalism while clothing them in conservative-sounding terminology. World War I, the rise of totalitarian states in Europe, and the Great Depression had raised serious questions about the old Liberalism's optimistic outlook in man's abilities. Archaeology and advances in textual research had done much to discredit the historical-critical method while strengthening the Fundamentalists' belief in the reliability of the Scriptures. For instance, archaeology proved that, contrary to what Liberals had asserted, the art of writing was commonly practiced in the time of Moses and that there was a great Hittite empire in ancient times, though it was previously known to history only from the Bible. Observing that many of the old liberal institutions were losing the support of orthodox-minded constituents, Harry Emerson Fosdick (1878-1969) delivered in 1935 the now famous sermon from his Riverside Church in New York City—"The Church Must Go Beyond Modernism." This was the historic beginning of Neo-liberalism, which indeed was not new but rather the same old Liberalism clothed in a more attractive garb, intended to be more palatable to the average lay person.

Neo-orthodoxy, whose founding father was Karl Barth (1896-1968), was ostensibly a modern restatement of the theology of the Protestant Reformers, but it simply preserves the basic tenets of the older Liberalism using extremely nebulous terminology. The foundation for its underlying philosophy, Existentialism, was laid by Sören Kierkegaard (1813-1855), Danish philosopher and theologian. Neo-orthodoxy and religious Existentialism (used interchangeably for practical purposes) developed as a reaction to the cold, dead rationalism of old-line Liberalism. Whereas René Descartes (1596-1650) had begun his philosophy with pure reasoning—"I think; therefore, I am"—Existentialism begins with present existence (living) as its first principle. The basic idea is that existence is prior to reasoning. Therefore, it is impossible to find ultimate truth and the real meaning of life speculatively. The true meaning (or mystery) of existence lies only in individual living. Human experience is the starting point of all understanding. Life has no objective or absolute meaning. A human being must create his own meaning, and he does this by looking within himself. Truth is purely *subjective*. This philosophy has permeated "evangelical" churches today. Even Christian young people, who would not commit certain acts themselves, often feel that if *others* want to do such things, it may be all right for them.

Accepting the liberal view of the Scriptures, Karl Barth attacked Fundamentalists for "worshipping a self-sufficient paper pope." While claiming to preserve the "message" of the

Bible, neo-orthodox men deny many of the literal *facts* of the Bible. Neo-orthodoxy's underlying principle is Immanuel Kant's theory that there is another realm of "things in themselves" which lies beyond the senses. This purely subjective "world of things in themselves" Neo-orthodoxy calls *Geschichte*. Opposed to *Historie* (literal history), *Geschichte* is the category to which the Neo-orthodox relegate any inconvenient biblical miracle or doctrine, such as the creation account, the fall of man, and the miracles of Christ. Such facts are "inconvenient" because like Modernism, Neo-orthodoxy is careful not to contradict modern man's denial that God can act contrary to natural "scientific" laws. To the Neo-orthodox, the Bible is still only a human book, and therefore a fallible one. It may be the means whereby man can encounter or "experience" God; but the Bible never actually becomes the absolute Word of God, because all true religious knowledge lies only in the "other world"—the *Geschichte*. Remember, Neo-orthodoxy rejects many of the historical accounts in the Scriptures.

Neo-orthodoxy is neither "new" nor "orthodox"; it is the old Liberalism in a new and subtle guise of philosophical-sounding terminology which has too often intimidated both pastors and laymen.

The Historical-Critical Approach to the Bible

In one sense, modern Liberalism is not different from any other philosophy or religion that man has devised since his rebellion in the Garden of Eden. It revives certain heresies that are remarkably like what the early Church encountered. However, part of Liberalism's success in capturing modern denominations is due to the destruction of confidence in Scripture through the historical-critical method, something relatively recent.

The origin of the method may be traced to the eighteenth century. A French physician, Jean Astruc, published a commentary on Genesis in 1753 which asserted that the book was not a single literary composition but rather a composite of two primary documents that are distinguishable by their use of different names for God—Jehovah and Elohim. Astruc speculated that Moses simply used and edited these two basic documents. During the same period, a German Protestant scholar, J. S. Semler, translated into German a seventy-year-old work by a Roman Catholic priest, Richard Simon, who on the basis of his own source analysis, or "source criticism," denied the Mosaic authorship of the entire Pentateuch.

Although higher critics did not fully develop the classic four-source (JEDP) hypothesis until the nineteenth century, the criteria for future documentary criticism appeared even in the eighteenth century. These included (1) the use of different names of God; (2) stylistic differences; (3) alleged discrepancies; (4) repetitions; and (5) alleged clues of a composite or editorial structure.

The exaltation of human reason, especially in the nineteenth century, led to further developments of source criticism. Because the criteria for distinguishing sources were purely subjective, it was inevitable that the number of the conjectured sources would multiply. Men such as J. G. Eichhorn (1752-1827), J. S. Vater (1771-1826), W. M. L. DeWette (1780-1849), and Hermann Hupfeld (1796-1866) championed source criticism. Evolutionary thought dominated the intellectual climate, and by the middle of the nineteenth century the alleged sources of the Pentateuch numbered four—JEDP. J represents the use of the name Jehovah; E is for Elohim; D stands basically for the book of Deuteronomy; and P is the priestly material which allegedly constitutes the framework of the entire Pentateuch.

The greatest development of source criticism came from K. H. Graf (1815-1869) and Julius Wellhausen (1844-1918). When Graf began to date the four sources, source criticism became "historical" criticism. The alleged dates are these: J—ninth century B. C.; E—eighth century B. C.; D—the time of Josiah (640-609 B. C.); and P—fifth century B. C. The implications are obvious: Moses could not have written the Pentateuch, even though Christ Himself ascribes it to him; Deuteronomy was a pious fraud passed off on the people of Josiah's day as an ancient work of Moses; and the historical accuracy of the Bible is out of the question. Wellhausen himself denied the historicity of Abraham, Noah, and other Bible characters.

R. K. Harrison, in his *Introduction to the Old Testament* (Grand Rapids: Eerdmans, 1969), concludes that Wellhausen "occupied a position in the field of Old Testament criticism analogous to that of Darwin in the area of biological science." Before his death, Wellhausen "conceded that the rationalism which he had embraced so avidly in earlier years had made havoc of his own faith in the authority and authenticity of the Old Testament" (pp. 21, 26).

S. R. Driver of Oxford University brought Wellhausen's destructive views to England, while Francis Brown and Charles

A. Briggs of Union Theological Seminary in New York sowed the same seeds in the soil of American religious thought. These same three men later collaborated on a revision of the Hebrew lexicon compiled by Semitic scholar F. H. W. Gesenius. Though now a standard reference work, this massive dictionary is saturated with the JEDP theory.

The Jewish scholar and philologist, Umberto Cassuto, shattered liberal assumptions in his *Documentary Hypothesis*, published in 1934. It was then that many of the old-line Liberals shifted some of their major emphases and attempted to camouflage their old ideas into a "neo-liberal" movement. They continue to employ the so-called historical-critical method.

It is ironic that while Liberals criticize conservatives for asserting the inerrancy of original manuscripts which no longer exist, they base their own claims upon alleged sources for which not a thread of archaeological evidence has ever been verified. The Bible teaches its own inerrancy, but the historical-critical method is merely a forced hypothesis. Both internal and external evidences teach the Mosaic authorship of the Pentateuch. Internal claims include these: Exodus 17:14; 24:4; 34:27; Numbers 33:1-2; Deuteronomy 31:9, 24. The phrase "Jehovah spake to Moses" occurs again and again in Leviticus. External evidences include these: Joshua 1:7f.; Judges 3:4; II Chronicles 25:4; Ezra 6:18; 7:6; Malachi 4:4; Matthew 8:4; Mark 7:10; 10:4-5; Luke 20:37; John 5:45-47; 7:19. (For further discussion of biblical inspiration and inerrancy from a conservative standpoint the reader should consult Stewart Custer, *Does Inspiration Demand Inerrancy?* (Nutley, N.J.: The Craig Press, 1968); Benjamin B. Warfield, *Inspiration and Authority of the Bible* (Philadelphia: Presbyterian and Reformed Publishing Company, 1948); and Edward J. Young, *Thy Word Is Truth* (Grand Rapids: Eerdmans, 1957).

Glossary

ACLU—The American Civil Liberties Union, founded in 1920 with headquarters in New York City, is an organization of 250,000 members divided into fifty state groups. It was founded by avowed socialists and Communists and has pushed these ideologies ever since. Though calling itself "the guardian of the Bill of Rights," the ACLU sets itself against all of the traditional values of the American people. For example, it uses court actions to support pornography, abortion, and drug use, and to oppose prayer and Bible-reading in the schools. The organization publishes a monthly paper called *First Principles* and a bi-monthly called *Civil Liberties*.

Allegorical—(Figurative). Some parts of the Bible are obviously allegory, including Psalm 80, which describes Israel as a vine, and Galatians 4:24, which Paul specifies as an allegory. However, influenced by ancient Greek philosophy, an extreme reliance on allegory entered the church in the second century A.D. Church leaders primarily from Alexandria, Egypt, rejected what they considered crude literalisms which would offend the philosophical Greek mind. These Alexandrian church fathers set forth three possible levels of Bible interpretation: the literal (or fleshly) sense; the moral (or practical) sense; and the spiritual (or allegorical, mystical) sense which they considered the only true approach to Scripture. Church leaders such as Jerome introduced extreme allegory into the Western Church. Beginning with the sixteenth-century Reformers, like Martin Luther and John Calvin, Protestants have rejected extreme allegory as too subjective and uncontrolled. Liberals often resort to extreme allegory in order to avoid a literal interpretation of such historical people and events as the creation, Adam and Eve, the fall of man, and the universal flood.

Apostasy—(from the Greek *apostasia*, which means a falling away, a revolt, or an abandonment). The word occurs only twice in the New Testament Scriptures. In Acts 21:21 it is rendered "forsake" in the King James Version. In II Thessalonians 2:3 it is a "falling away." Plutarch used it to describe a political revolt, and it occurs in I Maccabees 2:15 to describe the enforced apostasy under Antiochus Epiphanes (a falling away from

Judaism to paganism). In Joshua 22:22 the Hebrew word which is translated "rebellion" carries the same idea.

In the history of the Christian Church, *apostasy* refers to the willful abandonment of professed truth. First Timothy 4:1 says that "in the latter times some shall depart from the faith." Second Timothy 4:3-4 says "the time will come when . . . they shall turn away their ears from the truth." Hebrews 3:12 tells us, "Take heed, brethren, lest there be in any of you an evil heart of unbelief, in departing from the living God."

Confession of faith—See Creed.

Cooperative Program—The Cooperative Program of the SBC is the financial link between the state conventions and the SBC. It is the channel through which Southern Baptist churches support the official missions and educational institutions of the Convention.

Creed—The word *creed* is derived from the Latin verb *credo*, which means "I believe." A creed then is a summary of the beliefs of an organized group. There is only a shade of difference between the terms *creed* and *confession of faith*. Creeds are more formal and are primarily for instructional purposes, while confessions have a more public importance.

Baptists have generally preferred the term *confession of faith*, which carries the idea of being less binding than a formal creed. Historically, Baptists have been characterized by such strong individualism that they have generally avoided any appearance of usurping the authority of any particular local church. It is simply "understood," for example, that every Southern Baptist church agrees with the Baptist Faith and Message Confession, which the SBC adopted in 1925 and slightly revised and affirmed in 1963. It should become obvious after reading this book that for many the Baptist Faith and Message serves primarily as a window dressing.

Ecumenical movement—The ecumenical movement is a worldwide religious movement dedicated to uniting all religions. The method of accomplishing this includes dialogue—consultation or conversation emphasizing points of agreement and ignoring points of divergence. The word *ecumenical* is derived from the Greek *oikoumene*, which originally referred to "the inhabited world"—as in Caesar Augustus's decree in Luke 2:1.

Today, the word carries the basic idea of "uniting," and it was for this purpose that Liberals organized the Federal (now National) Council of Churches (NCC) in 1908 and the World Council of Churches (WCC) in 1948. This effort at ecumenicity will find its consummation in the one-world church of the future tribulation period described in Revelation 17 and 18.

Ecumenicity—See Ecumenical movement.

Errancy—Errancy is the belief that the Bible is a man-made, fallible book, which has in it a mixture of truth and error. Those who hold to this liberal position either believe that God cannot preserve His Word from error if it is given through human writers, or else, in spite of His frequent claims to the contrary, that He did not choose to do so.

Evolution—The word *evolution* is derived from the Latin *evolutio* ("the unrolling of a scroll"). In natural science, evolution is the hypothesis that all life and matter have resulted from a slow and continuous change from lower and simpler to the higher and more complex. This is a denial of the biblical account of creation found in Genesis 1 and 2 and Exodus 20:11. *Theistic evolution* is the position that the physical universe, including life, originated with God, who guided its development through eons of time. This is a variation of the so-called day-age or long-day view. Some refine this theory into *threshold evolution,* which teaches that at times during the evolutionary process, God stepped in and created some new thing to help evolution along.

Feminism—Feminism is the philosophy of the women's liberation movement, i.e., the rejection of social distinctions based on gender. It is a logical extension of secular humanism, insisting that it is unjust for man to have authority over woman and rejecting belief in a God who would ordain such a condition in society. Its major mouthpiece is the National Organization for Women (NOW), and its goals include the creation of a "just" national payscale enforced by the government, the guarantee of a woman's right to obtain an abortion for any reason, and (often) the freedom of choice in sexual preference (i.e., homosexuality and lesbianism). In liberal religious circles feminism emphasizes the promotion of women's ordination into the pastoral ministry contrary to the biblical teaching in I Timothy 2:12, I Corinthians 14:34-35, and Genesis 3:16.

Form criticism—The term *form criticism* refers to a type of higher criticism that the Germans call *Formgeschichte*, which means "form history." As with other types of higher criticism, it repudiates the doctrine that the Bible is the absolute, infallible Word of God. Form critics presuppose that the various categories of literary types found in any book of the Bible—miracle stories, proverbs, prophecies, liturgical formulas, etc.—existed as oral traditions before an uninspired editor brought them together to form a connected narrative. Hermann Gunkel (1862-1932) was one of the first to apply this method to the Pentateuch, while Martin Dibelius (1883-1947) and Rudolf Bultmann (1884-1976) were among the earliest to apply it to the New Testament. Describing the Gospels as a "heap of unstrung pearls," these Liberals attempted to "demythologize" these books by freeing them of supposed myths and legends. Form criticism then is the liberal attempt to reconstruct the alleged process by which biblical books evolved into their present form.

Fundamentalist—A Fundamentalist is one who defends the whole Bible as the absolute, inerrant, and authoritative Word of God and is committed to the biblical doctrine of holiness or separation from all apostasy and willful practices of disobedience to the Scriptures.

Gnosticism—*Gnosticism* is a term which designates a many-sided heresy which threatened the Christian church in the first three centuries. The term *Gnostic* comes from the Greek word *gnosis* which means "knowledge." The Gnostics claimed a special, higher knowledge to which "ordinary" people did not have access. This was a pseudo-intellectualism, in some ways like today's Liberalism. Gnosticism distinguished between what they called the human, historical Jesus and the heavenly Christ who supposedly descended upon Jesus at His baptism and departed before the crucifixion. Gnosticism was actually a blend of Greek philosophy with oriental mysticism, with elements of Judaism and Christianity added to make it attractive to the undiscerning Christian. Whereas ancient Gnosticism denied the humanity of Christ while seeking for deity, modern-day Liberalism denies the deity of Christ while searching for the historical, human Jesus.

Graf-Wellhausen hypothesis—Named after K. H. Graf (1815-1869) and Julius Wellhausen (1844-1918), this is the liberal conjecture that the Pentateuch evolved into its present form centuries after Moses. These Liberals began with the presupposition that the Bible is merely a human book which cannot be completely trusted as historically accurate. The method of theoretically reconstructing the Pentateuch into its alleged original form is known by such terms as *source criticism, higher criticism, higher textual criticism*, the *historical-critical method*, or simply the *JEDP hypothesis*. The letters JEDP represent the four primary conjectured sources of the Pentateuch: J represents the use of the name Jehovah; E is for the use of God's name, Elohim; D stands for Deuteronomy; and P is the priestly material. When the Liberals added dates to these supposed sources, source criticism simply became historical criticism.

Heresy—The Greek word *hairesis*, "heresy," comes from the word *haireomai*, which means "to choose." *Heresy* has three basic meanings in the New Testament: (1) a chosen way of life, i.e., a religious sect (not necessarily a bad one). It is used to describe the Sadducees (Acts 5:17), the Pharisees (Acts 15:5; 26:5), and even Christianity (Acts 24:5, 14; 28:22); (2) schism or discord within the Christian church (I Corinthians 11:18-19; Galatians 5:20; Titus 3:10); (3) destructive doctrine taught willfully by false teachers of perdition (II Peter 2:1). This last definition comes closest to what has become the standard usage in church history.

Higher criticism—See Graf-Wellhausen hypothesis.

Historical-critical method—See Graf-Wellhausen hypothesis.

Inerrancy—Inerrancy, or infallibility, is the doctrine that the original Scripture manuscripts were completely without any mixture of error. The relatively few scribal variations which later crept into the handwritten copies would equal about one-quarter to one-half page in a 500-page book, and these copyist variations affect no major doctrines whatsoever. It is providential that there are enough copies available that textual scholars can virtually get back to the original wording by comparing the manuscripts with one another. Perhaps God in His omniscient wisdom knew that if the original manuscripts were preserved men would worship them rather than Himself. Christians can rest assured, however, that they have the Word of God. Jesus said, "The scripture cannot be broken" (John 10:35).

GLOSSARY

JEDP—See Graf-Wellhausen hypothesis.

Left-wing—On the liberal side of political or religious issues.

Liberalism—Old Liberalism or Modernism is the theological position which rejects any or all of the Bible as the absolute, infallible, and authoritative Word of God; denies the supernatural elements of the Bible; denies the deity and substitutionary atonement of Christ; and perpetrates the anti-scriptural doctrines of the universal fatherhood of God, the universal brotherhood of man, and the social gospel as the answer to man's needs. (See also the glossary definitions of the other two branches of Liberalism—Neo-liberalism and Neo-orthodoxy).

Literalist—*Literalist* is a term used in derision by Liberals against those who embrace the doctrine of biblical inerrancy. Actually a so-called literalist is one who accepts the Bible at face value. While acknowledging the various symbolical, typological, and allegorical portions of Scripture, the "literalist" believes, along with mainline Protestantism since Luther's day, that the historical-grammatical method of Bible interpretation is normally the correct one. It is called the *historical-grammatical method* because it maintains that generally any statement should be interpreted as a person who lived in the period of history when it was written would have interpreted it. In other words, the literalist believes that the most natural method of interpreting any statement is generally a literal one, except where the context indicates otherwise.

Lower criticism—The science of lower biblical (or textual) criticism is the careful comparison of ancient manuscripts in order to determine what the author originally wrote before scribal mistakes crept into the text. This conservative study has contributed significantly to our understanding of passages whose manuscripts contain copyist variations. Men such as B. F. Westcott (1825-1901), F. J. A. Hort (1828-1892), and J. B. Lightfoot (1828-1889) did much to advance this worthwhile study.

Modalism—Modalism was a branch of the ancient (second-century) heresy of Monarchianism. One branch was called Dynamic Monarchianism, which denied Christ's deity and His

209

distinct personality. Modalistic Monarchianism, the other branch, affirmed the "divinity" of Christ, but simply identified it with the Father—the "Monarch." This heresy, which was sometimes called Patripassianism (from the Greek words for "father" and "suffering," because they believed the Father suffered on the cross) denied Christ's distinct personality. Its most popular teacher was Sabellius, from whom it also took the name Sabellianism.

Moderate—*Moderate* is a term which reporters and journalists often use to describe a Liberal. This, however, is extremely misleading. Most Neo-liberals and Neo-orthodox sympathizers do not desire these two labels because their own mission is to remain entrenched within institutions whose support comes primarily from a conservative constituency. The use of the word *moderate* in this way suggests to the undiscerning that the conservatives are immoderate or "ultra-conservative."

Modernism—See Liberalism.

NCC—National Council of Churches; see Ecumenical movement.

Neo-evangelicalism—See New Evangelicalism.

Neo-liberalism—Neo-liberalism, which emerged about 1935, is an attempt to preserve the basic tenets of the older Liberalism while clothing them in conservative-sounding terminology. The major difference between old and new Liberalism is their method of biblical studies. Whereas the older Liberalism was analytic, taking the Bible to pieces and analyzing its parts, Neo-liberalism is more synthetic, finding a degree of unity in the Bible. Although Neo-liberals have referred to themselves as the "biblical theology movement," they begin with the same old presuppositions, that the Bible is basically a human book and not the absolute, infallible Word of God. Neo-liberal spokesmen have included Harry E. Fosdick, John C. Bennett, Walter M. Horton, Henry P. Van Dusen, and Bishop G. Bromley Oxnam.

Neo-orthodoxy—Neo-orthodoxy, whose founding father was Karl Barth (1896-1968), is an attempt to preserve the basic tenets of the older Liberalism while clothing them in philosophical terminology. Much of its language is in the non-literal realm. The major difference between the older Liberalism and Neo-orthodoxy lies in the doctrine of God. Whereas the older Liberalism emphasized God's immanence (that He is so closely identified with the world that He never acts contrary to natural, physical laws), Neo-orthodoxy emphasizes God's transcendence (that He is totally different and remote from the physical world). The old-line Liberal's God was only an extension of man (pantheism). Barth, on the other hand, speaks of God as the "Wholly Other." Both groups deny the biblical doctrine of three distinct persons of the Trinity. To them, for example, the Holy Spirit is only a mode or expression of God and not a distinct Person of the Trinity. Neo-orthodox spokesmen have included Emil Brunner, Reinhold and Richard Niebuhr, Paul J. Tillich, and Rudolf Bultmann.

New Evangelicalism—New Evangelicalism is the religious mood or attitude which repudiates Fundamentalism's doctrine of separation from false teachers and advocates theological dialogue with Modernism and greater social involvement. Harold J. Ockenga coined the term *New Evangelical* in 1948 when he described the movement as a "new breed."

New left—The new (or evangelical) left is the segment of political and religious Liberalism which also identifies with traditionally conservative or evangelical groups. They attempt to make the tenets of Liberalism palatable to a larger segment of the mainline denominations. An advocate of the new left might attend a Southern Baptist revival meeting one day and lobby for the pro-abortion movement the next. Richard Quebedeaux, in his *Worldly Evangelicals* (1978) and *Young Evangelicals* (1974), discusses this group in much detail. (Harper and Row published both of these works).

Pragmatism—Pragmatism is the humanistic philosophy which maintains that ideas and doctrines can be judged properly only on the basis of how they actually work in the realm of human experience. In other words, to the pragmatist human experience is the test of doctrine. The Bible is not the ultimate authority. William James is often called the father of pragmatism.

Rationalism—*Rationalism* (from the Latin *rationales*, from *ratio*, which means "reason") is the view that human reason alone is sufficient to solve man's problems and to elevate man to his maximum potential.

Separation—Fundamentalists believe that the doctrine of separation (or sanctification) is inherently part of the scriptural teaching of God's holiness—separation from deeds of darkness (I John 2:15-17; II Corinthians 6:15-7:1; James 4:4); from false teachers (Matthew 7:15; Galatians 1:8-9; II John 9-11; I Timothy 6:20-21); and from professing Christians who willfully and continually walk in disobedience (Matthew 18:15-18; I Corinthians 5:1-13; II Thessalonians 3:6, 14-15). On the positive side, sanctification implies joyful and loving Christian fellowship with those who are "followers of God" and who "walk in love" (Ephesians 5:1-2).

Social gospel—The social gospel is the old liberal doctrine that sin is society's selfishness, not a personal reality, and that salvation is society's change from selfishness to concern for the poor. The goal of social-gospel advocates is "Christian socialism." Washington Gladden (1836-1918) is often considered the father of the social gospel, and Walter Rauschenbusch (1861-1918), author of *A Theology for the Social Gospel* (1917), is its theologian.

Source criticism—See Graf-Wellhausen hypothesis.

Symbolical—As applied to the interpretation of Scripture, the symbolical method as used by Liberals views the biblical narratives as not literally and historically true; they are merely literary devices used to convey a "deeper" message. According to this view, the stories of the Garden of Eden, the serpent and the fall of man, for example, are merely non-historical narratives containing moral lessons for man. This method is opposed to the *historical-grammatical method*, which takes the Bible at face value and accepts the literal meaning of the words unless there is something in the context to indicate that the author intended otherwise.

Textual criticism—See Lower Criticism; see also the glossary definition of the Graf-Wellhausen hypothesis, for a contrast between lower and higher biblical criticism.

Theistic evolution—See Evolution.

Unitarian—The Unitarian Church is a heretical, monotheistic religion which rejects the Trinity and therefore rejects the deity of Christ and of the Holy Spirit. In 1961 the Unitarian Church and the Universalist Church merged.

Universalism—Universalism is the heretical teaching that all mankind is or ultimately will be saved, and therefore there is no eternal punishment.

WCC—World Council of Churches; see Ecumenical movement.

Selected Bibliography

Periodicals

Adult Teacher (SBC Sunday school quarterly)
Annual (SBC, 1845-1984)
Arkansas Baptist Newsmagazine (Arkansas Baptist State Convention)
Atlanta Journal and Constitution
Baptist Challenge
Baptist Courier (newspaper of the General Board of the South Carolina Baptist Convention)
Baptist Program (SBC newspaper)
Baptist Standard (newspaper of the Baptist General Convention of Texas)
Baptist History and Heritage (a Southern Baptist journal)
Baptist Messenger (newspaper of the Baptist General Convention of Oklahoma)
Baptist Press (official news service of the SBC)
Baptist Record (newspaper of the Mississippi Baptist Convention)
Baptist Training Union Magazine (SBC)
Baptist and Reflector (newspaper of the Tennessee Baptist Convention)
Biblical Recorder (newspaper of the Baptist State Convention of North Carolina)
Birmingham News
California Southern Baptist (newspaper of the Southern Baptist General Convention of California)
Capitol Voice
Christian Century
Christian Citizen
Christian Index (newspaper of the Executive Committee of the Baptist Convention of the state of Georgia)
Christian News (all articles cited are Religious News Service releases)
Christianity Today
Chronicle of Higher Education
Church at Work
Context (collegiate Bible study in the Forefront series of the SBC Sunday School Board curriculum)
Convention Uniform Series (a SBC Sunday School Board quarterly series)
Dallas Morning News

Dallas Times Herald
Denver Post
Enquirer (Columbus, Georgia)
Eternity
Evangelical Newsletter
Facts and Trends (SBC publication)
The Faith and Southern Baptists (published by Southern Baptists)
FAITH for the Family
First Baptist Reminder (publication of First Baptist Church of Dallas, Texas)
Folio (newsletter of the women's movement within the SBC)
Fort Worth Star Telegram
Foundation
Free Inquiry
Fundamentalist Journal
General Information Guide (SBC Sunday School Board)
Greenville News
Greenville News-Piedmont
Greenville Piedmont
Guideposts
Houston Chronicle
Junior Teacher (SBC Sunday school quarterly)
Kansas City Star
Leadership
Light (publication of the SBC Christian Life Commission)
Lubbock Avalanche Journal
Maranatha Gospel Messenger
Moody Monthly
News Leader (Richmond, Virginia)
Newsweek
Outreach (SBC publication)
People's Baptist Sentinel
Perspectives in Religious Studies (publication of the Association of Baptist Professors of Religion—ABPR)
Plains Baptist Challenger
Primary Teacher (SBC Sunday school quarterly)
Reformed Journal
Religious Herald (newspaper of the Baptist General Association of Virginia)
Review and Expositor (journal of Southern Baptist Theological Seminary)
Review of the News
Richmond News Leader

Richmond Times Dispatch
Saturday Evening Post
SBC Today (published by Southern Baptists)
Searchlight (published by J. Frank Norris when he was a
     Southern Baptist)
Senior Adult Bible Study (SBC Sunday school quarterly)
Southern Baptist Advocate (published by Southern Baptists)
Southern Baptist Journal (published by Southern Baptists)
Span (a Golden Gate Baptist Theological Seminary publication)
St. Louis Post Dispatch
St. Petersburg Independent
St. Petersburg Times
Sunday School Board Annual Report (SBC)
Sword and Trowel (published by Charles H. Spurgeon)
Tarrant County Baptist (a Southern Baptist publication)
The Tennessean
Texas Monthly
The Tie (a Southern Baptist Theological Seminary publication)
Time
Times-Picayune/States-Item
Training Union Quarterly (SBC)
Tulsa Daily World
USA Today
Utah Evangel
Washington Post
Watchman-Examiner (newspaper formerly published by con-
     servatives within the Northern Baptist Convention)
Western Recorder (newspaper of the Kentucky Baptist
     Convention)
Western Reporter
Winston-Salem Journal
Witness (publication of the First Baptist Church of Atlanta,
     Georgia)
Word and Way (newspaper of the Missouri Baptist Convention)

Books

Allen, Clifton J., gen. ed. *Broadman Bible Commentary.* 12 vols.
     Nashville: Broadman Press, 1969-73.

Alley, Robert S. *Revolt Against the Faithful.* Philadelphia: J.
     B. Lippincott Company, 1970.

Baker, Robert A. *The Southern Baptist Convention and Its People: 1607-1972.* Nashville: Broadman Press, 1974.

Barnes, William W. *The Southern Baptist Convention, 1845-1953.* Nashville: Broadman Press, 1954.

Boyce, James P. *Abstract of Systematic Theology.* Philadelphia: American Baptist Publication Society, 1887.

―――――. *Three Changes in Theological Institutions.* Greenville, South Carolina: C. J. Elford's Book and Job Press, 1856.

Broadus, John A. *Commentary on the Gospel of Matthew.* Valley Forge, Pennsylvania: American Baptist Publication Society, 1886.

―――――. *Memoir of James Petigru Boyce.* New York: A. C. Armstrong and Son, 1893.

―――――. *Paramount and Permanent Authority of the Bible.* Philadelphia: American Baptist Publication Society, 1887.

Burton, Joe W. *Road to Nashville.* Nashville: Broadman Press, 1977.

―――――. *Road to Recovery.* Nashville: Broadman Press, 1977.

Bush, L. Russ, and Nettles, Tom J. *Baptists and the Bible.* Chicago: Moody Press, 1980.

Buttrick, George Arthur. *The Christian Fact and Modern Doubt.* New York: Charles Scribner's Sons, 1934.

―――――, ed. *The Interpreter's Bible.* 12 vols. Nashville: Abingdon Press, 1951-57.

―――――. *The Interpreter's Dictionary of the Bible.* 4 vols. Nashville: Abingdon Press, 1962.

Carroll, B. H. *Inspiration of the Bible: A Discussion of the Origin, the Authenticity and the Sanity of the Oracles of God.* Compiled and edited by J. B. Cranfill. New York: Revell, 1930.

————. *Interpretation of the English Bible*. Nashville: Southern Baptist Sunday School Board, 1913.

Christian, Curtis W. *Shaping Your Faith*. Waco, Texas: Word Books, 1973.

Clark, Theodore R. *Saved by His Life*. New York: Macmillan, 1959.

Claypool, John R. "The Problem of Hell in Contemporary Theology." Ph. D. dissertation, Southern Baptist Theological Seminary, 1959.

Conner, Walter Thomas. *The Faith of the New Testament*. Nashville: Broadman, 1940.

————. *Revelation and God: An Introduction to Christian Doctrine*. Nashville: Broadman, 1936.

Crapps, Robert W.; Flanders, Henry J., Jr.; and Smith, David A. *The People of the Covenant*. New York: Ronald Press, 1963.

Criswell, Wallie A. *Look Up, Brother!* Nashville: Southern Baptist Sunday School Board, 1970.

————. *These Issues We Must Face*. Grand Rapids: Zondervan, 1953.

————. *Why I Preach That the Bible Is Literally True*. Nashville: Broadman Press, 1969.

Dana, Harvey E. *The Authority of the Holy Scriptures: A Brief Story of the Problems of Biblical Criticism*. Nashville: Southern Baptist Sunday School Board, 1923.

Dilday, Russell H., Jr. *The Doctrine of Biblical Authority*. Nashville: Convention Press, 1982.

Draper, James T. *Authority: The Critical Issue for Southern Baptists*. Old Tappan, New Jersey: Revell, 1984.

Eighmy, John Lee. *Churches in Cultural Captivity.* Knoxville: The University of Tennessee Press, 1972.

Elliott, Ralph H. *The Message of Genesis.* Nashville: Broadman Press, 1961.

Ferré, Nels F. S. *The Christian Faith.* New York: Harper and Brothers, 1942.

————. *Christianity and Society.* New York: Harper and Brothers, 1950.

————. *The Christian Understanding of God.* New York: Harper and Brothers, 1951.

————. *Faith and Reason.* New York: Harper and Brothers, 1946.

————. *Pillars of Faith.* New York: Harper and Brothers, 1948.

————. *Return to Christianity.* New York: Harper and Brothers, 1943.

————. *The Sun and the Umbrella.* New York: Harper and Brothers, 1953.

Francisco, Clyde T. *Introducing the Old Testament.* Nashville: Broadman, 1950.

Garrett, James L.; Hinson, E. Glenn; and Tull, James E. *Are Southern Baptists "Evangelicals"?* Macon, Georgia: Mercer University Press, 1983.

Gatewood, Willard B. *Controversy in the Twenties: Fundamentalism, Modernism, and Evolution.* Nashville: Vanderbilt Press, 1969.

Gill, Everett. *A. T. Robertson: A Biography.* New York: Macmillan Company, 1943.

Green, Joseph F. *Bible's Secret of Full Happiness.* Nashville: Broadman Press, 1970.

————. *The Heart of the Gospel.* Nashville: Broadman Press, 1968.

Grindstaff, W. E. *Our Cooperative Program.* Nashville: Convention Press, 1965.

Hadden, J. K., and Swann, C. E. *Prime Time Preachers.* Reading, Massachusetts: Addison-Wesley Publishing Company, Inc., 1981.

Harrison, Roland K. *Introduction to the Old Testament.* Grand Rapids: Eerdmans, 1969.

Hinson, E. Glenn. *Jesus Christ.* [n.p.]: McGrath Publishing Company, 1977.

Hollyfield, Noel Wesley, Jr. "A Sociological Analysis of the Degrees of 'Christian Orthodoxy' Among Selected Students in the Southern Baptist Theological Seminary." Th.M. thesis, Southern Baptist Theological Seminary, 1976.

Honeycutt, Roy L. *To Your Tents O Israel! A Biblical Call to Duty, Unity and Honor.* Address delivered at Southern Baptist Theological Seminary's Convocation, Louisville, Kentucky, August 18, 1984.

Hull, William E. *The Integrity of the Theological Curriculum.* Louisville: The Southern Baptist Theological Seminary, 1969.

Humphreys, Fisher H. *The Death of Christ.* Nashville: Broadman Press, 1978.

Hyatt, Irwin T. *Our Ordered Lives.* Cambridge, Massachusetts: Harvard University Press, 1976.

Johnson, L. D. *Introduction to the Bible.* Nashville: Convention Press, 1969.

Keith, Billy. *W. A. Criswell: The Authorized Biography.* Old Tappan, New Jersey: Fleming H. Revell Company, 1973.

Kennedy, Gerald. *God's Good News.* New York: Harper and Brothers, 1955.

Lindsell, Harold. *The Battle for the Bible.* Grand Rapids: Zondervan, 1976.

————. *The Bible in the Balance.* Grand Rapids: Zondervan, 1979.

Lumpkin, William L. *Baptist Confessions of Faith.* Valley Forge, Pennsylvania: Judson Press, 1969.

McBeth, Leon. *The First Baptist Church of Dallas.* Grand Rapids: Zondervan, 1968.

Manly, Basil, Jr. *The Bible Doctrine of Inspiration Explained and Vindicated.* New York: A. C. Armstrong and Son, 1888.

Moody, Dale. *The Word of Truth.* Grand Rapids: Eerdmans, 1981.

Mueller, William A. *A History of Southern Baptist Theological Seminary.* Nashville: Broadman, 1959.

Mullins, E. Y. *Axioms of Religion.* Valley Forge, Pennsylvania: Judson Press, 1908.

————. *The Christian Religion in Its Doctrinal Expression.* Valley Forge, Pennsylvania: Judson Press, 1917.

————. *Christianity at the Cross Roads.* Nashville: Southern Baptist Sunday School Board, 1924.

————. *Freedom and Authority in Religion.* Philadelphia: The Griffith and Rowland Press, 1913.

Newport, John P. *Paul Tillich.* Waco, Texas: Word Books, 1984.

Powell, William A. *The SBC Issue & Question.* Buchanan, Georgia: Baptist Missionary Service, Inc., 1977.

Price, J. M. *Christianity and Social Problems.* Nashville: Southern Baptist Sunday School Board, 1928.

Robertson, A. T. *The New Citizenship: The Christian Facing a New World Order.* New York: Fleming H. Revell Company, 1919.

————. *Word Pictures in the New Testament.* 6 vols. Nashville: Broadman, 1930-33.

Routh, Porter. *Chosen for Leadership.* Nashville: Broadman, 1976.

Rowley, H. H. *The Unity of the Bible.* Philadelphia: Westminster Press, 1955.

Rust, Eric C. *Christian Understanding of History.* London: Lutterworth Press, 1947.

————. *Evolutionary Philosophies and Contemporary Theology.* Philadelphia: Westminster Press, 1969.

————. *Nature and Man in Biblical Thought.* London: Lutterworth Press, 1953.

————. *Salvation History.* Richmond: John Knox Press, 1962.

————. *Science and Faith.* New York: Oxford University Press, 1967.

Sampey, John R. *The Heart of the Old Testament: A Manual for Christian Students.* Nashville: Southern Baptist Sunday School Board, 1909.

————. *Southern Baptist Theological Seminary: The First Thirty Years—1859-1889.* Baltimore: Wharton, Barron and Company, 1890.

Scarborough, Lee R. *Gospel Messages.* Nashville: Southern Baptist Sunday School Board, 1922.

Schuller, Robert H. *Self-Esteem: The New Reformation.* Waco, Texas: Word Books, 1982.

Carroll, Benajah Harvey, 50-51, 52, 57 n.1
Carter, Jimmy, 149
Carver, W. O., 123
Cate, Robert L., 66, 69
Chafin, Kenneth L., 44, 54, 139, 144, 157-158, 164, 167, 180, 182
Chance, J. Bradley, 100
Christian, Curtis W., 92-93
Christian Fact and Modern Doubt (Buttrick), 60-61
Christian Faith, The (Ferré), 33
Christian Life Commission, 15, 57, 65, 71, 126, 132, 134-136, 139
Christian Religion in Its Doctrinal Expression, The (Mullins), 27
Christian Understanding of God (Ferré), 34
Christianity and Liberalism (Machen), 85, 199
Christianity and Social Problems (Rice), 52
Christianity and Society (Ferré),
Church of Christ, Scientist, 96
Clark, Theodore R., 61-62
Clarke, John, 11
Claypool, John R., 128
Clower, Jerry, 153
Coble, William B., 79-80
Cochran, Malone, 183
Coffin, Henry Sloane, 35
Cole, Harold, 182
Coleman, Larry, 158
Colson, Howard P., 124-125
Commentary on the Gospel of Matthew (Broadus), 24
Communism, 33, 60. See also Marxism; Socialism
Confessions of faith. See Creeds
Conner, Walter Thomas, 52, 123
Conventions (annual SB meetings), 14-15. See also Atlanta Convention (1978); Houston Convention (1979); Kansas City Convention (1980); Los Angeles

Convention (1981); New Orleans Convention (1982); Pittsburgh Convention (1983); St. Louis Convention (1980)
Cooperative Program, 13-15, 16 n.3, 19, 45, 47, 51, 64, 69, 72, 82, 84, 87, 88, 133, 139, 161, 165, 172, 175-176, 178, 187, 205
Cothen, Grady C., 84-85, 110, 134-135, 163
Cox, Harvey, 126
Crapps, Robert Wilson, 95-96
Creation. See Genesis, book of: Creation
Creeds, 11, 18, 56, 78, 104-109, 159-160, 165, 196-197, 205
Criswell, Wallie Amos, 1-2, 8 n.1, 61, 68, 85, 87-88, 99, 114, 133, 136 n.5, 139, 142-145, 150, 151 n.4, 154-155, 165, 171, 186

Dahlberg, E. T., 52
Dallas Baptist College, 108
Daniel, book of, 61, 96, 112, 126
Davies, G. Henton, 113, 114
Davis, D. Anne, 181
Davis, Earl, 158
Davis, Suzanne Martin, 72
Death of Christ, The (Humphreys), 62-63, 127
Deity of Christ. See Jesus Christ: Deity
Dilday, Russell H., Jr., 56, 176-177, 181
Doctrine of Biblical Authority, The (Dilday), 56
Dorr, Samuel F., 44
Dow, Grove S., 17, 18
Drake, Ed, 142
Draper, James T., Jr., 163-170
Drinking and alcoholism, 93, 100, 133, 135-136, 160, 163, 169 n.1, 177
Drug abuse, 133, 135-136, 177
Drumwright, Huber L., 56
Duke, David N., 100
Dunn, James, 65-66, 139, 169 n.4
Durham, John I., 70, 113

Sparkman, Temp. *Being a Disciple*. Nashville: Broadman, 1972.

————. *Salvation and Nurture of the Child of God: The Story of Emma*. Valley Forge, Pennsylvania: Judson Press, 1983.

Stagg, Frank. *New Testament Theology*. Nashville: Broadman, 1962.

Stanley, Charles F. *Wednesday Business Meeting*. Cassette. Atlanta: First Baptist Church, November 19, 1975.

Summers, Ray. *Worthy Is the Lamb*. Nashville: Broadman, 1951.

System Bible Study. Chicago: The System Bible Company, 1922.

Thompson, James J. *Tried As by Fire*. Macon, Georgia: Mercer University Press, 1982.

Torbet, Robert G. *A History of the Baptists*. Valley Forge, Pennsylvania: Judson Press, 1973.

Toy, C. H. *The History of the Religion of Israel*. Boston: Unitarian Sunday School Society, 1894.

Trueblood, Elton. *Essence of Spiritual Religion*. New York: Harper and Row, 1975.

————. *Future of the Christian*. New York: Harper and Row, 1971.

————. *Philosophy of Religion*. New York: Harper, 1957.

Unger, Merrill. *The Mystery of Bishop Pike*. Wheaton: Tyndale House, 1971.

Wahking, Harold L. *Being Christlike*. Nashville: Broadman, 1970.

Ward, Wayne E., and Green, Joseph E., eds. *Is the Bible a Human Book?* Nashville: Broadman Press, 1970.

Warfield, Benjamin B. *The Inspiration and Authority of the Bible.* Philadelphia: Presbyterian and Reformed Publishing Company, 1948.

Young, Edward J. *Thy Word Is Truth.* Grand Rapids: Eerdmans, 1957.

Index

Philadelphia Baptist Association, 11
Philadelphia Confession of Faith, 11
Phillips, John W., 19
Pike, James A. (Episcopal bishop), 65
Pillars of Faith (Ferré), 32-33
Pittsburgh Convention (1983), 166-167, 178
Playboy (magazine), 2, 93, 134
Pleitz, James L., 164
Poteat, Edwin McNeill, 34-35
Poteat, William L., 18
Powell, William A., Sr., 56, 69, 80, 89, 107, 148-149, 183
Power of Jesus Christ, The (Peale), 143
Pragmatism, 27, 211
Pressler, Paul, 86, 150-151, 154, 157, 171
Pressler-Patterson strategy, 150-151, 180
Price, J. M., 52

Ralph Elliott controversy, 15, 77-79
Ramm, Bernard, 4
Rationalism, 85, 202, 211-212
Rauschenbusch, Walter, 29
Resurrection of Christ. See Jesus Christ: Resurrection
Return to Christianity (Ferré), 33
Revelation, book of, 53, 61, 112
Revolt Against the Faithful (Alley), 98
Reynolds, Herbert H., 93, 94, 182
Rhodenhiser, O. William, 99
Roberts, C. A., 140
Robertson, Archibald Thomas, 29-30, 31 n.13, 32, 121
Rogers, Adrian P., 150, 153-155
Roman Catholics, 2, 54, 96, 139, 140-142, 143, 144, 195
Rowley, H. H., 38
Rust, Eric C., 36-38

St. Louis Convention (1980), 93, 133, 156-157

Salvation, 63, 81, 94; Eternal security, 43; Immortality, 55. See also Evangelism
Salvation and Nurture of the Child of God: The Story of Emma (Sparkman), 81-82
Samford University, 91
Sampey, John Richard, 28-29
Saved by His Life (Clark), 61-62
Scarborough, Lee Rutland, 17-18, 51, 52
Schuller, Robert, 54, 143-144
Screven, William, 11
Self, Bill, 158, 182
Self-Esteem: The New Reformation (Schuller), 54, 144
Separation, doctrine of, 4, 5, 6, 189-191, 193, 194, 212
Seventy-Five Million Campaign, 13, 15 n.2
Shaping Your Faith (Christian), 92-93
Sheen, Bishop Fulton J., 144
Sherman, Cecil, 157, 166-167, 176, 184 n.7
Silent majority, 6, 26, 188
Simmons, Paul D., 45, 132
Sinlessness of Christ. See Jesus Christ: Sinlessness
Sisk, Ronald D., 135-136
Situation ethics, 81, 134
Slatton, James, 158
Smith, Bailey, 156-162, 164, 167
Smith, David Anthony, 95-96
Smith, T. C., 72, 75 n.7, 94-95
Social gospel, 13, 29, 64, 212
Socialism, 33, 81, 122. See also Communism; Marxism
Song of Solomon, book of, 2
Source criticism. See Historical-critical method
Southeastern Baptist Theological Seminary, 21, 70-75, 79, 113, 164, 181
Southern Baptist Advocate, 135, 149
Southern Baptist Journal, 56, 67-68, 72, 93, 148-149, 183
Southern Baptist Theological

230